BRITISH BIRDS

Golden Eagle

BRITISH BIRDS

THE REV. F. O. MORRIS

A SELECTION FROM THE ORIGINAL WORK
EDITED AND WITH AN INTRODUCTION BY

TONY SOPER

ILLUSTRATED BY A. F. LYDON · ENGRAVED BY BENJAMIN FAWCETT

**SPRING
BOOKS**

First published in this form in Great Britain in 1981 by
Webb and Bower (Publishers) Ltd

This edition published in 1987 by Spring Books
An imprint of Octopus Publishing Group PLC
59 Grosvenor Street
London W1

Distributed by Hamlyn Publishing Group Ltd
Bridge House, London Road,
Twickenham, Middlesex, England

This redesigned one-volume edition with additional material
© 1981 Webb & Bower (Publishers) Ltd

ISBN 0 600 55410 4

Printed in Hong Kong

CONTENTS

INTRODUCTION

Tony Soper

FRANCIS ORPEN MORRIS was born 25 March 1810 at Cove, near Cork. His father was an Admiral in the Royal Navy, his grandfather saw active service as a naval captain in the American War of Independence. He was educated at Bromsgrove School in Worcestershire, where he first showed an interest in natural history, and after a period with a private tutor he went up to Worcester College, Oxford, where he graduated B.A. Taking Holy Orders, he progressed to the living of Nunburnholme in the East Riding of Yorkshire, where he spent the rest of his life. Married in 1835, he had three sons and six daughters.

He was a stalwart member of the Tory establishment, with decided views and a predeliction for writing to *The Times* about them. A kindly and enlightened landowner, he encouraged agricultural workers to better themselves through the virtues of self-help. Temperate and reasonable, his tolerance nevertheless strained easily when confronted with Christian back-sliders or the heresies of Darwinian natural selection.

In everyday life, his pastoral duties allowed him comfortable time to pursue his passion for ornithology, a study well regarded as a re-spectable branch of natural history. Gilbert White's *Natural History of Selborne*, 1789, inspired a generation of parsons to dream of adding their own volume of observations to the library of natural science, their wildlife field researches marching step by step and in harmony with their pastoral duties, since an understanding of wild nature was seen primarily as a path towards an understanding of the works of God.

In Morris's time the general attitude to animals was that as lesser creatures they were at Man's disposal. Most particularly, if they were edible they were to be eaten. These were after all the days when small birds like sparrows and yellowhammers were 'reckoned good eating', thrushes 'good birds to eat, often sold in the markets with their kindred species', and even starlings 'good to eat, but rather tough and slightly bitter'. And if birds of prey had the temerity to eat game birds, then they were to be destroyed. This in spite of the widely held belief that if Man didn't hold birds in check then they would quickly multiply till the world provided standing-room only.

Morris was well disposed towards sportsmen in their traditional sense, but hard on what he saw as butchery. He raised no objection to the management of game preserves, but inclined to the view that game-keepers were not the best judges as to which animals did harm and which did not. He disapproved of rows of defunct hawks strung up on a gibbet, though he acknowledges their value as an indicator of the local raptor population. He tells us, without comment, of the 'only Irish hobby' shot for identification, and of £1000 prices for a well-trained peregrine. (Curious that the black-market 1980s price is said to be just half as much again). He laments the persecution of owls, encroachment of agriculture on the buzzard's life-style, and the universal hostility to the heron.

Closer to his parish, the sea-birds of the cliffs of Scarborough and Bridlington were being systematically destroyed by shooting parties of 'gentlemen' who hired steamers to take them to the foot of the breeding colonies. One of his correspondents wrote of boats literally laden with sea-fowl, the boatmen sitting on them and the birds heaped up in the bow and stern above the gunwale. It transpired that this same persecution was going on at other sea-bird stations like the Bass Rock, the Isle of May, and the Pembrokeshire islands. Morris wrote letters to *The Times*, an association was formed (in 1869), public opinion stirred and a not entirely successful Sea-birds Act found its way to the Statute books. It was a beginning. And Morris became active in pursuit of protective legislation. He petitioned the House of Commons to institute a tax on guns, outlaw iron traps and license the use of clap nets. He argued that luxuries should be taxed before all else, that gamekeepers were luxuries and should therefore be heavily taxed at a suggested £20 each year.

In Victorian times birds were treated not only as pests or protein but also as objects of fashion. The skins of great crested grebes became an admired substitute for fur. Hats, bonnets and dresses were bedecked with stuffed kingfishers, ball-dresses covered with canaries ('I am glad to say the wearer of it, though handsome, had no partners'). Morris, encouraged by Lady Mount-Temple, established 'The Plumage League', whose object was to discourage the use of birds for adornment. Membership was restricted to ladies.

The Sea-birds Act clearly needed amendment and extension, and Morris added his determined and systematic agitation to the ground-swell moving in favour of close-season protection for all feathered friends. In 1880 the Wild Birds Protection Act set a pattern which was to endure for 75 years. A more enlightened and humane attitude towards birds infected the public, and nine years later the infant Royal Society for the Protection of Birds was formed. Morris carries a fair share of responsibility for these achievements, and the main expression of his influence was in the publication of *A History of British Birds*. It had been preceded by an honourable, and in many ways superior, succession of ornithological works, but there had been nothing so easily accessible to the public, or so successful.

Morris's first publication had been *A Guide to an Arrangement of British Birds* (1834), a catalogue intended for those labelling cabinets or collections. For this was the era of the collector. Shells, seaweeds, birds' eggs or butterflies, the mania was for a drawing-room display. Morris continued his interest in nomenclature, both scientific and vernacular, and he embraced a wide net of correspondents. But the 'history' resulted from his acquaintance with Benjamin Fawcett, a bookseller and printer who by good fortune lived in the market town of Driffield, Morris's next-door parish. Fawcett had illustrated some children's books, then collaborated with Morris in a bible natural history. They now discussed a major work on birds aimed at a large-scale popular readership.

Their plan was to break the existing pattern of expensive works, as exemplified by Gould, Montagu, Macgillivray, Bewick, Yarrell and Audubon, and to produce a long-running part-work. The arrangement they agreed was that they should deal with four species a month, Morris providing the text, Fawcett arranging the artistic and production work. After much debate the price was fixed at one shilling, a master stroke.

Morris wrote to order, as required by the schedule, without default. Working in the rectory drawing-room in the evenings, unmoved by general conversation or background music-making, he abstracted himself into a world of birds. Encouraged by his far-flung correspondents, and cheerfully, but uncritically, including almost anything anyone chose to write on the subject, his discursive pen ran away with him. From a narrowly scientific point of view much of the material may be open to question, but as enjoyable and pleasant bird-reading it warmed his readers' hearts. All the prejudices and received errors of the mid-nineteenth century are encapsulated here, fortified by the author's genuine and hearty sense of humour, and lightly salted with poetic references. He never misses an opportunity to ram home a campaigning point. He never hesitates to fire a broadside at anyone straying from the straight path of Christian principle. He does not fail to bring to our attention that, in accepting a lesser rock on which to build a nest when a more desirable and higher one is already taken, the cormorant shows that the more lowly of us must accept our allotted station in life without complaint. Some of his descriptions of birdsong are as lyrical as their subject; he clearly loved wild music and delighted to describe it. The volumes are full of life and bursting with human nature. Morris took special pleasure in recording the everyday names of his subjects, and pilloried those who sought to impose new-fangled names – see his defence of 'wagtail'. He was well aware that his 'old English' attributions were more than suspect, but included them just the same. And in this context, it is entirely in character that he much preferred to be called 'parson', rather than the newly fashionable 'clergyman'.

Some of the anecdotes stretch credulity, but the Victorian taste revelled in way-out natural history. The reader wanted not only information, but an insight into the strange, the bizarre and wonderful. Stirred with a strong dose of moral rectitude, it was a heady brew, reinforcing the superior attitudes of those made in God's image, and firmly relegating lesser animals to their place.

Benjamin Fawcett deserves much of the credit for the commercial success of the series. With a great capacity for work and business, coupled with an independence of character, he master-minded the long-running production. His main illustrator was A.F. Lydon, but some of the working drawings were by the Reverend Richard Alington, rector of Swinhope, Lincs, an old and valued schoolfriend of Morris. His drawings aimed at being lifelike. None was more heatedly discussed than that of the kestrel, reckoned by some to be a bold and clever attempt to depict the hawk in its typical attitude of hovering, and by others to be an unfortunate headless bird.

The crucial task of engraving the wood-blocks was undertaken by Fawcett himself. He developed his own printing process and in due course his establishment became famous in the trade. As the work gathered momentum he moved to larger premises. The printed pages of bird drawings were coloured individually, by hand. Thirty to forty colourists, mostly female, filled their allotted areas with water-colour, sitting in rows and working on a production line. Some specialized in foliage, some in skies, most dabbed the colours by numbers on to the required portion of the bird's anatomy.

The first part emerged from his printshop to be published at the beginning of June, 1850, by Groombridge and Sons of London, at the agreed retail price of one shilling. Without fail, subsequent parts, each of twenty-four pages and dealing with four birds, complete with four hand-coloured pictures, were issued each month, for seven years. Queen Victoria, having graciously accepted the dedication, regularly received the monthly offering. Prince Albert subscribed for an additional two copies. The publishers, having cautiously advised a print run of 1000 copies, underestimated demand by a handsome margin which must have at once delighted and exasperated Morris. Thousands of pounds of profit were made, the work quickly swept the market, was promptly reissued three times, with four revised editions and two cabinet editions over the years till 1888, only to be overtaken and humbled in due course by yet another parson, the Reverend C.A. Johns.

Without much doubt, the price was a major factor in its success; it put the work well within the reach 'of all classes'. Morris succeeded in his aim of presenting, not a scientific treatise, but a popular, readable and comprehensive treatment, well illustrated and with ample letter-press, aimed at creating a widespread taste for the natural history of birds. The parts were assiduously collected, bound and preserved. Predictably, the bird establishment looked askance and down its nose at this popularization. Professor Alfred Newton, the great ornithologist, regarded the volumes as inferior to anything that had preceded them. He ventured to hope, of his *Dictionary of Birds*, issued as a part-work from 1893, that it might serve as a corrective to those 'indifferent to Natural History, except when highly-coloured pictures are presented to them by popular writers of superficial pretensions'.

In fact Morris lacked literary or scientific pretension; he identified his target audience with precision and wrote for it with skill. He was over-generous with his contributors and he perpetuates the conventional myths and wisdoms. Much of his information came from unreliable and inaccurate sources, so his work was never destined for the shelves of ornithological professors. The pages abound with errors and mistakes and records accepted without discrimination, yet they charmed and delighted their readers, and offered the decided advantage of being almost the only work of moderate price to give a fairly accurate and coloured plate for every species then on the British list.

The volumes succeeded in their aim of converting large numbers to the enjoyment of science, albeit at a modest level. They were employed as text-books by several generations of teachers and advanced students. The coloured plates served innumerable plagiarists, and apparently taxidermists used them as guides to set their specimens for over half a century. For at least the same span local observers used the volumes as identification and field-character guides, and recorded their material accordingly. So Morris found his niche in British ornithological history.

Unfortunately, on the rare occasions when a complete set finds its way to the bookshops, it fetches hundreds of pounds. So the object of this present celebration of Morris's work must surely have found his approval. For the aim is to offer a generous selection of his essays, complete with the finest reproduction of his original plates, at a price which, part for part, and taking honest account of the inflation which would have shocked him profoundly, matches his original offer to the public. Inevitably, much of his voluminous writing has had to be reduced to manageable proportions, but I have carefully tried to cut only the repetitious and totally out-of-date material on distribution, with its interminable references to gentlemen who shot such-and-such a bird on such-and-such a date in such-and-such a county. I have tactfully tidied away some of the more tedious of his correspondents. And I have omitted the plumage descriptions since they do not make for enjoyable reading and are, of course, better available in modern text-books.

Since Morris, surprisingly in view of his declared interests and maritime forbears, is least forthcoming on marine species, it has been possible to leave some of his accounts exactly as written. For the un-expurgated experience, see for instance his entry for the shag (green cormorant), skua, shearwater or fulmar. I hope you will then feel a merciful release applies to earlier pages. The gamebirds and waterfowl are poorly represented, because they are to be the subject of a companion volume, but apart from these it has been the intention to provide a representative selection of Morris's birds, complete with all the flavour and pleasure of his writing. I have deleted long lists of alternative scientific names, retaining only his chosen nomenclature and, incident-ally, his order of classification, plus his translations from the Latin, and his interesting common names, as he would undoubtedly have come back to haunt me if they had been omitted. But I have to say again that his 'old English' names must be taken with a pinch of sea salt, and that no one in his right mind would use this volume as a field guide for late twentieth-century ornithology. Its value is in the nostalgic revelation of bygone attitudes and understanding.

Morris laboured, with love, for over seven years on this project. It must have been with great sadness, mixed no doubt with a measure of relief, that he reached his final bird. And it is abundantly clear that he was loth to quit when he came to the storm petrel (will anyone be surprised that the tidal currents and tempests of scientific classification have moved this inoffensive little bird so that it now occupies one of the *first* pages of the handbooks!). He lingers with pardonable fondness and spills the words in this farewell passage on his well-loved theme. He worked hard, and his work bore a great deal of fruit. His obituary, in the British Ornithologists' Union journal of 1893, says, 'He made no claim to be a scientific ornithologist, but was passionately devoted to the study of our native birds, and took a leading part in the well-justified agitation that has lately spread so far for their protection.'

TO

THE QUEEN'S

MOST GRACIOUS MAJESTY.

———

MADAM,

THE Author of these volumes ventured to solicit for them Your Majesty's patronage, being persuaded that Your Majesty felt interest in a study which both tends to promote the refinement of those who apply themselves to it, and bears witness to the Glory of GOD.

However imperfectly the work has been executed, it cannot but in some degree, from the very nature of the subject, advance these ends.

It is, therefore, humbly dedicated to Your Majesty, in accordance with the permission so graciously given.

Your Majesty's

Loyal and Dutiful Subject and Servant,

FRANCIS ORPEN MORRIS.

PREFACE TO THE FIRST EDITION.

'It is from the great book of Nature, the same through a thousand editions, that I have venturously essayed to read a chapter to the public.'—WAVERLEY.

THE anomaly of custom demands that that which has to be written on the completion of a work, should be made a preface to it, and that an author's last words should be his first.

The several objects had in view in these volumes have been—

First, to collect together, as far as I could, all the known facts respecting the Natural History of each and every British Bird, so that my work might contain a greater number of such facts than any previous one.

Secondly, to produce at the same time a readable book.

Thirdly, to give correct and life-like figures of the several species.

And, fourthly, to bring out the work at such a price as to place it within the reach of every class, whose taste might happily lead them to the study of Natural History.

I have endeavoured also throughout to impart a religious character to this treatise on some of the most interesting works of the CREATOR, as indicated from the very first page by the motto 'Gloria in excelsis Deo' prefixed to the account of the 'birds of the air,' and subsequently by the kindred one 'De profundis ad Dominum' attached in like manner to that of the water-birds, whose home is more or less on the 'great deep.'

How far I have succeeded in each or either of the first-named objects proposed it is for my readers to say, by a comparison of mine with other previous works on the British Birds; in fact, they have already said, as presently alluded to, and I thankfully acknowledge the commendations of those whose praise is a valued reward.

With regard to the last-named particular, the price of the work; this has all along been the great difficulty. The plates could have been executed in a much more highly-finished manner if more had been charged for them, but under the circumstances it was absolutely impossible. Each number contained four coloured plates, every one done by hand, and, excepting the last half-dozen—when materials in the shape of information about the birds had run short —twenty-four well and handsomely printed pages for a shilling, making the book, as far as I know, the cheapest ever brought out in this country.

The critics, and those some of the leading ones, who have already given their opinions of the work while it was in progress, have expressed themselves without exception so favourably, that I trust still to be found to have merited a continuation of their kindness.

In describing the specific characteristics of the birds, I have endeavoured to give an outline of their more prominent features, leaving out those more recondite ones which some authors have gone into. In like manner in the description of the colours I have omitted such names used by other writers as would not, I am sure, be generally understood by the class of readers whom I have especially had in view. It has been my aim, as I have before remarked, to make a readable book, one which should in some distant degree engraft the attractiveness of such writers as Gilbert White, on the necessary details required in the description of species, and I have endeavoured to make the most of the limited space at my disposal, and at all events to convey through the work a sense of some of those delights of the country which, as I enjoy with the utmost thankfulness myself, I feel must be still more valuable on any occasional opportunity to those whose lot has unhappily been cast in towns.

It would not be dutiful in me to conclude without expressing my deep gratitude to Her Most Gracious Majesty the Queen for her condescending patronage, enhanced by the manner in which the favour was communicated by her illustrious husband the Prince Consort. The desire to do a kindly action must, I feel, have been the prevailing motive with Her Majesty, but the work itself, however unworthy, is none the less under obligation for the benefit conferred.

My thanks are likewise due, and are respectfully offered to His Grace the Archbishop of York, who by his considerate sympathy with, and support of my undertaking, has added to former acts of kindness in word and deed.

To the public I am also largely indebted, and I cannot withhold my grateful acknowledgment of the extensive support they have given to my 'History'—some fifty-fold more than my excellent publishers, duly and properly cautious, suggested in the first instance should be provided for. Especially have I to thank those very numerous correspondents, in every rank of life, whose approval, expressed in the most flattering manner, from all parts of the United Kingdom, has afforded me the greatest encouragement while endeavouring to make my labours worthy of their approbation.

But lastly, and above all, let me render thanks and praise where they are most due. Seven years and a half, short as they are to look back upon, are long to look forward to, and are in themselves no inconsiderable proportion even of a longer life than mine; and having been permitted for this lengthened space of time, without let or hindrance, free from accident or disease, to supply regularly month by month the materials for each successive number of my work, I feel that it would not be fitting were I not, now that the task has been completed, to record my grateful sense of the mercy of the Great Author and Preserver of all, without whom not even a sparrow falleth to the ground, and to set forth whose Power and Goodness has not been lost sight of in these volumes. Unless He protect, it is but lost labour to rise early, and late take rest, and eat the bread of carefulness, and in His name all our works should be begun, continued, and ended.

Nunburnholme Rectory, September 14th., 1857.

GOLDEN EAGLE.

RING-TAILED EAGLE. BLACK EAGLE.

ERYR MELYN, OF THE ANCIENT BRITISH.

Aquila chrysaëtos, SELBY. SHAW. JENYNS.

Aquila—An Eagle, possibly from *Aquilus*—Dark—sunburnt.
Chrysaëtos. Chrusos—Gold. *Aietos*—An Eagle.

THE Golden Eagle is so called from the golden red feathers on the
head and nape of the neck. It seems to have established a prescriptive
right, though on what exclusively sufficient grounds it might be difficult
to say, to the proud appellation of the king of birds, as the Tiger, in
the corresponding predatory class among quadrupeds, has obtained that
of 'Royal.' The epithet would however be more appropriately conferred
upon the Lion, 'huic des nominis hujus honorem,' to whom many
noble qualities, to be looked for in vain either in the Tiger or the
Eagle, have in all ages been attributed, though whether even in his
case justly, is more than doubtful.

The flight of the Golden Eagle when not pursuing its prey, is at
first slow and heavy like that of a Heron, and when sailing in the
air much resembles that of the Common Buzzard. In beating a small
space of ground it flies about in circles, alternately sailing and flapping
its wings, the wings seeming as if rather turned upwards during the
former. It prowls generally along the sides of hills, but often ascends
to a vast height when looking out for food, and on perceiving its
quarry, descends upon it like a flash of lightning, though sometimes
in doing so, it will make several spiral turns at intervals, as if to
break the extreme violence of the shock of its fall. The impetus,
aided by the weight of the bird, must be very great. If it does not
then at once discern its victim, which has, perhaps, attempted to hide
itself, it peers about with its outstretched neck in every direction,
when, if it again catch a glimpse of it, as it is almost sure to do, it
is down upon it directly with extended legs, and scarce seeming to
touch it, bears it off in triumph. It usually thus secures the animal,
seizing it before it can even attempt to escape, or perhaps paralyzed
through fear, but occasionally, as in the instances hereafter stated,
follows in pursuit. One is mentioned which was seen hovering above
a hare, which it frightened from bush to bush, until at last it forced

it to leave its cover, and attempt escape, when it was almost immediately overtaken and pounced upon.

It is a curious fact that two Eagles will sometimes course a hare together—one flying directly over it, and the other following it near the ground; and one has been known to stoop at a hare pursued by the hounds, and to carry it off, a hundred yards before them—a singular realization of the fable of Tantalus.

The female is noisy and clamorous at the approach of spring, and also before wet or stormy weather.

The food of the Eagle consists principally of the smaller animals, such as sheep, lambs, dogs, cats, fawns, hares, mountain hares, rabbits, and rats, as also of birds, both old and young, the latter even from the nest, such as blackcock, grouse, ptarmigan, among which it makes great havoc, sea-gulls, and even gannets. It does not hesitate, however, on occasion, to attack larger game, but assails with characteristic resoluteness even roebucks and other deer. It is said to fix itself on the head of the victim it has aimed at, and to flap with its wings in the animal's eyes, until in distraction it is driven over some precipice, or into some morass, where it then becomes a secure and easy prey.

One was seen flying in one of the Orkney Islands with a pig in its talons, which it dropped alive when fired at. Another, in Ireland, alighted and carried off a lamb, with which it flew in a straight direction towards its haunt in the Mourne Mountains. There arrived, it was seen to soar upwards, probably towards its nest, but dropped the lamb at the edge of a wood, and it was recovered unhurt—the distance flown was reckoned to be more than two miles with this burden to support. There are at least three authenticated instances of their having carried off children in this country—one of these in one of the Orkney Islands, and another in the Isle of Skye, but both, providentially, were rescued.

A third instance of the kind is mentioned by Bishop Stanley, but as it happened in one of the Ferroe Islands, it is, at the least, possible that the bird may have been a Sea Eagle. It is said that the child was carried to a precipice so tremendous, that no one, even of the daring climbers of those parts, had ever ventured to ascend it, but the unfortunate mother of the unfortunate child attempted and scaled it, alas! alas! too late. It is melancholy indeed to even think of so sad a chapter in human woe. One can easily believe the truth of another record of a similar event, said to have occurred in Sweden. A mother saw her child, which had been laid down at some distance from her in the fields, carried off by an Eagle, and heard its cries for some time in the air, till it was taken beyond her hearing and sight. She lost her reason, and became an inmate of a lunatic asylum—an asylum truly, for unless the mercy of Providence had thus shrouded her with the mantle of forgetfulness, had provided this anodyne for such heart-rending grief as hers, surely the last cry of her child must for ever have echoed in her ears.

The numbers of animals and birds destroyed by Eagles must be very great: the remains of three hundred ducks and forty hares were found in the eyrie of one. in Germany; and it is on record that a peasant in the county of Kerry, and another in the county of Antrim, supported their families for a considerable time, by means of the animals brought by parent Eagles to their nests. In a nest found by Willughby lay a lamb, a hare, and three heath-poults. In another in Scotland were found a number of grouse, partridges, hares, rabbits, ducks, snipes, ptarmigan, rats, mice, etc., and sometimes kids, fawns, and lambs. With these the house of the owner of the property where the nest was built was frequently supplied. They are very careful in watching, feeding, and defending their young.

The Golden Eagle never feeds on carrion, or fish cast up, unless forced by hunger, when unable to meet with prey to kill for itself.

When the Golden Eagle has pounced upon its victim, it kills it, if small, by a stroke with its talons behind the head, and another at the region of the heart. It seems not to use the bill for slaughter, but only for tearing up its prey when killed. It generally, in spite of its care and skill in skinning or plucking, swallows part of the fur or feathers, or small bones, or part of the bones of the animal or bird it has seized, and these it afterwards disgorges from its mouth in large pellets. It rarely drinks, but is fond of washing itself.

The note is a clear, loud, and sharp cry, of two tones, repeated many times in succession.

Nidification commences towards the beginning of March.

The nest, which is very large and flat, and has no lining, according to some authors, but is stated by others to be lined a little with grass or wool, and where these cannot be procured, or not in sufficient plenty, with small sticks, twigs, rushes, sea-weed, or heather, is generally built on high and inaccessible thunder-blasted rocks, and precipices, or the stump of some tree projecting from them, or the lofty trees of the forest. It builds, however, less frequently on the latter than in other situations, but is said to alight on trees more frequently than the Sea Eagle. It is always, where possible, rebuilt of the same materials—the accustomed eyrie being made use of for many successive years, or, most likely, from the most favourable locality as to food and security combined having been chosen, for many generations, if its owners are not driven from it by their only superior enemy, man.

OSPREY.

FISHING HAWK. FISHING EAGLE. BALD BUZZARD. FISHING BUZZARD.

PYSG ERYR, AND GWALCH Y WEILGI, OF THE ANCIENT BRITISH.

Pandion haliaëtus,   SAVIGNY. VIGORS. SELBY.

Pandion—The name of a Greek hero, changed into a bird of prey.
Haliaëtus. *(H)als*—The sea. *Aietos*—An Eagle.

IT is not every one who has had the fortune—the good fortune—to visit those scenes, where, in this country at least, the Osprey is almost exclusively to be met with. In these, which may in truth be called the times of perpetual motion, there is indeed hardly a nook, or mountain pass, which is not yearly visited by some one or more travellers. Where shall the most secure dweller among the rocks be now free from the intrusion of, in ornithological language, at least 'occasional visitants?' Still the case is not exactly one to which applies the logical term of 'universal affirmative.' Though every spot may be visited, it is not every one who visits it. How many of those who shall read the following description of the Osprey, have taken the 'grand tour' of Sutherlandshire?

In that desolate and romantic region, though even there at wide intervals, and 'far between,' and in a very few other localities, the Fishing Hawk may yet be seen in all the wild freedom of his nature. There it breeds, in the fancied continuance of that safety which has for so many ages been real. You may see, even in the year eighteen hundred and fifty, an occasional eyrie on the top of some rocky islet in the middle of the mountain lake.

The Osprey being so strictly a piscivorous bird, is only met with in the immediate neighbourhood of water; but salt and fresh water fish are equally acceptable to it; and the bays and borders of the sea, as well as the most inland lakes, rivers, and preserves, are its favourite resort: when young, it may even, it is stated, be trained to catch fish.

The Osprey is in some degree, or rather in some situations, a gregarious bird. As many as three hundred pairs have been known to build together in America, which, as before remarked, seems to be by far its most abundant habitat. It is a very frequent circumstance for several pairs thus to congregate, the similarity of their pursuit by no means seeming to interfere with that harmony which should ever prevail among members of the same family. They sometimes unite in a general attack on their common enemy, the White-headed Eagle, and union being strength, succeed in driving him from their fishing grounds, of which they then maintain the peaceable possession.

The flight of the Osprey, though generally slow and heavy like that of the Buzzard, and performed with a scarcely perceptible motion of the wings, and the tail deflected, is strikingly easy and graceful. It rises spirally at pleasure to a great height, darts down perhaps at times, and then again sails steadily on. When looking out for prey, on perceiving a fish which it can strike, it hovers in the air for a few moments, like the Kestrel, with a continual motion of its wings and tail. Its stoop, which follows, though sometimes suspended midway, perhaps from perceiving that the fish has escaped, or to 'make assurance doubly sure,' is astonishingly rapid.

If the fish it has pounced on be at some distance below the surface, the Osprey is completely submerged for an instant, and a circle of foam marks the spot where it has descended: on rising again with its capture, it first, after mounting a few yards in the air, shakes its plumage, which though formed by nature extremely compact for the purpose of resisting the wet as much as possible, must imbibe some degree of moisture, which it thus dislodges. It then immediately flies off to its nest with a cry expressive of success, if it be the breeding season, or to some tree if it is not, and in that situation makes its meal. When this is ended, it usually, though not always, again takes wing and soars away to a great height, or else prowls anew over the waters—unlike the other Hawks, which, for the most part, remain in an apathetic state, the result apparently of satisfied hunger: thus continues the routine of its daily life. Sometimes it is said to devour its food in the air, but I cannot think this; also at times on the spot; if the fish be too large for bearing conveniently away, the prey is held with the head forward. The audacious White-headed Eagle often robs the too patient Osprey of it hardly-toiled-for prey before it has had time to devour it itself, forcing it to drop it in the air, and catching it as it falls.

The Osprey seldom alights on the ground, and when it does so, its movements are awkward and ungainly. It is not in its element but when in the air: occasionally however it remains for several hours together in a sluggish state of repose, perched on some mountain side, hill, rock, or stone.

It builds at very differnt times, in different places—in January, February, March, April, and the beginning of May: the latter month appears in this country to be the period of its nidification. It repairs the original nest, seeming, like many other species, to have a predilection from year to year for the same building place. The saline materials of which it is composed, and perhaps also the oil from the fish brought to it, have the effect, in a few years, of destroying the tree in which it has been placed. The male partially assists the female in the business of incubation, and at other times keeps near her, and provides her with food—she sits accordingly very close. Both birds, when the young are hatched share the task of feeding them with fish, and have even been seen to supply them when they have left the nest, and have been on the wing themselves; they both also courageously defend them against all aggressors, both human and other. They only rear one brood in the year. If one of the parents happen to be killed, the other is almost sure to return, ere long, with a fresh mate: where procured, as in other similar cases, is indeed a mystery.

The nest of the Osprey is an immense pile of twigs, small and large sticks and branches, some of them as much as an inch and a half in diameter—the whole forming sometimes a mass easily discernible at the distance of half a mile or more, and in quantity enough to fill a cart. How it is that it is not blown down, or blown to pieces by a gale of wind, is a question which has yet to be explained. It occasionally is heaped up to the height of from four or five feet to even eight, and is from two to three feet or four in breadth, interlaced and compacted with sea-weed, stalks of corn, grass, or turf; the whole, in consequence of annual repairs and additions, which even in human dwellings often make a house so much larger than it was originally intended to be, not to say unsightly, becoming by degrees of the character described above. It is built either on a tree, at a height of from six, seven, or eight to fifteen feet, and from that to fifty feet from the ground, on a forsaken building, or the ruins of some ancient fortress, erected on the edge of a Highland Loch, the chimney, if the remains of one are in existence, being generally preferred, or on the summit of some insular crag; in fact, it accommodates itself easily to any suitable and favourable situation. Bewick, erroneously following Willughby, (and Mudie him,) says that the Osprey builds its nest 'on the ground, among reeds'— it very rarely indeed does so. It is a curious fact that smaller birds frequently build their nest in the outside of those of the Osprey, without molestation on the one hand, or fear on the other. Larger birds also build theirs in the immediate vicinity, without any disturbance on the part of either.

BUZZARD.

BOD TEIRCAILL, OF THE ANCIENT BRITISH.

Buteo vulgaris,   FLEMING.

Buteo—............   *Vulgaris*—Common.

DR. JOHNSON assigns as the meaning of the word Buzzard, 'a degenerate or mean species of Hawk,' but being by no means one of the admirers of the author of the Dictionary, I shall take leave to differ as much from the present as from another well-known definition of his touching the 'gentle art,' of which for many years I have been a professor.

The Buzzard is plentifully distributed over nearly the whole of the continent of Europe, and is also found in North America, and in the more northern parts of Africa. It inhabits Spain and Italy, Denmark, Sweden, Norway, and Russia, Holland and France, but does not appear to be known in the Orkney or Shetland Islands. In England, Scotland, Wales, and Ireland, it is sufficiently abundant, affecting both the wildest and the most cultivated districts, but in both taking a more than ordinary care to choose such situations as will either exempt it from the intrusion, or enable it to have timely notice of the approach of an enemy. The Rev. George Jeans informs me of one formerly seen for some time at Egham. Still, with all its precautions, and with every aid that its own instinct and the most retired or the most rugged localities can afford, it, like too many others of our native birds, is gradually becoming more rare. The advancement of agriculture upon grounds heretofore wild and uncultivated, the natural consequence of an increase of population within a fixed circumference, and other causes, contributing to this fact, which at all events a naturalist must lament.

The Buzzard is found in a variety of situations, such as rocky cliffs, chases, parks where timber abounds, or in 'ci devant' forests. It remains in England throughout the year, but nevertheless, is partially migratory: this in small companies, frequently, as hereafter stated, in company with the Rough-legged Buzzard.

I am much indebted to my liberal-minded friend, Arthur Strickland, Esq., of Bridlington-Quay, for the following striking notice of the fact of its migration in this country, communicated to him in the year 1847, by his brother, then residing at Coleford, in the Forest of Dean, in Gloucestershire. I must observe that the letter was not originally intended to be published.

'Coleford, 1847.

I have a curious circumstance in ornithology to tell you. There is no account that I have heard of relating particularly to the migration of some of the Hawks, proving them to assemble in flocks for the purpose of migration, and going off together in large parties like Swallows, but of this I have positive proof in the Common Buzzard. On the 2nd. of August, 1847, just at sunset, we were assembled in the yard to the number of five persons; we were busily engaged talking on a fine bright evening: the air was filled as far

Osprey

Buzzard

as we could see, (about forty yards to the north, and one hundred to the south,) with great Hawks, all proceeding together steadily and slowly to the westward. Those immediately above us were within gunshot of the top of the house—with large shot I might have brought some down from where I stood. The man called them Shreaks—a common name for the Wood Buzzard. The evening was so bright, and they were so near, that I saw them as plain as if they were in my hand. They were flying in little parties of from two to five, all these little parties flying so close together that their wings almost touched, whilst each little party was separated from the next about fifteen or twenty yards: fourteen parties passed immediately over us that I counted, but as I did not begin to count them at first, and as I have no doubt the flock extended beyond the boundary of our view, I cannot tell how many the flock consisted of. On this day a remarkable change occurred in the weather, which may have caused an early migration.'

Even when high in the air, particularly on a bright and sunny day, the bars and mottled markings on the wings and tail, the motions of which latter are also clearly discernible in steering its course, appear visibly distinct.

The flight of this species appears heavy, but it is not so in reality: a series of sweeps, when, in piscatorial language, the bird is on the feed. It rises slowly at first, more after the manner of an Eagle than a Falcon, and, when on the wing, proceeds sedately in quest of its prey, which when it perceives, halting sometimes for a moment above, it darts down upon, and generally with unfailing precision. Its quarry is then either 'consumed on the premises,' or carried of for the purpose to some more convenient or more secure place of retreat, or to its nest, to supply the wants of its young. It does not continue on the wing for a very long time together. When not engaged in flight, it will remain, even for hours together, in the same spot—on the stump of a tree, or the point of a cliff, motionless, as some have conjectured, from repletion; and others from being on the look out for prey, at which, when coming within its ken, to stoop in pursuit. It frequents very much the same haunts, and may often be seen from day to day, and at the same hour of the day, beating the same hunting ground.

I am inclined to think that the species of prey most naturally sought by the Buzzard is the rabbit. It feeds, however, for necessity has no law, on a great variety of other kinds of food. It destroys numberless moles, of which it also seems particularly fond, as well as field mice, leverets, rats, snakes, frogs, toads, the young of game, and other birds, newts, worms, and insects. The latter, of the ante-penultimate kind mentioned, it seems to have been thought to have obtained, by some means or other from their pools, but such a supposition is by no means necessary, for those little animals, like many other water reptiles, are often to be found wandering on dry land—out of, and far away from their more proper element. The way in which the Buzzard procures moles is, it is said, by watching patiently by their haunts, until the moving of the earth caused by their subterraneous burrowings, points out to him their exact locality, and the knowledge of it thus acquired he immediately takes advantage of to their destruction. The feet, legs, and bill being often found covered with earth or mud is thus accounted for, and not by his ever feeding on any such substance.

The note of the Common Buzzard is wild and striking, its shrillness conveying a melancholy idea, though as every feeling of melancholy produced by any thing in nature must be, of a pleasing kind—when heard in the retired situations in which this bird delights. One of its local names is the Shreak, evidently derived from the sound of its note.

The Buzzard builds both in trees, and in clefts, fissures, or ledges of mountains and cliffs, and if the latter are chosen, in the most secure and difficult situations. One in particular I remember in a most admirable recess, out of all possible reach except by being lowered down to it by a rope. The nest is built of large and small sticks, and is lined, though sparingly, with wool, moss, hair, or some other soft substance. Not unfrequently, to save the trouble of building a nest of its own, it will appropriate to itself, and repair sufficiently for its purpose, an old and forsaken one of some other bird, such as a Jackdaw, a Crow, or a Raven, and will also occasionally return to its own of the preceding year.

PEREGRINE-FALCON.

HEBOG TRAMOR, CAMMIN, OF THE ANCIENT BRITISH.

Falco peregrinus,   LATHAM. FLEMING.

Falco—To cut with a bill or hook.   *Peregrinus*—A stranger or foreigner—
a traveller from a distant country.

THE Peregrine-Falcon has always been highly prized both living and dead, in the former case for its value in falconry, on account of its courageous spirit and docility, combined with confidence and fearlessness, and in the latter for its handsome and fine appearance. It used to be trained for flying at Herons, Partridges, and other large birds, and in the time of King James the First as much as a thousand pounds of our money was once given for a well-trained 'cast' or pair.

The Peregrine is widely distributed, being found throughout the whole of North America, and in parts of South America, even as far south as the Straits of Magellan, and northwards in Greenland; in Africa, at the Cape of Good Hope; in most countries of Europe, particularly in Russia, along the Uralian chain, Denmark, Norway, Sweden, and Lapland; in Siberia and many parts of Asia; and also in New Holland. The rocky cliffs of this country have hitherto afforded it a comparative degree of protection, but 'protection' seems exploded—explosion in fact sounding the knell of the aristocratic Peregrine.

Strange to say these birds have been known to take up a temporary residence on St. Paul's Cathedral, in London, anything but 'far from the busy hum of men,' preying while there on the pigeons which make it their cote, and a Peregrine has been seen to seize one in Leicester Square.

It is a shy species, and difficult to be approached. It retires to roost about sunset, choosing the high branch of a lofty tree, or the pinnacle of a rocky place. 'Sometimes he is seen in the open fields, seated upon a stone, rock, or hillock, where he quietly waits, watching for his prey.' 'He displays both courage and address in frequent contests with his equals.'

Its flight is extremely rapid, and is doubtless well described by Macgillivray, as strongly resembling that of the Rock Pigeon. It seldom soars or sails after the manner of the Eagles and Buzzards. It does so, indeed, occasionally, but its usual mode of flying is near the ground with quickly repeated beatings of its wings. Montagu has calculated the rate of its flight at as much as one hundred and fifty miles an hour, and Colonel Thornton at about sixty miles. An average of one hundred may I think be fairly estimated. Meyer says that it never strikes at prey near the ground, through an instinctive fear of being dashed to pieces; but the contrary is the fact, its upward sweep preserving it generally from this danger. The recoil, as it were, of the blow which dashes its victim to the earth, overpowers in itself the attraction of gravity, and it rises most gracefully into the air until it has stayed the impetus of its flight. Instances however have been known where both pursuer and pursued have dashed against trees, or even a stone on the ground, in the ardour of pursuing and being pursued, and each has been either stunned for the time, or killed outright by the violence of the blow. Sometimes, in pursuit of its prey, the Peregrine will 'tower' upwards until both are lost to sight. In the breeding season also, both birds may now and then be seen soaring and circling over the place chosen for the nest, and at this period they will seize and hold and convey off to their young the prey they have struck, not dashing it to the ground, a quarry not too large being accordingly singled out. They will at times attack even the Eagle. On alighting they often quiver the wings and shake the tail in a peculiar manner, and when standing frequently nod or bow down the head quickly. They are fond of basking, lying down at full length on the ground, and at times resting in a perfectly sitting posture, with the legs flat under them.

The food of the species before us consists principally of birds, such as the larger and smaller sea-gulls, auks, guillemots, puffins, larks, pigeons, ptarmigan, rooks, jackdaws, woodcocks, land-rails, wild geese, and even at times the Kestrel, partridges, plovers, grouse, curlews, teal, and ducks; but it also feeds on hares, rabbits, rats, and other small quadrupeds, as well as at times on larger ones, such as dogs and cats, and also occasionally on fish. The plumage of its feathered game is carefully plucked off before they are eaten. It is said to harass the grey crows, but not to use them for food. Some cases have been known of Peregrines having fallen into the sea, and been drowned, together with birds which they had struck when flying over it: the more remarkable as the prey so seized were only small, and far inferior in size to themselves: probably they had been in some way hampered or clogged, as a good swimmer may be by a drowning boy, so that although if they had fallen on the land, they might have extricated themselves, yet such opportunity has been lost by their mischance of dropping into the sea, and they have met with a watery grave.

It is very curious how these and all the other birds which form the food of the one before us, live in its immediate vicinity, without any apparent fear or dread. They seem patiently to 'bide their time,' and take their chance of being singled out from their fellows. Perhaps with equal wisdom to that of the followers of the Prophet, they are believers in fatalism, and, content with the knowledge that whatever

Peregrine-Falcon

is, is, and whatever will be, will be, live a life of security, and resign it at the 'fiat' of the Peregrine, as a matter of course. This applies to cases where both are residents together; where however, strange to say, the Peregrine is only a straggling visitor, his presence but for a day or two has the effect of dispersing the flocks of birds which had been peacefully enjoying themselves before his arrival. Its mode of striking its prey has been variously described. It has by many been supposed to stun its victim by the shock of a blow with its breast, and by others it has been known to rip a furrow in its quarry completely from one end of the back to the other, with its talons or bill. In the former case it is said to wheel about, and return to pick up the quarry it has struck. It is, as may be supposed, the terror of all it pursues, which, rather than venture again on the wing while it is in the neighbourhood, will suffer themselves to be taken by the hand.

Feeding as the Hawks do, on birds and animals, they have the habit, partaken of likewise by several other genera of birds, of casting up the indigestible part of their food, which in the present case consists of fur and feathers, in small round or oblong pellets.

The note of the Peregrine is loud and shrill, but it is not often heard except in the beginning of the breeding season.

The nest, which is flat in shape, is generally built on a projection or in a crevice of some rocky cliff. It is composed of sticks, sea-weed, hair, and other such materials. Sometimes the bird will appropriate the old nest of some other species, and sometimes be satisfied with a mere hollow in the bare rock, with occasionally a little earth in it. It also builds in lofty trees.

A simple but ingenious way of catching the young of these and other Hawks, is mentioned by Charles St. John, Esq., in his entertaining 'Tour in Sutherlandshire.' A cap or 'bonnet' is lowered 'over the border' of the cliff, down upon the nest; the young birds strike at, and stick their claws into it, and are incontinently hauled up in triumph.

The eggs are two, three, four, or, though but rarely, five in number, and rather inclining to rotundity of form. Their ground colour is light russet red, which is elegantly marbled over with darker shades, patches, and streaks of the same.

KESTREL.

WINDHOVER. STONEGALL. STANNEL HAWK.

CUDYLL COCH, CEINLLEF GOCH, OF THE ANCIENT BRITISH.

Falco Tinnunculus, MONTAGU. SELBY.

Falco—To cut with a bill or hook.
Tinnunculus, Conjectured from *Tinnio*—To chirp.

THIS species is in my opinion, not only, as it is usually described to be, one of the commonest, but the commonest of the British species of Hawks. It is found in all parts of Europe—Denmark, France,

Italy, Spain, Norway, Sweden, Lapland, Greece, and Switzerland; and also in Asia in Siberia; in Central Africa, and at the Cape of Good Hope; so too, according to Meyer, in America. It is easily reclaimed, and was taught to capture larks, snipes, and young partridges. It becomes very familiar when tamed, and will live on terms of perfect amity with other small birds, its companions. One of its kind formed, and perhaps still forms, one of the so-called 'Happy Family,' to be seen, or which was lately to be seen, in London. The Kestrel has frequently been taken by its pursuing small birds into a room or building. It does infinitely more good than harm, if indeed it does any harm at all, and its stolid destruction by gamekeepers and others is much to be lamented, and should be deprecated by all who are able to interfere for the preservation of a bird which is an ornament to the country.

Other species of Hawk may be seen hovering in a fixed position in the air, for a brief space, the Common Buzzard for instance, but most certainly the action, as performed by the Kestrel, is both peculiar to and characteristic of itself alone, in this kingdom at least. No one who has lived in the country can have failed to have often seen it suspended in the air, fixed, as it were, to one spot, supported by its out-spread tail, and by a quivering play of the wings, more or less perceptible.

The food of the Kestrel consists of the smaller animals, such as field mice, and the larger insects, such, namely, as grasshoppers, beetles, and caterpillars: occasionally it will seize and destroy a wounded partridge, but when seen hovering over the fields in the peculiar and elegant manner, so well illustrated by my friend the Rev. R. P. Alington in the engraving which is the accompaniment of this description, and from which the bird derives one of its vernacular names, it is, for the most part, about to drop upon an insect. Small birds, such as sparrows, larks, chaffinches, blackbirds, linnets, and goldfinches, frequently form part of its food, but one in confinement, while it would eat any of these, invariably refused thrushes; one, however, has been seen, after a severe struggle to carry off a missletoe thrush. The larvæ of water insects have also been known to have been fed on by them, and in one instance a leveret, or rabbit, and in another a rat. Slow-worms, frogs, and lizards are often articles of their food, as also earth-worms, and A. E. Knox, Esq. possesses one shot in Sussex in the act of killing a large adder. Thirteen whole lizards have been found in the body of one. Another has been seen devouring a crab, and another, a tame one, the result doubtless of its education, as man has been defined to be 'a cooking animal,' a hot roasted pigeon. 'De gustibus non disputandum.'

'The Kestrel,' says the late Bishop Stanley, 'has been known to dart upon a weasel, an animal nearly its equal in size and weight, and actually mount aloft with it. As in the case of the Eagle, it suffered for its temerity, for it had not proceeded far when both were observed to fall from a considerable height. The weasel ran off unhurt, but the Kestrel was found to have been killed by a bite in the throat.'

It is a curious fact that notwithstanding their preying on small birds, the latter will sometimes remain in the trees in which they are, without any sign of terror or alarm. They have been known to carry off young chickens and pigeons. When feeding on insects which are of light weight, they devour them in the air, and have been seen to take a cockchaffer in each claw. Bewick says that the Kestrel swallows mice whole, and ejects the hair afterwards from its mouth, in round pellets —the habit of the other Hawks. Buffon relates that 'when it has seized and carried off a bird, it kills it, and plucks it very neatly before eating it. It does not take so much trouble with mice, for it swallows the smaller whole, and tears the others to pieces. The skin is rolled up so as to form a little pellet, which it ejects from the mouth. On putting these pellets into hot water to soften and unravel them, you find the entire skin of the mouse, as if it had been flayed.'

The note of the Windhover is clear, shrill, and rather loud, and is rendered by Buffon by the words 'pli, pli, pli,' or 'pri, pri, pri.' It is several times repeated, but is not often heard except near its station, and that in the spring.

I am indebted to my obliging friend, the Rev. J. W. Bower, of Barmston, in the East-Riding, for the first record that I am aware of, of the breeding of the Kestrel in confinement. The following is an **extract from his letter dated November 30th., 1849**, relating the circumstance:—'A pair of Kestrels bred this summer in my aviary. The female was reared from a nest about four years ago, and the year after scratched a hole in the ground, and laid six or seven eggs, but she had no mate that year. Last winter a male Kestrel pursued a small bird so resolutely as to dash through a window in one of the cottages here, and they brought the bird to me. I put him into the aviary with the hen bird, and they lived happily together all the summer, and built a nest or scratched a hole in the ground, and she laid five eggs, sat steadily, and brought off and reared two fine young ones.' Some pairs of Kestrels seem to keep together throughout the winter. About the end of March is the period of nidification. The young are at first fed with insects, and with animal food as they progress towards maturity. They are hatched the latter end of April or the beginning of May.

The nest, which is placed in rocky cliffs on the sea-coast or elsewhere, is also, where it suits the purpose of the birds, built on trees, in fact quite as commonly as in the former situation; sometimes in the holes of trees or of banks, as also occasionally on ancient ruins, the towers of churches, even in towns and cities, both in the country and in London itself, and also in dove-cotes. Sometimes the deserted nest of a Magpie, Raven, or Jackdaw, or some other of the Crow kind is made use of. 'Few people are, indeed, aware,' says Bishop Stanley, 'of the numbers of Hawks existing at this day in London. On and about the dome of St. Paul's, they may be often seen, and within a very few years, a pair, for several seasons, built their nest and reared their brood in perfect safety between the golden dragon's wings which formed the weathercock of Bow Church, in Cheapside. They might be easily distinguished by the thousands who walked below, flying in and out or circling round the summit of the spire, notwithstanding the constant motion and creaking noise of the weathercock, as it turned round at every change of the wind.' When built in trees, the nest is composed of a few sticks and twigs, put together in a slovenly manner, and lined with a little hay, wool, or feathers: if placed on rocks, hardly any nest is compiled—a hollow in the bare rock or earth serving the purpose.

Kestrel

Sparrow-Hawk

SPARROW-HAWK.

PILAN, GWEPIA, OF THE ANCIENT BRITISH.

Accipiter fringillarius,   SHAW. SELBY.

Accipiter—Accipio—To take.   *Fringillarius—Fringilla*—A Finch.

'TAKE it for all in all,' there is perhaps no bird of the Hawk kind more daring and spirited than the one before us—next to the Kestrel the most common of the British species of that tribe. It hunts in large woods, as well as in the open fields, and may frequently be seen sweeping over hedges and ditches in every part of the country. In the winter the males and females, like the chaffinches, appear to separate: the motive is of course unknown.

It prefers cultivated to uncultivated districts, even when the latter abound in wood, though wooded districts are its favourite resorts. The Rev. Leonard Jenyns says that in Cambridgeshire the males are much less frequently seen than the females, and this observation appears to be also general in its application, not as we may suppose from any disparity in numbers between the two, but from the female being of a more bold, and the male of a more shy and retiring disposition.

The organ of combativeness, according to phrenologists, would appear to be largely developed in this bird: it seems to have universal letters of marque, and to act the part of a privateer against everything that sails in its way—a modern specimen of 'Sir Andrew Barton, Knight.' It will fearlessly attack in the most pugnacious manner even the monarch of the air—the Golden Eagle, and has been known so far to obtain the mastery, as to make him drop a grouse which he had made a prize of: one has been seen after a first buffet, to turn again and repeat the insult; and another dashed in the same way at a tame Sea Eagle which belonged to R. Langtry, Esq., of Fortwilliam, near Belfast.

The Sparrow-Hawk occasionally perches on some projection or eminence of earth, stone, or tree, from whence it looks out for prey. If successful in the ken, it darts suddenly off, or if otherwise, launches into the air more leisurely. When prowling on the wing, it sweeps along, apparently with no exertion, swiftly, but gently and stealthily, at one moment gliding without motion of the wings, and then seeming to acquire an impetus for itself by flapping them, every obstacle in the way being avoided with the most certain discrimination, or surmounted with an aërial bound. Sometimes for a few moments it hovers over a spot, and after flying on a hundred yards or so, repeats the same action, almost motionless in the air. Its flight is at times exceedingly rapid, and it was formerly employed in the art of falconry, for hunting partridges, landrails, and quails.

Unlike the Kestrel, which has a predilection for quadrupeds, the food of this species consists principally of the smaller birds, and some that are larger—snipes, larks, jays, blackbirds, swallows, sparrows, lapwings, buntings, pigeons, partridges, thrushes, pipits, linnets, yellowhammers, bullfinches, finches, as also, occasionally, mice, cockchaffers and other beetles, grasshoppers, and even sometimes when in captivity, its own species; small birds are devoured whole, legs and all; the larger are plucked. Of two which I lately had in my possession, kept in an empty greenhouse belonging to a friend, one was found dead one morning, and partly devoured; and I have heard of another similar instance. Whether it had died a natural or a violent death is uncertain, but as they quarrelled over their food—they were both females—the latter is the most probable. Mr. Selby says that he has often known such cases. The first blow of the Sparrow-Hawk is generally fatal, such is the determined force with which with unerring aim it rushes at its victim; sometimes indeed it is fatal to itself. One has been known to have been killed by dashing through the glass of a greenhouse, in pursuit of a blackbird which had sought safety there through the door; and another in the same way by flying against the windows of the college of Belfast, in the chase of a small bird. The voracity and destructiveness of this species is clearly shewn by the fact, witnessed by A. E. Knox, Esq., of no fewer than fifteen young pheasants, four young partridges, five chickens, two larks, two pipits, and a bullfinch, having been found in and about the nest of a single pair at one time. One was shot in Scotland which contained three entire birds, a bunting, a sky lark, and a chaffinch, besides the remains of a fourth of some other species. The young appeared to have been catered for in the place of their birth by their parents, even after they were able to fly to some distance from it. A pigeon has been known to have been carried by a female Sparrow-Hawk a distance of one hundred and fifty yards.

Small birds in their turn sometimes pursue and tease their adversary in small flocks, but generally keeping at a respectful distance, either a little above, or below, or immediately behind: their motive, however, is at present, and will probably remain, like many other arcana of nature, inexplicable. A male Sparrow-Hawk which had a small bird in its talons, has been seen pursued by a female for a quarter of an hour through all the turns and twists by which he avoided her, and successfully, so long as the chase was witnessed.

'In pursuit of prey,' says Bishop Stanley, 'they will not unfrequently evince great boldness. We knew of one which darted into an upper room, where a goldfinch was suspended in a cage, and it must have remained there some time, and continued its operations with great perseverance, as on the entrance of the lady to whom the poor bird belonged, it was found dead and bleeding at the bottom, and its feathers plentifully scattered about.' See, however, the effect—the good effect—of education. 'Even the Sparrow-Hawk,' says the same kind-hearted writer, 'which by some has been considered of so savage and wild a nature as to render all means for taming it hopeless, has, nevertheless, in the hands of more able or more patient guardians, proved not only docile, but amiable in its disposition. About four years ago, a young Sparrow-Hawk was procured and brought up by a person who was fond of rearing a particular breed of pigeons, which he greatly prized on account of their rarity. By good management and kindness he so far overcame the natural disposition of this Hawk, that in time it formed a friendship with the pigeons, and associated with them. At first the pigeons were rather shy of meeting their natural enemy on such an occasion, but they soon became familiarized, and approached without fear. It was curious to observe the playfulness of the Hawk, and his perfect good humour during the feeding time; for he received his portion without any of that ferocity with which birds of prey usually take their food, and merely uttered a cry of lamentation when disappointed of his morsel. When the feast was over, he would attend the pigeons in their flight round and round the house and gardens, and perch with them on the chimney-top or roof of the house; and this voyage he never failed to take early every morning, when the pigeons took their exercise. At night he retired and roosted with them in the dove-cote, and though for some days after his first appearance he had it all to himself, the pigeons not liking such an intruder, they shortly became good friends, and he was never known to touch even a young one, unfledged, helpless, and tempting as they must have been. He seemed quite unhappy at any separation from them, and when purposely confined in another abode he constantly uttered most melancholy cries, which were changed to tones of joy and satisfaction on the appearance of any person with whom he was familiar. The narrator of the above concludes his account by adding, that he was as playful as a kitten and as loving as a dove.'

The nest, which has frequently been the previous tenement of a crow, magpie, or other bird, is built in fir or other trees, or even bushes of but moderate height, as also in the crevices or on ledges of rocks, and on old ruins. It is large in size, flat in shape, and composed of twigs, sometimes with, but often without a little lining of feathers, hair, or grass. This species seems, however, to be but seldom its own architect, but the same nest is sometimes resorted to from year to year; in fact, it is the opinion of Mr. Hewitson, no mean one, that the Falcons very rarely make a nest for themselves; an action of ejectment is commenced in person against some other tenant at its own will of its own property —no notice to quit having previously been given—and, notwithstanding this legal defect, forcible possession proves to be nine points of the law, and 'contumely' is all the satisfaction that 'patient merit of the unworthy takes.'

TAWNY OWL.

DILLYAN FRECH, DILLUAN RUDD, ADERYN Y CYRPH, OF THE ANCIENT BRITISH.

BROWN OWL.

Ulula stridula,   SELBY.

Ulula. Ululare—To howl like a wolf.   *Stridula*—Harsh—grating—creaking.

HERE is another victim of persecution! Were it not for the friendly shelter of the night, and the fostering care of some few friends, where is the Owl that would be able to maintain a place among the 'Feathered Tribes' of England? Their 'passports' are invariably sent to them in the form of cartridge paper; a double-barrelled gun furnishes a ready 'missive;' their 'congè' is given with a general 'discharge,' and the unoffending, harmless, nay, useful bird, is ordered for ever to 'quit.' His family are not permitted to hold their own, but are themselves outlawed and proscribed; their dwelling is confiscated, a 'clearance' is effected; and if there are a wife and children, 'alack for woe!' They are carried into captivity. You have my pity, at all events, 'Bonny Brown Owl;' and, believe me, I would that the expression of it might do you a kindness; but I have sad misgivings —you are a marked bird—they have given you a bad name, and the proverb tells you the fatal consequence.

The Tawny Owl, or Brown Owl, is known in many countries of Europe—Lapland and Scandinavia generally, Russia, Spain, Italy, and others; as also in Asia Minor and Japan. One is mentioned by Bishop Stanley as having alighted on the main-top-gallant yard of a ship he was on board of in the Mediterranean, at a distance of eighty miles from land. It is a common species in England, but is more rare in Scotland, especially in the northern parts, and the Orkney Islands: two have been met with in the Queen's County, in Ireland. In Yorkshire near Barnsley, Huddersfield, and Halifax, the 'Manufacturing Districts,' it is but rarely seen, but in other parts of the country not unfrequently, at least such was once the case. Wooded districts are its resort, and from these it only issues, voluntarily, at night, which, as with our antipodes, is its day. In the winter, when the trees ordinarily no longer afford it a covert, it secretes itself in old buildings, or the hollows of trees, or in evergreens, such as firs and holly, and in ivy.

If disturbed during the day-time, and frightened from its retreat, it flies about in a bewildered manner, the light doubtless being unnatural and uncongenial to it. It may easily, in this state, be overtaken and knocked down with sticks and stones. One was shot in the middle of Romney Marsh near noon of day in 1860. The twilight of morning and evening is the time to see it enjoying its fitful flight.

The following anecdote of a bird of this species is related by Mr. Couch, in his 'Illustrations of Instinct:'—'A Brown Owl had long been in the occupation of a convenient hole in a hollow tree; and in it for several years had rejoiced over its progeny, with hope of the pleasure to be enjoyed in excursions of hunting in their company: but, through the persecutions of some persons on the farm, who had watched the bird's proceedings, this hope had been repeatedly disappointed by the plunder of the nest at the time when the young ones were ready for flight. On the last occasion, an individual was ascending their retreat to repeat the robbery, when the parent bird, aware of the danger, grasped her only young one in her claws, and bore it away, and never more was the nest placed in the same situation.' These birds are easily tamed, and become quite domestic. 'They are at first,' says Montagu, 'very shy, but soon become tame if fed by hand. If put out of doors within hearing of the parent birds, they retain their native shyness, as the old ones visit them at night, and supply them with ample provision.' Even if taken in the mature state they may be tamed without difficulty. They have never been known to drink. So I wrote in my first edition of this work, but since writing the above Mrs. Gwilt, of Hereford Square, South Kensington, has written of a tame one she has:—'There is a large cage for him with a zinc bath, which about once in ten days he enters in the morning on a dry day, and on those days never goes to sleep as on others. When drinking he as it seems 'scoops' up the water about three times and seems to enjoy it.' Also, Mr. M. C. Cooke informs me that he has known a tame one which used to drink repeatedly, as well as to wash itself, holding up its head after each draught, as a fowl does. The following curious account has been furnished to me by Mr. Chaffey, of Doddington, Kent: —'My old Owl, a brown one, I had in my possession twenty-six years. When she was about sixteen years old, she laid two eggs, and sat upon them some time before I discovered it; as soon as I did I took them away, and replaced them with two bantam's eggs, upon which she sat about a fortnight, and then forsook them. Last year she again laid two eggs, one of them only having a hard shell; she sat upon the one egg for about a fortnight, when I removed it and found it addled. I then took it away, and procured a hen's egg which had been sat upon about the same time, and which in due time she hatched. Never in my life did I see any bird half so tender and careful of their young as she was. For the first four days she hardly let it have time to feed, taking it by the neck out of my hand, and running with it into the dark corner where it was hatched. After a short time it would eat as freely as the old one. When the chicken was about three months old, the poor old Owl choked herself by swallowing part of a fowl which I had given her for her supper. I had turned the male Owl out as the chicken was hatched. He used to come every evening to the place and remain there for hours, till the death of the other bird, after which I saw or heard nothing more of him. The chicken grew up a very fine bird.'

The flight of the Brown Owl is rather heavy and slow, particularly at its first entering on the wing.

The food of this species consists of leverets, young rabbits, moles, rats, mice, and other small quadrupeds; birds of various kinds, frogs, beetles, and other insects, worms, and even fish.

Every one must love the whooping of the 'Madge Howlett.' The note resembles the syllables 'hoo-hoo-hoo,' 'to-hoot,' 'to-hoo,' and it also occasionally utters a harsh scream. The former is as if the letter O were long produced in a loud and clear tone, and then after short intermission repeated in a tremulous manner, and the latter has been likened by Waterton to the word 'quo-ah.' I may here observe, in reference to the generic name prefixed to this species, that the name of the Owl is probably a corruption of the word 'howl.' Meyer describes the note as resembling a satirical laugh.

Nidification commences in March. The nest, if it deserves the name, is formed of a few soft feathers, some straws, or a little moss, sometimes merely of the decayed wood in the hollow of the tree in which it is placed; and one has been observed so low down that a person could see into it from the ground; occasionally it is built in rocks, sometimes it is said, in barns or the like buildings, or even in the deserted nests of other birds, such as buzzards, crows, and magpies. The young are hatched in April: they continue to perch among the branches of trees in the neighbourhood of the nest before finally taking their leave of it, and are fed during this interval by the parent birds.

The eggs are white, and from two or three to four or five in number: the first is sat on as soon as laid, and the young are hatched in about three weeks: they are blind for some days, and their red eyelids look as if inflamed.

WHITE OWL.

DILLYAN WEN, OF THE ANCIENT BRITISH.

YELLOW OWL.   BARN OWL.   SCREECH OWL.   GILLI-HOWLET.   HOWLET.
MADGE OWL.   CHURCH OWL.   HISSING OWL.

Strix flammea,   PENNANT.   MONTAGU.

Strix—Some species of Owl.   *Flammea*—Of the colour of flame—yellow.

THIS bird, a 'high churchman,' is almost proverbially attached to
the Church, within whose sacred precincts it finds a sanctuary, as others
have done in former ages, and in whose 'ivy-mantled tower' it securely
rears its brood. The very last specimen but one that I have seen was
a young bird perched on the exact centre of the 'reredos' in Charing
Church, Kent, where its ancestors for many generations have been
preserved by the careful protection of the worthy curate, my old en-
tomological friend, the Rev. J. Dix, against the machinations of mis-
chievous boys, and the 'organ of destructiveness' of those who ought
to know better.

One of these birds after having been tamed for some time, was found
to be in the habit for some months, of taking part of its food to a
wild one, which overcame its shyness so far as to come near the house,
and it would then return to the kitchen and eat the remainder of its
portion. Another of them is described by Meyer, as so tame 'that it
would enter the door or window of the cottage, as soon as the family
sat down to supper, and partake of the meal, either sitting upon the
back of a chair, or venturing on the table; and it was sometimes seen
for hours before the time watching anxiously for the entrance of the
expected feast. This exhibition was seen regularly every night.' If
captured when grown up, it sometimes refuses food, and its liberty in
such, indeed in any case, should be given it. In cold weather a
number of these birds have been found sitting close together for the
purpose of keeping each other warm. The male and female consort
together throughout the year. If aroused from their resting-place
during the day, they fly about in a languid, desultory manner, and
are chased and teased by chaffinches, tomtits, and other small birds,
by whom indeed they are sometimes molested in their retreat, as well
as by the urchins of the village.

The flight of this bird, which is generally low, is pre-eminently soft,
noiseless, and volatile. It displays considerable agility on the wing,
and may be seen in the tranquil summer evening turning backward
and forward over a limited extent of beat. It also, its movements
being no doubt directed by the presence or absence of food, makes
more extended peregrinations in its 'night-errantry.' If its domicile
be at some distance, it flies regularly at the proper time, which is
that of twilight, or moonlight, to the same haunt. During the day it
conceals itself in hollow trees, rocks, buildings, and evergreens, or
some such covert. It is a bird of a cultivated taste, preferring even
villages and towns themselves, as well as their neighbourhoods, to the
mountains or forests, and frequents buildings, church steeples, crevices,
and holes in walls, for shelter and a roosting place, as also, occasionally,
trees in unfrequented spots. Montagu says that it sometimes flies by

day, particularly in the winter, or when it has young. When at rest it stands in an upright position.

Moles, rats, shrews, and mice, are extensively preyed on by the bird before us: as many as fifteen of the latter have been found close to the nest of a single pair, the produce of the forage of one night, or rather part of the produce, for others doubtless must have been devoured before morning. He who destroys an Owl is an encourager of vermin—nine mice have been found in the stomach of one—a veritable 'nine killer.' It is very interesting to watch this bird, when hunting for such prey, stop short suddenly in its buoyant flight, and drop in the most adroit manner to the earth, from which it for the most part speedily re-ascends with its booty in its claws; occasionally, however, it remains on the spot for a considerable time, 'and this,' says Sir William Jardine, 'is always done at the season of incubation for the support of the young.' It also occasionally eats small birds— thrushes, larks, buntings, sparrows, and others, as also beetles and other insects. A tame one kept in a large garden, killed a lapwing, its companion.

The White Owl is said to collect and hoard up food in its place of resort, as a provision against a day of scarcity. It seizes its prey in its claw, and conveys it therein, for the most part, when it has young to feed; one however has been seen to transfer it from its claw to its bill while on the wing; but, as Bishop Stanley observes, 'it is evident that as long as the mouse is retained by the claw, the old bird can- not avail itself of its feet in its ascent under the tiles, or approach to their holes; consequently, before it attempts this, it perches on the nearest part of the roof, and there removing the mouse from its claw to its bill, continues its flight to the nest. Some idea may be formed of the number of mice destroyed by a pair of Barn Owls, when it is known that in the short space of twenty minutes two old birds carried food to their young twelve times, thus destroying at least forty mice every hour during the time they continued hunting, and as young Owls remain long in the nest, many hundreds of mice must be destroyed in the course of rearing them.'

The note of this species is a screech—a harsh prolongation of the syllables 'tee-whit,' and it seldom, if ever, hoots. It has been asserted that it never hoots, but 'never's a bold word:' Sir William Jardine is not the man to misstate a fact. What if the White Owl should be to be added to the number of mocking birds? The Rev. Andrew Matthews' reasoning on this subject is somewhat obscure: he is of opinion that the White Owl does not hoot, and in corroboration thereof, says that while a tame Brown Owl lived, the large trees round the house were nightly the resort of 'many wild birds of this species,' who left no doubt about their note, but after his death, though the screeching continued, the hooting ceased.

If attacked, these birds turn on their backs, and snap and hiss. The young while in the nest make an odd kind of snoring noise, which seems to be intended as a call to their parents for food.

The White Owl builds its nest, for the most part, in old and deserted, as well as in existing buildings and ruins, chimneys, caves, or mouldering crevices, barns, dove-cotes, church steeples, pigeon lofts, and, but very rarely, in hollow trees, also in rocks, where none of the former are to be had. With the pigeons, if there are any in the place, they live in the most complete harmony, and often unjustly

Tawny Owl

White Owl

bear the blame of the depredations committed by jackdaws and other misdemeanants, both quadruped and biped.

The nest, if one be made at all, for oftentimes a mere hollow serves the purpose, is built of a few sticks or twigs, lined with a little grass or straw, or, though but seldom, with hair or wool, and this is all that it fabricates, and to but a small extent either of bulk or surface.

The appearance of this Owl, owing to its somewhat wedge-shaped face, is very singular, especially when asleep, as it is then even more elongated. The whole plumage is beautifully clean and pure.

BLUE TIT.

Y LLEIAN, LLYGODEN Y DERW, OF THE ANCIENT BRITISH.

BLUE-CAP. BLUE-BONNET. NUN. TOMTIT. BLUE MOPE. BILLY-BITER. HICKMALL.

Parus cœruleus,	MONTAGU. BEWICK. SELBY.
Parus—...........?	*Cœruleus*—Blue—azure.

FROM the window of my study, in which, 'ubi quid datur' (or rather detur) 'oti,' the 'midnight oil' is burned, by which 'illudo chartis'— in plain English, in which this work is written, I have almost daily opportunities of watching the interesting actions of this pretty little bird, which I shall accordingly describe.

They are not migratory, but in or before hard weather they move southwards, to escape the severity of the north, returning when that cause is removed. In the autumn, after the cares of bringing up a family are over, they often approach nearer to houses and gardens, and may be seen on almost every hedge.

These birds are of a pugnacious disposition, and frequently quarrel with their neighbours, as well as among themselves: the Robin, however, is quite master of the field. Two were once observed so closely engaged in combat, that they both suffered themselves to be captured by a gentleman who saw them. They are very bold and spirited, and are caught without difficulty in traps. They often assail their enemy, the Hawk—the destroyer of their species, chasing him in the same way that Swallows do; as also Magpies, Thrushes, and any other suspicious characters, and the Owl they are particularly inveterate against. They bite severely if caught, and the hen bird in like manner will attack any one who molests her when sitting, in the discharge of which duty she is so devoted that she will sometimes suffer herself to be taken off the nest with the hand; otherwise, if the nest be disturbed in her absence, she forsakes it. One has been known to sit still while a part of the tree which guarded the entrance of her retreat was sawn off.

When the young are hatched, both birds become very clamorous, and have even been known to fly at and attack persons approaching the nest. They pass most of their time in trees, after the manner of the other Titmice, often frequenting the same locality from day to day for some time, in search of food. 'So nimble are they,' says J. J. Briggs, Esq., 'in this operation, that having once alighted on the stem of a plant, be it ever so fragile, and though it bends from its perpendicular until the end almost touches the roots, the bird rarely quits his hold until he finishes his examination of the leaves.' They also alight on the ground, or in a stubble field, to pick up what they may meet with there, and cling with perfect ease, for the like purpose, to the smooth bark of a tree, a wall, or a window-frame, when they sometimes tap at the window, like the familiar Redbreast, possibly looking at the reflection of themselves: from these habits their claws are often much worn. All their motions are extremely quick, nimble, and active. In the spring they are mostly seen in pairs, in the summer in families, and later on in the year, occasionally, in small flocks. They frequent cultivated districts, and are to be seen in any and every place where timber abounds or hedgerows exist, in greater or less abundance. They roost at night in ivy, or the holes of walls and trees, and under the eaves of thatched places, or in any snug corner. They are the most familiar, and perhaps the most lively of the genus. In severe winters they often perish from cold.

The flight of this species is rather unsteady, executed by repeated flappings, and if lengthened is undulated.

The Blue-cap seems to be omnivorous in its appetite. Its principal food consists of caterpillars, spiders, moths, and other insects, and their eggs. In quest of these it plucks off numberless buds, but it is at least questionable whether the remedy is not even in this case far better than the disease, for doubtless the insects or their eggs, which it thus destroys, would eventually otherwise consume those very leaves, now, though prematurely, 'nipped in the bud.' 'In what evil hour, and for what crime,' says Mr. Knapp, 'this poor little bird could have incurred the anathema of a parish, it is difficult to conjecture. An item passed in one of our late churchwardens' accounts, was 'for seventeen dozen of Tomtits' heads.'' A few peas are the extent of its depredations. Grain, especially oats, which they hold between their claws, and pick at until they twitch them from the husk, seeds, and berries, they likewise feast on; they are fond also of animal food, and will, occasionally, so some say, destroy other small birds. They have been observed by J. J. Briggs, Esq., to carry food—a caterpillar, or an insect, to the young, three or four times every ten minutes. Mr. Weir communicated to Mr. Macgillivray his observations on their feeding their young, from a quarter-past two in the morning, to half-past eight in the evening, and found that they did so in that period, on the average of the different hours, four hundred and seventy-five times, each time bringing at least one caterpillar, and sometimes two or three, so that probably this one pair of birds destroyed six or seven hundred in the course of a single day. The destruction of the Blue-cap by the farmer or gardener is an act of economical suicide. Well has the author of the book of Ecclesiasticus written, 'all things are double one against another, and GOD has made nothing imperfect.'

Meyer renders the note of the Blue Tomtit by the words 'zit, zit;' 'tzitee,' and 'tsee, tsee, tsirr,' which is, I think, as near as it can be approached; and shews that a comparison of it by one of my school-fellows to the words in the Latin Grammar 'me te se, præter que ne ve,' was far from being inapt, as in truth it is not. Macgillivray gives us 'chica, chica, chee, chee,' as also 'chirr-r-r.' It has also a sort of scream—a signal of alarm, and the hen bird, when sitting on the nest, hisses at any enemy, and spits like a kitten, ruffling up her feathers at the same time. 'Many a young intruder,' says Mr. Knapp, 'is deterred from prosecuting any farther search, lest he should rouse the vengeance of some lurking snake or adder.' In the spring of the year I have heard this bird utter a very pleasing and decided song, though of weak sound. My brother, Beverley R. Morris, Esq., M.D., has also related a similar instance in the 'Naturalist,' volume ii, page 108.

The nest, which is composed of grass and moss, and lined with hair, wool, and feathers, and is built in March or April, is usually placed in a hole of a tree, about half a dozen or a dozen feet from the ground, or even close to it. I have seen one myself near the top of a thick quickset hedge, in my own garden, about four feet from the ground. 'If the hole is small, the nest consists only of a few feathers or tufts of hair; if large, the foundation is of moss, grasses, and wool. The nest is well constructed.' One, containing young birds, was found so late as October 10th., 1839, by the Rev. George Jeans, in the Blowwell Holt, Tetney, in Lincolnshire. Frequently a hole in a wall is made use of, sometimes the top of a pump, though the bird may be continually disturbed, or the nest even in the first instance destroyed by the action of the handle, the entrance being the cleft for the handle to work in.

The eggs are generally seven or eight or more in number, but have been known as few as six, and as many as sixteen, and some have said even eighteen or twenty; the usual number being from eight to twelve. They are of a delicate pink white, more or less spotted, and most so at the larger end, with clear rufous brown.

LONG-TAILED TIT.

Y BENLOYN GYNFFONHIR, OF THE ANCIENT BRITISH.

LONG-TAILED TITMOUSE. MUM RUFFIN. BOTTLE TIT. LONG TOM.
LONG-TAILED PIE. BOTTLE TOM. POKE PUDDING. LONG POD.
HUCK-MUCK. LONG-TAILED MAG. MUFFLIN. LONG-TAILED MUFFLIN.

Parus caudatus, PENNANT. MONTAGU.

Parus—............ ? *Caudatus—*Tailed.

'How pleasant it is,' says Macgillivray, 'to gaze upon these little creatures, streaming along the tops of the tall trees by the margin of the brook, ever in motion, searching the twigs with care, and cheeping their shrill notes as they scamper away, one after another.' This is from the life. Thus have I often seen them jerking off from tree to tree, or branch to branch, and pleasant they are to behold. Mr. Hewitson also well observes, 'I have never met with the Long-tailed Titmouse

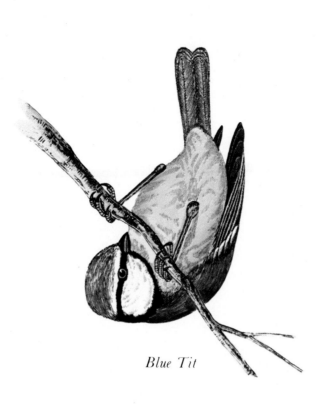

Blue Tit

Long-Tailed Tit

so common, or seen them so often, as to destroy the novelty and interest which their appearance never fails to excite, as they come flitting across my path in rapid succession.'

This species is a common one in this country, frequenting plantations, woods, thickets, shrubberies, and tall hedges. It is to be met with throughout England and Wales, as also in Ireland, but not very numerously there, and in Scotland in abundance, except in the northern parts. It remains with us the whole year.

The habits of this little bird resemble those of the rest of the family, of which it is the miniature, but it is, if possible, still more active, from the very first peep of day till the sun has again gone down, being incessantly occupied in quest of food. The young consort with their parents during the first autumn and winter, and early spring, and when roosting at night, huddle up all close together, as if one mass of feathers, probably for the sake of warmth. In April, the different members of the family separate, to become in their turns the founders of other branches. While engaged in nidification, they attack with the utmost fearlessness any birds that approach their nest, even if three or four times larger than themselves.

In flying, as they do from tree to tree, in an irregular string, these little birds have a singular appearance; they seem also so light, and, as it were, overburdened by the length of their tails, that but a moderate gust might be thought to be too much for them. 'Constantly in motion,' says Meyer, 'from tree to tree, and flying in a straight line with much rapidity, they remind the spectator of the pictured representation of a flight of arrows.' 'Away,' says Mr. Knapp, 'they all scuttle to be first, stop for a second, and then are away again, observing the same order and precipitation the whole day long.'

Their food consists entirely, or almost entirely, of insects and their larvæ: seeds have been found in them, but so very few, that possibly they may, I think, have been swallowed accidentally with their other food.

That which Shakespeare truly describes as so pleasing in a woman, a 'small voice,' goes to the heart of the naturalist when uttered by the tiny bird before us. It is the very embodiment of gentleness, weakness, and tenderness. I have but lately been listening to it, in the woods of Swinhope, in company with the Rev. R. P. Alington, my friend of the 'joyous days of old,' in whom, as in myself, the love of nature is inborn, inbred, and inwrought, so as that no time nor circumstances can eradicate it. It has, however, a second note—a louder twitter, and a third chirp, still hoarser. This is heard in the spring. Macgillivray describes it by 'twit, twit,' and 'churr, churr,' and Meyer by 'te, te,' and 'tse-re-re;' others by 'zit, zit.' In the same season it even attains to somewhat of a low and pleasing, though short, song.

Nidification commences early in March.

The nest of the Long-tailed Titmouse, the situation of which is repaired to frequently from year to year, is beautiful, and I may say wonderful. It is a hollow ball, generally nearly oval, with only one orifice; some have said two, to account for the location of the tail, which is said to project through one of them; and Mr. Hewitson describes one that he saw which had two openings, leaving the top of the nest like the handle of a basket, but such must be exceptional or accidental cases. A French writer has explained that one orifice is intended for a front and the other for a back door! Mudie writes as follows:—'They, in the case of two apertures, sit with the head of the male out at the one, and the tail of the female out at the other, so that both the apertures are partially closed, and the male is ready to start out as soon as there is light enough for hunting,' 'the male going out first in the morning, and the female last at night!' (Bewick says that the male has his head and the female her tail out of the one hole.) There being, however in reality, but one orifice, through which they 'have their exits and their entrances,' will perhaps be a sufficient answer to both these theories. How the birds manage, is another question, but certain it is that it is so. The nest is so admirably adapted, by the lichens or moss it is elegantly covered with, to the appearance of the tree it is built on, as to make it oftentimes very difficult to be detected. It is generally placed between the branches of a tree, unlike those of the other Titmice, and frequently not far from the ground, or firmly fixed in a bush; is composed of moss, small fragments of bark and wool, compacted with gossamer-like fibres, and the cocoons of spiders' eggs, and of the chrysalides of moths, and plentifully lined with feathers, so much so, as in some parts of the country to have acquired for it the 'sobriquet' of 'feather-poke;' one, on their being counted, was found to contain two thousand three hundred and seventy-nine. It is, as may be supposed, waterproof and very warm.

It is from five to seven inches long, by three or four wide, and the aperture about an inch and a half in diameter, and the same distance from the upper end. The elasticity of the materials of the nest tend to keep it rather closed. One has been seen in which a feather of the lining acted as a valve or door, but I think that this was probably accidental. The fabrication of the nest occupies from a fortnight to three weeks; and the credit of the handiwork belongs to both the male and female, she not being, as has been asserted, the sole architect. They both, as it were, knead it during its formation, with their breasts and the shoulders of their wings, aided by every variety of posture of the body.

A writer in the Penny Cyclopædia observes, 'we have seen in a nursery garden in Middlesex, a whole family of them within a few yards of the nurseryman's cottage, and close to his greenhouse, which visitors were constantly entering; and we have found its exquisitely-wrought nest in a silver fir about eight feet high in a pleasure ground, in the same county, little more than a hundred yards from the house.'

The eggs are from ten to twelve in number, occasionally, but very rarely, as many as sixteen. In reference to these cases, Mr. H. Horsfall, of Calverley House, near Bradford, Yorkshire, writes as follows in the 'Zoologist,' page 2567:—'I suspect where the greater number is found, there will be more than one pair of birds attached to the same nest. I have known several instances where a considerable number of birds have had one nest in common: in one instance there were nine.' They are sometimes entirely white, or with the spots almost obsolete, but are generally spotted a little with pale red. They are, as may be imagined, very small, being not much bigger than a large pea, sometimes even smaller.

SPOTTED FLYCATCHER.

Y GWYBEDOG, OF THE ANCIENT BRITISH.

BEAM BIRD. RAFTER. COB-WEB BIRD. BEE BIRD. CHERRY CHOPPER.
POST BIRD. WALL BIRD. CHERRY SUCKER. CHANCHIDER.

Muscicapa grisola,   MONTAGU. PENNANT.

Muscicapa. Musca—A fly. *Capio*—To catch or take.   *Grisola*—......?

THIS bird is common throughout Europe, as far north as Norway and Sweden; as also in Africa, along the whole of the western coast, from the north to the south. It is well known in England and Wales, Ireland and Scotland; but least so in the extreme north. It frequents walled and other gardens, orchards, lawns, shrubberies, and pleasure grounds.

The Spotted Flycatcher is, with us, a summer visitant, but unusually late in its arrival, which varies in different localities and seasons, from the 7th. to the 20th. of May, and it departs similarly about the end of September, and even as late as the middle of October.

This familiar bird is very noticeable for a solitariness and depression of appearance, as well as for its habit of perching on the point of a branch, the top of a stake, a rail, or a projection of or a hole in a wall, from whence it can 'comprehend all vagroms' in the shape of winged insects that come within its ken. You seem to think that it is listless, but on a sudden it darts off from its stance, sometimes led a little way in chase in an irregular manner like a butterfly; a snap of the bill tells you that it has unerringly captured a fly, and it is back to its perch, which it generally, but not invariably, returns to after these short sorties. It has a habit of flirting its wings aside and upwards a little, while perched, every now and then. Although so quiet a little thing, it will sometimes daringly attack any wanderer who seems likely to molest its 'sacred bower,' signifying first its alarm by a snapping of the bill. It is, like many other harmless birds, under the ban of the ignorant, and though its whole time is taken up in destroying insects that injure fruit, which it scarcely ever touches itself, it is accused of being a depredator, and too often suffers accordingly. It must, however, on the other hand, be admitted that some very trifling damage may be done by its destruction of bees, from which it has been given one of its trivial names. White, of Selborne, says that the female, while sitting, is fed by the male as late as nine o'clock at night, and I have verified the observation myself on more than one occasion.

The following curious circumstance has been recorded of some young Flycatchers, which had been taken from a nest, and placed in a large cage, with some other birds of different species, among which was a Robin. The young birds were fed regularly by one of their parents —the female, while her mate, who accompanied her constantly in her flight, used to wait for her, outside the window, either upon the roof of the house, or on a neighbouring tree. Sometimes the little birds were on the top perch in the cage, and not always near enough to the wires to be within reach of the parent, when she appeared with

Spotted Flycatcher

food; but the Robin, who had been for some time an inhabitant of the cage, where he lived in perfect harmony with all his associates, and had from the first taken great interest in the little Flycatchers, now perceiving that the nestlings could not reach the offered food, but sat with their wings fluttering, and their mouths open, anxious to obtain it, flew to the wires, received the insects from the mother bird, and put them into the open mouths of the nestlings. This was repeated every succeeding day, as often as his services were required.

Its food consists almost exclusively of insects, which after capturing in the manner already described, it generally holds for a short time in its bill before devouring; any large ones are frequently taken to the ground to be eaten. Occasionally a few cherries are consumed, but so seldom, that it is almost the most that can be said, that it makes 'two bites' of them. In feeding its young, two or three insects are frequently brought at a time. I have observed them continue to feed them until even after nine o'clock at night.

Nidification commences immediately after the arrival of the birds; they almost seem to have paired before their migration, or if not, at all events they do so at once when here.

The nest, which is built at the beginning of June, is composed of various materials, such as small twigs, catkins, and moss, lined with feathers, hair, down, and cobwebs. The same situation is resorted to year after year, and scarce any attempt is made at concealment. A pair, which built in the trellis-work close to the drawing-room window of a house I once resided in, not being disturbed, returned there three successive summers, and I hope that they, or their descendants, do so still. Another pair have now for three seasons built in the same way in the trellis-work over the drawing-room window of Nafferton Vicarage, in which this account of it was written. Another since, in a thorn tree in the garden of Nunburnholme Rectory, in a most clever situation, in the hollow of the branches first diverging from the trunk. Although quite open, and only four feet and a half from the ground, and though I had seen the bird fly to the spot in a way which made me think she had a nest there, and though I searched for it at once, I could not at first find the nest, but one of my children discovered it afterwards. A favourite resort is such a place, or a tree trained against a wall, on account of the support afforded by it. A pair made their nest on the hinge of an out-house door in a village, which people were continually passing and repassing; another couple placed theirs in a tree, immediately over an entrance door, which, whenever it was opened, caused them to fly off; another pair on the angle of a lamp-post in Leeds; and another on the ornamental crown of one in London. Trees are also built in, ledges of rocks, holes in walls, the exposed roots of trees over a bank, the side of a faggotstack, or a beam in an out-building, whence, no doubt, one of its provincial names—the 'Beam Bird,' and also, indeed, probably another, namely, 'Rafter,' and possibly also 'Cobweb Bird.'

Two broods are not uncommonly reared in the year; the first being hatched early in June; but the second may be only the consequence, at least in some cases, of the first one having been destroyed.

The eggs, four or five in number, are greyish or greenish white, spotted with pale orange-coloured brown; in some the broad end is blotted with grey red. After the young have quitted the nest they are very sedulously attended by their parents.

HOOPOE.

Y GOPPOG, OF THE ANCIENT BRITISH.

COMMON HOOPOE.

Upupa Epops,   PENNANT. MONTAGU.

Upupa—A Hoopoe, (Latin.) *Epops*—A Hoopoe, (Greek.)

THE elegant Hoopoe is a native of North Africa, from Egypt to Gibraltar; of Asia, where it occurs in Asia Minor; and also in the south of Europe; it goes northwards in summer as far as Denmark, Sweden, Tartary, Russia, and Lapland. In Germany, France, Italy, Holland, and Spain, it occurs in small flocks; also, I believe, in Madeira.

In Yorkshire, one of these birds was shot at Buckton, in the East-Riding, in May, 1851; and several had been procured in other parts previously—one of them taken while alighting on a boat in Bridlington Bay. Another at Bedale wood, near Cowling Hall; two near Doncaster; and another seen in 1836, in Sir William Cooke's wood; one at Armthorpe; another at Pontefract; one at Eccup, a young bird, by the Hon. Edwin Lascelles, October 8th., 1830; one at Low Moor, near Bradford; one at Skircoat Moor, near Halifax, September 3rd., 1840; one, a female, at Ecclesfield, near Bradford, April 9th., 1841; one at Coatham, near Redcar; and one near Scarborough. Two at Saltburn, near Redcar, in 1837 or 1838, as Captain E. H. Turton, of the Third Dragoon Guards, has informed me, and one at Wombwell Wood, near Barnsley, of which Mr. J. Lister, Postmaster of Barnsley, has written me word. It has also occurred in Sussex, Surrey, Kent, Suffolk, Norfolk, and Lincolnshire. One at Wilford, near Nottingham, in 1853. One was shot near London in April, 1852, and about the same time two were seen near Ipswich, Suffolk, as Claude A. Lillingston, Esq. has informed me, one of which was shot. Another was obtained near Ingham, in Norfolk, by R. Whaites, Esq. In Hampshire, one at Mopley, in the parish of Fawley, near Southampton, on the 14th. of April, 1854; one was shot near Esher, in the summer of 1855; also in Wiltshire, one on Salisbury Plain; and specimens have frequently occurred in Devonshire and Cornwall. Two were shot in the latter county that seemed to have paired, and one was seen in the autumn of 1836; another at Morval, the seat of John Butler, Esq., the 9th. of March, 1862; also in Scilly. In Northumberland one was caught near Bamborough Castle; and in Durham, one killed at Bedlington.

The figure before us is coloured from a specimen in my own collection, which was shot some years ago on the south-western border of Dorsetshire. Not a year passes in which one or more of these birds do not arrive in this country, and the same remark applies to Ireland. Mr. Thompson gives an accurate register of such in nine successive years, from 1833 to 1842, inclusive, with the exception of 1836, in which none were known to have been observed. In Scotland too, it sometimes occurs; in Sutherlandshire rarely: one was caught near Duff House, Banff, in September, 1832; so, too, in Ayrshire, and one near Porto Bello; also in the Orkney Islands.

Occasionally it has even been known to breed here, and doubtless would oftener do so, were it not incontinently pursued to the death at its first appearance. In Sussex, a pair built at Southwick, near Shoreham, and reared three young, and another pair close to the house at Park-End, near Chichester, in the same county. Montagu mentions that a pair in Hampshire forsook a nest which they had begun; and Dr. Latham had a young bird sent to him on the 10th. of May, 1786. In 1841, a pair built near Dorking, in Surrey, but the eggs were taken. A pair also frequented a garden near Tooting, in the same county, in the summer of 1833.

The Hoopoe is a migratory bird, at least to some extent, and one has been met with, seemingly unfatigued, half way across the Atlantic. It appears, however, that some of them do not change their quarters, while others do; and it is also related that the latter do not associate with the former when they arrive among them; their 'Travellers' Club' being like its London namesake, an exclusive one, save for such as have visited foreign parts. They migrate by night, and move singly or in pairs, unless, as is stated, the young brood follows close in the rear of its parents. They move but slowly in their peregrinations, attracted probably by the presence of food.

These birds pass much of their time on the ground in search of insects, which, however, they also take among the branches of trees, and seem to prefer low moist situations near woods. They are said to fight furiously among themselves, but as most quarrelsome people are, to be at the same time very cowardly, crouching to the ground in a paroxysm of terror, with wings and tail extended, at sight of a Hawk, or even a Crow. They are very shy also at the appearance of mankind. These birds are easily tamed when young, and follow their owner about. 'The greatest difficulty in preserving them during confinement, arises from their beaks becoming too dry at the tip, and splitting in consequence, whereby the birds are starved, from their inability to take their food.'

The flight of the Hoopoe is low and undulated, and the crest is kept erect or lowered at the pleasure of the bird, as it is excited or not. It is said to perch low. Its walk is described as something of a strut, and it keeps nodding its head as if vain of its gay top-knot.

Their food consists of beetles, other insects, and caterpillars; superfluous food they hide, and resort to again when hungry.

The note, from whence the name of the bird, resembles the word 'hoop, hoop, hoop,' 'long drawn out,' yet quickly, like the 'gentle cooing of the Dove.' It has also another note, 'tzyrr, tzyrr'—a grating hissing sort of sound, when alarmed or angry. It seems to utter its call with much exertion.

The nest, built in May, is placed in the hollow of a tree, or a crevice of a wall, and is composed of dry stalks of grass, leaves, and feathers.

The eggs vary from four to seven in number, and are of a uniform pale bluish grey, faintly speckled with brown.

Incubation lasts sixteen days. After the young leave the nest, they assemble in the immediate vicinity, and are long and sedulously attended to by their parents.

Hoopoe

CHOUGH.

BRAN BIG-COCH, OF THE ANCIENT BRITISH.

RED-LEGGED CROW. CORNISH CHOUGH. CORNISH DAW. KILLIGREW.
CORNWALL KAE. MARKET-JEW CROW. CHAUK DAW. CLIFF DAW.
HERMIT CROW. RED-LEGGED JACKDAW. GESNER'S WOOD-CROW.

Pyrrhocorax graculus,　　　　FLEMING.

Pyrrhocorax. Pyrrhos—Red.　　　　*Corax*—A Crow.
Graculus—A Chough, Jackdaw, or Jay.

ALTHOUGH generically distinct, yet, both in song and story 'the Chough and Crow' seem fated to be associated together.

This bird is a native of the three continents of the old world. It is known to inhabit France, the mountains of Switzerland, Spain, the island of Crete, Egypt, and the north of Africa, the mountains of Persia, the southern parts of Siberia, and the Himalayan Mountains in India. With us they frequent the cliffs of the coast.

In Yorkshire, one was killed by the gamekeeper of Randall Gossip, Esq., of Hatfield, near Doncaster. Two others are spoken of, one as having been shot near Sheffield, and another mentioned by Mr. J. Heppenstall to Mr. Allis; but it seems doubtful whether the accounts are not referable to one and the same specimen.

In Cornwall, the Chough has formerly been plentiful, but seems to be getting rare: that county, in fact, would seem to have been its main stronghold, the name of 'Cornish Chough' appearing to have been used as a term of reproach, as, for instance, to Tressilian, in 'Kenilworth:' they have been numerous on the cliffs at Perran. The Dover cliffs, and those of Beachy Head, Newhaven, and Eastbourne, in Sussex, the Isle of Purbeck, in Dorsetshire, Devonshire, and the Isle of Wight, it has also frequented a score of years ago, but a war of extermination has been carried on against it, and the consequence I need not relate. Whitehaven, in Cumberland, has been another of its resorts. In August, 1832, a Red-legged Crow was killed on the Wiltshire Downs, between Marlborough and Calne. It has also been seen on Mitcham Common, in Surrey. In November, 1826, one was shot at Lindridge, in Worcestershire.

In Wales, it has occurred in the cliffs of Glamorganshire, and is common in those of Pembrokeshire, from Tenby to St. David's Head, on Caldy Island, and also in Flintshire, the Isle of Anglesea, and Denbighshire. In the latter place a pair bred for many years in the appropriate ruins of Crow Castle, in the inland and beautiful vale of Llangollen; but one of them being killed by accident, the other continued to haunt the same place for two or three years without finding another mate, which was certainly a 'singular' circumstance: they are met with also in the Isle of Man, and breed on the Calf of Man.

In Ireland, according to Mr. Thompson, of Belfast, it is to be found in suitable localities all round the island, in some parts, particularly near Fairhead, in considerable abundance, the basaltic precipices of those parts being peculiarly suited to it: a pair were seen at Belfast, after a storm of wind from the south, on the 5th. of March, 1836.

In Guernsey and in Jersey it occurs in considerable numbers.

In Scotland, it has been known on the rocky cliffs between St. Abb's

Head and Fast Castle, at Coldingham, and near Berwick-on-Tweed; in Sutherlandshire, at Durness, and other precipitous parts, but rarely; Portpatrick, Wigtonshire; Ballantrae Castle, Ayrshire; and the coast; as also in the Hebrides, in the island of Barra, and in Galloway.

These birds, which are very easily tamed, and become extremely docile, exhibit all the restless activity, prying curiosity, and thievish propensities of their cousins—the Crows: they have in sooth a 'mono-mania' for petty larceny, especially of glittering objects; and it is said that houses have been set on fire by lighted sticks which they have carried off. In their wild state they are very shy, but in the breeding season they have allowed themselves to be approached within half a dozen yards. In the autumn and winter they keep in families, and are of gregarious habits. The following particulars are related of one kept tame by Colonel Montagu:—It used to avoid walking on grass, preferring the gravel walk; (Mr. Thompson, however, quotes from Dr. J. D. Marshall's 'Memoir of the island of Rathlin,' that there they frequent the pasture fields even more than the shores,) was fond of being caressed, but, though attached to them, was pugnacious even to its best friends if they affronted it: children he excessively disliked, was impudent to strangers, and roused by the sight of them to hostility even to his friends. One lady he was particularly friendly with, and would sit on the back of her chair for hours. He showed a great desire to ascend, by climbing up a ladder or stairs, would knock at a window with his bill until he was let in, and would pull about any small articles that came in his way.

Bishop Stanley says, 'on a lawn, where five were kept, one par-ticular part of it was found to turn brown, and exhibit all the appearance of a field suffering under severe drought, covered, as it was, with dead and withering tufts of grass, which it was soon ascer-tained the Choughs were incessantly employed in tearing up the roots of, for the purpose of getting at the grubs. The way they set about it was thus:—They would walk quietly over the surface, every now and then turning their heads, with the ear towards the ground, listening attentively in the most significant manner. Sometimes they appeared to listen in vain, and then walked on, till at length, instead of moving from the spot, they fell to picking a hole, as fast as their heads could nod.' They were often successful in their search, so that this account, in two respects, both as to their food and their going on the grass, militates against that of Montagu.

The flight of this species is described as resembling that of the Rook, but is said to be quicker, and occasionally to be performed in airy circles, with little motion of the wings. They generally fly high, in an irregular manner, with slow beats of the wings, and when it so pleases them to perform various gambols and evolutions in the air, 'they flap their wings, then sail on forty or fifty yards, and so on gradually, until they alight.' They do not alight on trees, but perch on the stones or rocks, and their gait is stately and graceful. The feathers of the wings are much expanded in flying, as in others of the Crow tribe, giving the wing a fringed appearance.

The food of the Chough consists principally of grasshoppers, chaffers, caterpillars, and other insects, in search of which it some-times follows the plough like the Rooks; and crustacea, but it also eats grain, seeds, and berries, and certainly carrion sometimes. Smaller insects are devoured whole; the larger it holds in its feet to peck at.

'It seldom attempts to hide the remainder of a meal.' These birds drink much.

The note is shrill, but is said to be lively and not disagreeable, which is, however, but negative praise. It somewhat resembles that of the Jackdaw, but may be distinguished from it, and is rendered by Meyer by the words, 'creea, creea,' and 'deea.' It has also a chatter, like the Starling.

The nest is made of sticks, and is lined with wool and hair. It is placed in the most inaccessible clefts, caverns, and cavities of cliffs, or in old church or other towers, or buildings, generally in the neighbourhood of the sea, but not always, as will have appeared from the previous and other statements.

The eggs, four or five in number, commonly five, are dull white, sprinkled and spotted with grey and light brown, most at the thicker end.

RAVEN.

BRAN, CIGFRAN, OF THE ANCIENT BRITISH.

CORBIE. CORBIE CROW. GREAT CORBIE-CROW.

Corvus corax,   PENNANT. MONTAGU.

Corvus—A Crow, (Latin.)   *Corax*—A Crow, (Greek.)

THE geographical distribution of the Raven is soon described. He is a 'Citizen of the world.' His sable plumage reflects the burning sun of the equator, and his dark shadow falls upon the regions of perpetual snow; he alights on the jutting peak of the most lofty mountain, and haunts the centre of the vast untrodden plain; his hoarse cry startles the solitude of the dense primeval forest, and echoes among the rocks of the lonely island of the ocean: no 'ultima Thule' is a 'terra incognita' to him; Arctic and Antarctic are both alike the home of the Corbie-Crow.

'In the best and most ancient of books,' says Wilson, 'we learn, that at the end of forty days, after the great flood had covered the earth, Noah, wishing to ascertain whether or no the waters had abated, sent forth a Raven, which did not return into the ark.'

It has been said, Miss Edgeworth tells us, of sailors, that they think every woman handsome who is not as old as Hecuba, and as ugly as Caifacaratataddera. The Raven is famed for longevity, and the 'Raven's wing' for blackness; but the eye of the naturalist perceives even here the 'line of beauty;' and, like Balbinus of old, he admires that which to others may seem only a defect.

But however the naturalist may look with complacency on the exterior of the Raven, yet it must be admitted that, judging by the standard of our own morality, his internal character corresponds there-with in blackness. But in truth we must not so judge him. He

Chough

Raven

fulfils, and no doubt perfectly fulfils, his allotted place in creation, and has, moreover, more than one redeeming feature, even in the view of an oblique censorship.

The union of the male and female Raven is for life, and his affection for her and his young is very great: they are generally seen singly, or in pairs, but occasionally in small flocks of about a score. They defend their young with great courage against the attacks of other birds, even those that are much their own superiors in size, though they tamely suffer them to be kidnapped by men or boys.

Ravens often fly at a considerable height in the air, and perform various circling evolutions and frolicsome somersets: the sound produced by the action of their wings is heard at some distance. Their flight is commonly steady and rather slow, made with regular flappings, the head and legs being drawn back, but on occasion they can fly at a great pace, and venture abroad in the heaviest gale. They hop on the ground in a sidelong sort of manner, and make rapid advances, if in haste, leaping and making use of the help of the wings, and at other times walk sedately.

The present is a very voracious bird, and whatever the sense be by which the Vultures are attracted to their food, by the same, in equal perfection, is the Raven directed to its meal, with unerring precision. It too is as patient of hunger as they are, but when an abundance of food comes in its way, like Captain Dalgetty, it makes the most of the opportunity, and lays in a superbundant stock of 'provant.' It performs the same useful part that those birds do, in devouring much which might otherwise be prejudicial.

Live stock as well, however, it stows away; weak sheep and lambs, as also poultry, it cruelly destroys: hence its own destruction by shepherds and others, and hence again its own consequent shyness and resort to some place of refuge. The eggs of other birds it likewise eats, watching its opportunity when the birds are absent, and makes free with those of hens and other poultry when the back of the housewife is turned; it transfixes them with its bill, and thus easily conveys them away: those of Cormorants even, it has been seen flying off with. Leverets, rabbits, rats, reptiles, young grouse, ducks, geese, pheasants, moles, mice, sea-urchins, shell-fish, which, Wilson says, it drops from a considerable height in the air on the rocks, in order to break the shells, worms, insects, caterpillars, and sometimes, it is said, barley, oats, and other grain, and carrion, whether 'fish, flesh, or fowl,' it likewise devours. I have often seen these birds searching the sea shore for any such 'waifs and strays.' They will feed on any common carrion with a dog or an otter, but will drive away the Hooded Crow and the Gull, only yielding place to the Eagle, when on the ground—'Gare le Corbeau' has no heed from him. In the case, however, of a large carcase there is room enough and plenty enough for both, and they feed in common.

The note is, as is so well known, a harsh croak, sounding like curreq, cruck, crock, or cluck, a gulping sort of a note, or rather 'craugh,' which former word it resembles, and is doubtless the origin of. It has also a different sound, uttered when manœuvring in the air, and others rendered by 'clung,' 'clong,' or 'cung,' and 'whii-ur.' In all countries, and in remote ages, his unearthly sepulchral voice and mourning garb fitting in with and confirming the superstition, the Raven has been supposed, excepting, it is said, by the American

Indians, to be the harbinger of death, as gifted with the faculty of anticipating what to him might prove a feast, and with the same motive to be a 'camp follower' on the battle-field, as the shark, the like omen to sailors, follows in the wake of the ship, from which some lifeless body may have to be committed to the 'great deep.'

Nidification commences early, even in the coldest climates: here sometimes so soon as January, and the eggs have been taken in the middle of February, in which month the nest is more usually begun. Incubation lasts about twenty days: the male and female both sit, and the former feeds and attends upon the latter. The Raven sometimes nestles not far from the Eagle, but is wont to harass him, so far as pestering him is concerned, but it is doubtful whether 'assault and battery' is actually committed. Shepherds encourage them on the above account.

Many a tree is well known in village chronicles as the Raven's tree, and many a hill as the Raven's hill. If one of the parent birds be destroyed, a new partner is quickly obtained, some 'Matrimonial Agency' being at work whose ways are utterly inscrutable to us. In one instance, the male being shot in the morning a new mate was found by the widow by three o'clock in the afternoon, and he duly performed the part of step-father to his step-children. Had he been a widower himself? How did the female find out this his condition? or he hers? Where had he been living in the single state, and how did the female manage to leave her own young, or did she communicate with him without doing so? These are questions more easily asked than answered.

The nest, which is large, and composed of sticks, cemented together with mud, and lined with roots, wool, fur, and such materials, is placed in various situations—the clefts of the branches of tall trees, church towers, caves, cliffs, and precipices.

The eggs are four or five, six or seven, in number, of a bluish green colour, blotted with stains of a darker shade, or brown. The young are generally fledged about the end of March or beginning of April. They are abroad by the middle of May, even in the extreme north.

CROW.

BRAN DYDDYN. BRAN DYFYN, OF THE ANCIENT BRITISH.

CARRION CROW. GOR CROW.
GORE CROW. BLACK NEB. FLESH CROW.

Corvus corone,   PENNANT. MONTAGU.

Corvus—A Crow, (Latin.)   *Corone*—A Crow, (Greek.)

THE Carrion Crow is a small edition of the Raven. The Italian proverb tells us that, 'chi di gallina nasce convien che rozole,' 'as the old Cock crows, so crows the young;' and thus do we find it to be with these two birds, the one, as it were, a derivative of the other, the major comprehending the minor.

These birds keep in pairs the whole year, and are believed to unite for life: more than two are seldom seen in company, unless it be when met over a carrion, or while the brood remain together; the contrary, however, is sometimes the case. In their wild state they have been known occasionally to pair with the Hooded Crow; in one instance for two or three years in succession. It does not appear for certain what the progeny are like, but one nest was said to contain some young birds resembling one of the parents, and some the other. The male spiritedly defends the female when sitting, and both bravely repel any bird, though much larger than themselves, that may show symptoms of having a design upon their·young. They fearlessly assail the Raven, the Kite, the Buzzard, and even the Peregrine, but the last-named frequently makes them pay their life as the forfeit of their temerity: they roost in trees and on rocks.

'The Carrion Crow,' says Mr. Weir, in a communication to Mr. Macgillivray, 'is very easily tamed, and is strongly attached to the person who brings him up. I kept one for two years and a half. It flew round about the neighbourhood, and roosted every night on the trees of my shrubbery. At whatever distance he was, as soon as he heard my voice, he immediately came to me. He was very fond of being caressed, but should any one, except myself, stroke him on the head or back, he was sure to make the blood spring from their fingers. He seemed to take a very great delight in pecking the heels of bare-footed youths. The more terrified they were, the more did his joy seem to increase. Even the heels of my pointers, when he was in his merry mood, did not escape his art of ingeniously tormenting. His memory was astonishing. One Monday morning, after being satiated with food, he picked up a mole, which was lying in the orchard, and hopped with it into the garden. I kept out of his sight, as he seldom concealed anything when he thought you observed him. He covered it so nicely with earth, that upon the most diligent search I could not discover where he had put it. As his wings had been cut to prevent him from flying over the wall into the garden, he made many a fruitless attempt during the week to get in at the door. On Saturday evening, however, it having been left open, I saw him hop to the very spot where the mole had been so long hid, and, to my surprise, he came out with it in the twinkling of an eye.' A single Crow has been known to drive away three Ravens.

Its flight is not lofty, and is generally sedate and direct, performed by regular flappings. Its walk too resembles that of the Raven.

The Crow feeds on all sorts of animal food, alive and dead, and its sense of perception, whatever it be, is as acute as that of the Raven. It is a most predaceous bird, and a fell and relentless destroyer of any creature it can master, young lambs, among which it often does much damage, leverets, young rabbits, pigeons, ducks, and the young of game and poultry, crustacea, fish, shell-fish, which it breaks open by letting fall from a height upon the rocks, and if it does not succeed the first time, it goes up higher and drops it again, as instinctively conscious of the greater effect—the result of the attraction of gravity; as also at times fruit, vegetables, grain, berries, potatoes, tadpoles, frogs, snakes, insects, eggs of all birds, which it either transfixes with, or holds in its bill, and so removes, walnuts, in fact anything. They frequently collect great heaps of shells on their favourite hillocks, which are often at some distance from the sea. One which carried off

Crow

Rook

a duckling from a pond, in its bill, was observed to kill it by walking forwards and backwards over it; another was seen to seize and kill a Sparrow engaged at the moment in inducing its young ones to fly; Montagu saw one chase and pounce at a Pigeon, like a Hawk, and strike another dead from the roof of a barn. These birds will hide any redundant food for a future occasion, and Colonel Montagu noticed a pair of them thus removing small fish left by the tide above high water mark. He also saw another make repeated pounces in a field where the grass was long at some animal, which raised itself on its hind legs, and defended itself stoutly; it proved to be a leveret: a small one has been seen to be carried off in the air by one of these birds. Mr. Hogg saw one dart out at, and chase, but unsuccessfully, a Grouse, which his approach had been the means of rescuing from the talons of a large Hawk. Bishop Stanley also records an instance of a rabbit, which weighed from half to three-quarters of a pound, having been caught up and carried away across two or three fields. Two Crows will often contend together for a prize which one of them has found, its discovery not being kept secret, but loudly proclaimed.

The Crow is often garrulous like the Magpie, and its note is a croak like that of the Raven, but hoarser. It caws on moonlight nights.

Nidification begins the end of February, or beginning of March, both birds helping to make the nest. They begin building almost before daylight, and only work for an hour or two, and then stop for the day. They are from four to six days in making the nest.

The nest is built in rocks or in trees, generally high up, and is made of sticks, firmly cemented with clay, and lined with roots, and again with straw, wool, moss, fur, hair, or anything else that is soft: the latter the Crows pull for the purpose from the backs of animals. It is almost always lined with cow-hair, and is built of the materials just mentioned, or strong heath, if it can be had, in preference to sticks. They never use the same nest twice. They are very careful in approaching it, and do so by four or more separate flights, first to a tree near the side of the wood parallel to the tree it is on, some three hundred yards off; then after a few moments to another a good way nearer, and so gradually edge in to the nest.

It is usually concealed as much as may be, for instance, among the topmost branches of a larch fir tree, but if not, it is placed on some bough near to the trunk of the tree, or in the cleft formed by the main branches. The Rev. R. P. Alington has sent me a drawing of one. A pair built on the ground in one of the Fern Islands, and their nest was made of pieces of turf laid one upon another, and lined with wool, all brought from the mainland four or five miles distant. The Rev. W. Waldo Cooper has known a nest repaired the second year. The same spot is regularly revisited year after year and century after century by generation after generation. When the young have been fully fledged and are able to provide for themselves, the parent birds drive them away from the neighbourhood.

The eggs, four to six in number, are pale bluish green, spotted and speckled with grey and brown: some are pale blue undertinted with grey. James Dalton, Esq., of Worcester College, Oxford, has one of a bright blue, without any spots, all the others in the nest having been of the usual colour.

ROOK.

YDFRAN, OF THE ANCIENT BRITISH.

Corvus frugilegus,   LINNÆUS. GMELIN.

Corvus—A Crow.   *Frugilegus. Fruges*—Fruits.   *Lego*—To collect
or gather.

Rooks are strictly gregarious in all their habits, and are thus identified with the 'corvus' of the Romans: they build together in trees,
and consort in like manner in search of food throughout the year.
They mix freely when feeding with Jackdaws, and even Gulls, as also
with Starlings, Fieldfares, and Missel Thrushes. The same colonies,
however, admit of no influx of strangers; none but natives born are
made free of their society—their freedom is that of birth. They breed
on the same trees, and occupy the same nests from year to year; if,
however, the trees give symptoms of decay, they are quitted for sounder
ones, and it has even been observed that they have forsaken some, the
bark of which had been peeled off preparatory to their being felled.
Strange stories are told, one in my neighbourhood, of their following
the fortunes of owners who have left their dwelling-places, and of their
having through some mysterious instinct, abandoned their rookeries
near a mansion when the house was about to be pulled down, or even
to be left untenanted. It is related in Evelyn's 'Memoirs,' that in
the winter of 1658, the severest ever known in England, some of these
birds were taken with their feet frozen to their prey.

It is a pleasant sight in the country to see at a certain hour every
evening, later or earlier, gradually, day by day, the rooks returning
in 'measured time' to their roost, 'going home,' keeping to the self-
same track through the air, varied only according to the season of the
year, a little on this side or on that, and when they do arrive at
their journey's end, if you have been beforehand to watch them,
what a deafening cawing is there, and what a variety of sounds,
what a dashing about in every direction, what a wheeling and diving,
what a contention, apparently for places, what order among seeming
disorder, what a certain settlement in the end of every dispute about
a place. Is the vocabulary of their language understood among themselves, and how is the government of their community managed; who
is the leader, and which are the led?

In the latter part of the year they may at times be seen diving
down in a frantic frolicsome manner from a great height in the air, with
closed wings, sweeping out when approaching a tree or the ground, as if
just in time to save themselves from being dashed to pieces. The rushing
sound of the pinions of a number together, for the manœuvre is performed in companies, being audibly heard, seeming at times like the
noise of a sudden gust of wind, is almost startling. This movement, I
believe, is popularly considered to betoken and to be the forerunner
of rain, but it certainly is not always followed by this consequence,
at all events not immediately. Frequently, however, high winds are
thus as it were foreshown.

The food of the Rook consists of the larvæ of cockchaffers, and those of other insects, beetles, moths, and wire-worms, snails, slugs, and worms, as also beech nuts, seeds, berries, roots of grasses, newly-planted potatoes, and other fruits and grains: 'fruges consumere nati,' as their specific name imports, and in hard weather, turnips, as likewise shell-fish, crustacea, and lizards. In the autumn they pluck and frequently bury acorns in the earth, and probably walnuts and fir cones, which they likewise carry off, provident, it is thought, of a season of want. 'Deus pascit corvos.' A few cherries and walnuts will at times be pilfered, and newly-sown grain requires to be well looked after, as they burrow it out when sprouting, leaving the braird to perish.

The 'caw' of the rook needs no description. There is something singularly pleasing in the harsh sound in the beautiful sunny days of September and October, whether it be from a peculiar state of the air in the still time, or an inflection of the note itself, I know not, but certain it is that so it is, to me at all events, and I doubt not to other observers; but plain as it is, who is there that does not love to hear it? Who does not bring back pleasant old thoughts of days gone by in unison with it, monotonous though it be?

In the autumnal months you may hear a passing bird uttering a note that resembles the bark of a small dog, and also at times perched on the bough of a tree one may be heard mumbling a very curious language, and at the same time bowing and bending in a most grotesque manner. So, too, when engaged with their young, they murmur a variety of soft notes, expressive no doubt of their feelings at the time. Rooks caw when engaged in building their nests, even on moonlight nights. They have considerable powers of mimicry; Hewitson heard one take off the notes of the Jackdaw, and Mr. Macgillivray mentions having repeatedly listened to another which imitated so remarkably well the barking of several dogs in the village, that had it been placed out of view it would have been impossible to have discovered the deception.

Early in March, after a previous preparation in February, the nests of the previous year are begun to be repaired, and some new ones are necessarily built by the young of that date. Repairs indeed, though without any definite object, so far at least as appears to us, are made months before, even in the late autumn and winter. They have been known to begin to build on the 16th. of February. Two Rooks have frequently been seen carrying a stick between them for the nest; but only when near it, so as for neither to be absent more than a minute or two, in order that they may not be robbed by others of their place. The male diligently feeds the female, and occasionally takes her place on the eggs. The young are hatched by the middle of April, and fledged by the latter end of May, about the 20th., or the beginning of June; and second broods are produced as late as November, but possibly they should be considered rather as early than late ones.

These birds having been considered obnoxious to the pheasants in a wood at Kilnwick Percy, near Pocklington, Yorkshire, the beautiful seat of my neighbour, Admiral the Hon. Arthur Duncombe, M.P., it was determined to dislodge them, and this was carried into effect by continual discharges of guns, day after day. At length one Sunday the desired result being supposed to have been obtained, the keepers left the wood and went to church, but during their temporary absence no fewer than forty nests were run up.

Magpie

Jay

Rooks build for the most part in the vicinity of old mansions or other buildings, chiefly, as I imagine, on account of ancient and full-grown trees being the accompaniments of these; but they by no means make exclusive choice of such situations; I have seen their nests in perfectly isolated places, and they have been known in several instances to build on trees of low growth; as for example on young oaks, only ten or twelve feet high in the grounds of the Duke of Buccleuch at Dalkeith Palace, although large trees were all around them. They have occasionally been known to domicile even in the midst of cities, and that not only on trees, as in the very heart of Edinburgh, where there are several small rookeries, but in other and the most unlikely places. Three pairs built on some low poplars, in a central part of the town of Manchester, and returned to them the following year: another pair on the crown which surmounts the vane of St. Olave's church, London; and another between the wings of the dragon on Bow church, and there they remained, clearly 'within the sound of Bow bells,' till the spire required to be repaired.

The eggs, four or five in number, are of a pale green ground colour, blotted over with darker and lighter patches of yellowish and greenish brown: they vary much.

MAGPIE.

PIOGEN. Y BI, OF THE ANCIENT BRITISH.

COMMON MAGPIE. PIANET. MADGE.

Pica caudata,   FLEMING. SELBY. GOULD.

Pica—A Pie—A Magpie.   *Caudata*—Tailed, (a factitious word.)

IF I remember aright, in the great French Revolution, the zeal of the people for 'liberté' was so great, that they opened the doors of all the cages, and let the birds fly out. I should have enjoyed the sight, though some of the captives would perhaps have preferred remaining where they were, and so did not value the unwonted freedom which they had never known the possession of, even as the poor prisoner who returned to the dungeon, with whose walls he had become familiar: to him the world was become the prison, the spider a more agreeable companion than his fellow-man: certainly he had found the one more friendly than the other. Nothing is to me more miserable than to see a bird in a cage, and, with reference to the species before us, who can tell what a Magpie is, either in character or in beauty, from only seeing him thus confined? He is, when himself, a brilliant—a splendid bird, gay alike in nature and in plumage.

The Magpie is met with in Europe, Asia, Africa, and America, being found in Spain, France, Italy, Belgium, Sweden, Russia, Lapland, Norway, and Greece, Asia Minor and Siberia, India, China, and Japan; also in the United States.

It is common in all the wooded parts of the three kingdoms of England, Ireland, and Scotland, but is unknown, except as a straggler, in the Orkneys, the Hebrides, or the Shetland Islands. Sly and wary, it keeps at a secure distance from the gunner, and so, though a marked bird, for the most part contrives to save itself; but many a one garnishes the gable-end of the gamekeeper's house. Nevertheless, if unmolested, it would naturally frequent the habitations of men, and even as it is many a nest is built contiguous to a farmsteading. Mr. Hewitson says, a contrast to the state of the case with us, 'The Magpie is one of the most abundant, as well as the most attractive of the Norwegian birds; noted for its sly cunning habits here, its altered demeanour there is the more remarkable. It is upon the most familiar terms with the inhabitants, picking close about their doors, and sometimes walking inside their houses. It abounds in the town of Drontheim, making its nest upon the churches and warehouses. We saw as many as a dozen of them at one time seated upon the gravestones of the churchyard. Few farmhouses are without several of them breeding under the eaves, their nest supported by the spout. In some trees close to houses, their nests were several feet in depth, the accumulation of years of undisturbed and quiet possession.' With us how different; and no wonder, for every gun is aimed at the Magpie, the extremest cunning and most wary shyness alone protecting those that yet survive.

It is a crafty, noisy, artful bird, and its chatter set up at the sight of almost any creature, proclaims and calls forth at once a mutual hostility. One has been seen to chase away a full-grown hare. Magpies continue in pairs throughout the year, but several are often seen together, probably the family party in general, but sometimes as many as a score. If taken young they are very easily tamed, and learn to imitate many words, and to perform various tricks. Thieving is as natural to them as to the rest of their tribe, and anything shining, in particular, they cannot resist the instinct to purloin, as most pleasantly illustrated in Miss Edgeworth's story of 'Old Poz.'

Their flight is made with quick vibrations, as if with some effort: on the ground this bird advances either by hopping or walking. It sometimes hops or leaps in a sidelong manner. If alarmed it flits by the side of hedges or walls, or shifts from tree to tree, and at length flies off to a distance.

The Magpie's appetite is omnivorous; young lambs, and even weakly sheep, leverets, young rabbits, young birds, game, eggs, fish, carrion, insects, crustacea, shell-fish, fruit, and grain, all meet its requirements. They often hunt for insects on the backs of sheep, who may be seen quietly standing the while. The Rev. George Jeans has written me word of one he saw repeatedly stooping at a Wagtail after the manner of a Falcon. 'Per contra,' at Walton Hall, Yorkshire, the seat of the late Charles Waterton, Esq., a Wood Pigeon built in a tree only four feet below the nest of a Magpie; both lived in the greatest harmony, hatched their eggs, and reared their young.

Its note is a harsh chatter.

Nidification begins early in the spring. The nest is begun early in March, sometimes they begin several before they are suited, more than one or even two being first built and then left, for reasons best known to the birds themselves, in the same way as is done by the Wren. When once approved of, it is maintained in use. One is known to have been repaired and inhabited for six years in succession, until having been made extraordinarily large, it was blown down by a high wind. Another, built in a gooseberry tree in the north of Scotland, was likewise domiciled in for several years, and was so well barricaded, not only the nest, but the bush itself, all round, with briars and thorns, that even a man, without a hedge-knife or something of that kind, could not get at it without much pains and trouble, much less a fox, cat, or hawk. It was thus fortified afresh every spring.

If one of the pair happen to be killed, another partner is incontinently obtained. One thus thrice a widower procured a fresh helpmate each time in not more than two or three days. Six others in succession sat on the same set of eggs in the parish church of Midcalder.

The nest, which is resorted to from year to year, is placed in the top of a tall tree, whether ash, beech, or willow sometimes, or occasionally in a lower one, or it may be in a bush or hedge, if otherwise suitably protectant, as also in woods and plantations, shrubberies, and even in a gooseberry bush one has been known for several successive seasons. Sometimes in the top of a larch or other fir. It is rather large, of an oblong shape, built of strong sticks, twigs, and thorns, cemented together with mud, and lined with fibrous roots and grass: an aperture just sufficient to admit the bird is left on one side or both, and from this loop-hole any approaching danger is descried, in order to a timely retreat; when in it the bird must keep its tail erect or bent forwards over the back; the top is covered over. I am informed by W. F. W. Bird, Esq., that the Magpie builds in Kensington Gardens.

The eggs are from three to six or seven, rarely eight in number, pale bluish or greenish white, spotted all over with grey and greenish brown, more or less dark.

JAY.

SCRECH Y COED. PIOGEN Y COED, OF THE ANCIENT BRITISH.

Garrulus glandarius,   FLEMING. SELBY.

Garrulus—Chattering, as birds. *Glandarius*—Of or belonging to acorns.

THE plate, if I may be pardoned a brief record of a pleasing reminiscence, is coloured from a specimen in my collection, the first stuffed bird I ever possessed, which was brought to me by my father from York, just after I had gone to school.

The Jay, one of our gaudiest birds, is found in all the temperate parts of Europe, in Denmark, Sweden, Norway, Switzerland, Germany, Spain, France, Holland, Belgium, Italy, Greece, Crete, and the Ionian Islands, in Asia Minor, and in Africa, in Barbary and Egypt. The Greeks eat it as food.

In this country it is sufficiently common, and would doubtless be much more so were it not so unrelentingly pursued as a 'vermin.'

This bird is exclusively addicted to woods and their immediately neighbouring trees for its habitat.

Jays, if not actually birds of passage, yet are decidedly of a roving disposition. 'When they are obliged, during migration, to cross a wide open country, they fly quicker, for fear of being attacked by birds of prey, and their fear may be perceived by their frequently turning back to their starting point, before they finally undertake the journey, and then it is performed in haste, one flying behind another in a singular manner.' Dr. Stanley, Bishop of Norwich, has recorded in his 'Familiar History of Birds,' that 'some gentlemen near Tunstall, in Suffolk, who were out shooting about five miles from the sea, observed an extraordinary flight of Jays passing in a single line from seaward towards the interior. The line extended further than the eye could reach, and must have consisted of some thousands; there could be no doubt of their being Jays, as several were killed as they passed.' 'During their migration the Jays alight on the first tree they meet with, and from thence utter their harsh note of joy, on having thus far travelled in safety. They never sit long on one branch, but shift and change continually, and when on the ground they hop about very awkwardly.'

Jays continue together long after the young have left the nest; indeed frequently until the following spring; sometimes small flocks of from twenty to forty collect together. They are easily tamed if brought up from the nest, and become very familiar, playful and impudent, imitating, as presently stated, all sorts of sounds in a facile manner. They are most restless birds, ever changing their position, raising and lowering their crests, and ever and anon uttering some outlandish note.

The flight of the Jay is very observable, as heavy and irregular, effected with some degree of apparent difficulty, and in a scurrying sort of manner, as if conscious that it was a proscribed bird, and doomed to destruction for either real or supposed faults; it is a series of quick beats, with occasional short cessations. They seldom settle on the ground; they glide cleverly through woods and thickets, and keep flitting along hedge sides.

As imported by its specific name, the acorn is the most choice 'morceau' of the Jay, and for this he even searches under the snow; but he also feeds on more delicate fruit, such as beans, peas, and cherries, as well as on beech-mast, nuts, grain, seeds, garden and wall fruit, berries, corn, worms, snails, cockchaffers, and other insects, larvæ, frogs and other reptiles, and mice, and is deterred by no scruples or qualms from making away with young birds, even partridges, and eggs. These birds are said, in the autumn, to hide portions of food for winter use, under leaves in some secure place, and in holes of trees.

Their true note is singularly harsh, and almost startling, resembling the syllables 'wrak, wrak,' but they have a decided talent for mimicry, and both in their wild and their tame state have been heard exhibiting their acquired and varied accomplishments, in imitating the bleating of a lamb, the mewing of a cat, the hooting of an owl, the neighing of a horse, the shriek of the Buzzard, the song of the Greenfinch, the human voice, the note of the Kite, the warbling of birds, the crowing of a Cock, the bark of a dog, and the calling of fowls to their food, and Bewick says, 'we have heard one imitate the sound of a saw so exactly, that though it was on a Sunday, we could hardly be persuaded that there was not a carpenter at work in the house.' They are said to have a low song in spring, soft and not unpleasing.

The nest is placed in a tall bush or hedge, generally at a not greater elevation than about twenty or thirty feet from the ground, and sometimes less. It is of an open shape, formed of twigs and sticks, and well lined with small roots, fibres, straws, grasses, and horse-hair. Some are much more cleverly constructed than others.

The eggs, five or six in number, are pale dull bluish green, greenish or yellowish white, freckled all over with two shades of light yellowish brown or purple. There are generally one or two small black streaks on them, and there is not unfrequently a ring near the larger end, but sometimes near the smaller, of darker spots. They vary occasionally both in size and in degree of polish.

GREEN WOODPECKER.

CNOCCELL COED. DELOR Y DERW, OF THE ANCIENT BRITISH.

LARGE GREEN WOODPECKER. WOODSPITE.
HIGH HOE. HEW-HOLE. PICK-A-TREE. ECLE. POPINJAY. RAIN-BIRD.
RAIN-FOWL. WHITTLE. AWL-BIRD. YAPPINGALL. YAFFLE.
YAFFER. NICK-A-PECKER.

Picus viridis, LINNÆUS.

Picus—A bird that makes holes in trees, supposed to be the Woodpecker.
Viridis—Green.

THOUGH to man it is a difficulty to make even a copy without some variation from the original, yet, to strike out a fresh design is by no means so easy as it might therefore be thought. Let the thoughtful artist then devoutly wonder at the unspeakable beauty of the varieties which the hand of Almightly power and wisdom has pourtrayed in the 'fowls of the air,' as in all the other 'wonderful works' of nature 'which God created and made.'

This handsome species is a native of Europe, being found in more or less plenty, according to the suitableness of the locality, in Russia, Spain, Greece, Italy, Scandinavia, France, and Holland; in Asia, even in Siberia; also in Africa, in Egypt, according to Meyer.

It is common throughout England, and, according to Selby, in Scotland, that is to say, in all the wooded districts. It is, however, greatly reduced in numbers in many or most parts. Thus Mr. Allis reports of it,—'Common about Doncaster, occasionally seen near Leeds and York, not common near Sheffield, nearly extirpated in the vicinity of Halifax, rarely met with at Hebden-Bridge, very rare near Huddersfield, though formerly more plentiful, frequently met with in the wooded districts near Barnsley, numerous near Thirsk.' The like remark would apply to the county generally. I have had them close to my own house at Nunburnholme, and have seen them near Crambe Vicarage, where they then bred, as also in Howsham wood near there, the seat of Colonel Cholmley. So too in the neighbourhood of Barnsley, in Stainborough Park, Lund wood, Ethersley wood, and Norroyds. In Cornwall it is not common: recently one was shot at Enys, and another at Sparnon plantation. In Ireland its occurrence has not yet been authenticated. It is stated, however, to have occurred in Kildare since the first edition of this work was published.

These birds roost early, and repose in their holes at night. The

Green Woodpecker

young run on the trees before they are able to fly, and if then captured are easily tamed.

Like the rest of its tribe, this species only ascends, for the most part obliquely, on the trees; any descent is performed by a retrograde motion. It alights near the base, and, tapping at intervals to alarm any hidden insects, quickly makes its way to the higher part of the bole, from which it flies downwards to another tree, or to another part of the same one, to commence again 'de novo.' Occasionally it may be seen in strong hedges, and has been noticed, so says Sir William Jardine, Bart., among gorse bushes. In severe weather it approaches villages and farms, searching for its food in the walls of old buildings and barns, as well as in the neighbouring trees.

The flight of this bird is generally short, from tree to tree, heavy and laboured, the wings being rapidly fluttered, and producing a rustling noise; it gains a long reach by the impetus it has acquired, and then drops, the effort requiring to be renewed. On the ground it walks horizontally, the tail dragging after it.

The 'laugh' of the Green Woodpecker, for so is its harsh note of 'glu, glu, glu, gluck' designated, is supposed to prognosticate rain; hence one of its trivial names. It is almost startling if suddenly and unexpectedly heard.

Its hard and wedge-shaped bill enables it without difficulty to procure its food by boring into the decayed wood of trees, even through any sound exterior part, and with its long and extensile tongue it extracts the insects and their eggs, spiders and caterpillars, on which it lives, from the crannies in the bark in which they lie concealed, and ants and their eggs from their hills. In searching for these it is frequently seen on the ground, and, Bewick says, uses not only its bill, but its feet: failing such a supply it will eat nuts. The tongue is a most wonderful organ, as in the rest of the Woodpeckers. 'It has the appearance of a silver ribbon, or rather, from its transparency, a stream of molten glass, and the rapidity with which it is protruded and withdrawn is so great that the eye is dazzled in following its motions: it is flexible in the highest degree.'

Preparations for building are commenced even so early as February, and the old nest is frequently repaired to and repaired. The nest, if decayed wood-dust may be called such, is placed at a height of fifteen or twenty feet from the ground, in a sound hole in a tree, and it is said that the birds carry away the chips and fragments of wood to a distance, as if afraid that they might lead to a discovery of their retreat. If necessary, it perforates a hole, or else suits one to itself, with its trenchant bill, the strokes of the active worker being so incessantly repeated, that the head can hardly be perceived to move: the sound of the 'Woodpecker tapping the hollow beech tree,' may be distinctly heard, it is said, at a distance of half a mile.

The eggs, four or five to six or eight in number, are bluish white in colour. In the 'Zoologist,' page 2229, Alfred Newton, Esq. mentions his having met with five eggs of this bird in a nest at Elveden, near Thetford, Norfolk, which were blotted and spotted with reddish brown and tawny yellow; and at page 2301, he speaks of having been informed of two other similar instances, one, or both of them, in the same neighbourhood.

The young are hatched in June. The parents are sedulously devoted to them, and, when fully fledged, they all quit together in company.

GREAT SPOTTED WOODPECKER.

Y DELOR FRAITH, OF THE ANCIENT BRITISH.

WHITWALL. WITWALL. WOODWALL. WOODNACKER. WOODPIE.
FRENCH PIE. PIED WOODPECKER. GREATER SPOTTED WOODPECKER.
GREAT BLACK AND WHITE WOODPECKER. FRENCH WOODPECKER.

Picus major,   PENNANT. MONTAGU.

Picus—A bird that makes holes in trees, supposed to be the Woodpecker.
Major—Greater.

THIS species is found over the whole of the European continent, from Russia to Italy, Sweden to France, Denmark and Norway to Germany, and other countries. In Asia Minor it has been noticed by H. E. Strickland, Esq.; and, Meyer says, is found in America also.

In this country it is of local distribution, dependent entirely on the nature of the locality, and nowhere to be called common. Wooded districts are, of course, its resort; and it is most frequent in the midland counties, in parks, forests, and woods, and is occasionally to be seen in gardens. It becomes much less numerous farther north.

Mr. Selby considers that these birds are probably migratory, as he has met with them in Northumberland in the months of October and November, generally after storms from the north-east. They, at all events, wander about more in the autumn than in any other part of the year.

This species naturally displays the capabilities of climbing which distinguish its race. With the most easy adroitness, it runs in all upward directions over the branches and trunks of trees, seeming at the same time to prefer having the latter between you and it, should you approach. Sometimes they will run up to the top of the tree, and then fly off. They seldom alight on the ground, and their movements then are neither quick nor graceful. The old birds shew great attachment to their young. Montagu mentions one instance in which 'notwithstanding that a chisel and mallet were used to enlarge the hole, the female did not attempt to fly out till the hand was introduced, when she quitted the tree at another opening.' The Greater Spotted Woodpecker is a courageous, active, strong, and lively bird, but unsociable with strangers, and defensive of its brood.

The flight of this Woodpecker is straight and strong, but short and curved; the wings being quickly moved from, and brought close back again to the body.

Their food consists of insects and caterpillars, seeds, fruits, and nuts. Mr. Gould observes that they 'sometimes alight upon rails, old posts, and decayed pollards, where, among the moss and vegetable matter, they find a plentiful harvest of spiders, ants, and other insects; nor are they free from the charge of plundering the fruit trees of the garden, and, in fact, commit great havoc among cherries, plums, and wall fruit in general.' They alarm the insects from their recesses by the noise made with their bills upon the trees, which is audible at the distance of half a mile. Meyer says that they do not cat ants, but he adds the eggs of insects, nuts, the seeds of fir-cones, and other seeds to the above bill of fare, and he also remarks, though I own I cannot think it a circumstance of very common occurrence, 'the jealousy of this bird leads it into danger, as it is sure to take notice if any one taps against a tree; and approaches sometimes near enough to be caught with the hand.'

In the spring these birds produce a like jarring noise to that made by the Green Woodpecker; and their note is expressed by Meyer by the syllables 'gich,' and 'kirr,' uttered only once at a time, at long intervals; perched, when wooing, at the top of a tree.

About the end of March, or beginning of April the nidification of this species commences.

No nest is formed; the eggs are laid on the dust that lodges at the bottom of the hole, at a depth of six or seven inches, but sometimes as much as two feet or even nearly three from the orifice. A pine tree seems to be preferred, but the oak and others are also made available; a pre-existing hole being adapted to their wants, or if there be none such, a new one is scooped out of the most unsound part of the tree. There is frequently a second hole, which facilitates the escape of the bird in case of danger. If the entrance be over large she reduces its size by filling it in.

The eggs are four or five in number, white and glossy, and are hatched after an incubation of fifteen or sixteen days.

I am much indebted to W. F. W. Bird, Esq., for a careful 'resumé' of the various authorities 'pro and con,' on the subject of a supposed occurrence of another species of Woodpecker; from which, on the whole, it seems to be incontestably established that it is only the young of the one before us; though, as Hunt remarks in his 'British Ornithology,' 'it is certainly a curious circumstance that the beautiful scarlet on the head of the young, is next to the white forehead, whilst in the old bird, the scarlet is at the back of the head, and the black next to the white forehead;' and also, that in the case of a nest of three young birds and an old one, sent to him by the Rev. Mr. Whitear, one of the young ones weighed more than its parent; but 'maternal solicitude' may have been the cause both of the one and the other effect.

CUCKOO.

COG, OF THE ANCIENT BRITISH.

COMMON CUCKOO. GOWK.

Cuculus canorus,   LINNÆUS. MONTAGU.

Cuculus—A term of reproach.   *Canorus*—Musical.

'A HORSE, a horse, my kingdom for a horse!' cried Richard at Bosworth, and much would the author of the 'History of British Birds' give for more discursive opportunities when he has arrived at so wide a field as the mysterious Cuckoo opens out.

Pleasant is every thought associated with the 'Cuckoo's time o' coming;' two opinions there will not be about this.

Great Spotted Woodpecker

The general appearance of the Cuckoo is strikingly like that of the female Sparrow-Hawk. It frequents localities of the most opposite description, the dreary fen and the wild heath of the open treeless moor, as well as those in which brushwood abounds, and the well-wooded hedgerows of the best cultivated districts.

It need hardly be mentioned that the Cuckoo is a migratory bird: 'in April come he will,' and that about the middle of the month—generally on the 17th.; it has been heard on the 15th.; once on the 13th., as mentioned by Mr. Thompson, of Belfast, but frequently not until one or other of the days between these dates and the 30th. The males arrive a day or two before the females; and the old birds leave the country in the autumn before the young ones. The general time for the former to depart is in the end of July or beginning of August; but it would appear as if, though they commence their outward-bound movement from north to south, about this time, they do not finally quit the land until rather later. They travel by night. It would seem that they return to the same station again and again.

Not only is the Cuckoo when come to maturity a bird of marvel, but even from the very first the chapter of its strange proceedings commences.—The instinctive propensity of the young one to turn out of the nest, by forcible ejectment, any other occupants, its lawful tenants by right of primogeniture, who may have been preserved from previous expulsion, is well known.

The young Cuckoo is for the most part hatched before the eggs of its foster-parent, if any have been left to be incubated, and in the latter case it loses no time in asserting its usurped rights, but generally on the very day after it is hatched its might takes the place of right, and one by one the true-born birds are thrown out, to be killed by the fall, or by any other mishap that may befal them. If it should happen that one or more of the little birds should, by some means or other, be preserved in the nest, their parent feeds them and the interloper with the like attention; making it to appear that she cannot discriminate between them: 'Tros Tyriusve' share equally her maternal care; and this even after leaving the nest, both on the ground and in trees.

As before hinted, the adult Cuckoo occasionally herself destroys, by throwing out, one or more of the eggs of the bird into whose nest she surreptitiously introduces her own. But how does she introduce them? Here again is another singularity! It is perfectly certain that in some instances she conveys them in her bill into the other birds' nests. Mr. Williamson, the curator of the Scarborough Museum, found the egg of one in a nest which was placed so close under a hedge, that the Cuckoo could not possibly have got into it; and T. Wolley, Esq., records another similar instance, communicated to him by Mr. Bartlett, of Little Russell Street, London, in which he found one in the nest of a Robin, which was placed in so small a hole that the same mode must have been resorted to. So again, Dr. Jenner has related an instance in which the egg was placed in the nest of a Wagtail, built under the eaves of a cottage. Here it is plain who has been the 'eaves dropper.' The Cuckoo has been seen removing the egg of a small bird from a nest, in which she had just placed her own changeling, by the same mode by which in cases where she could otherwise, if not in all, she introduces her own, namely in her bill. Cuckoos do not pair, but are polygamous, the reason of which has been suggested to be that parental care is not required for the young.

The flight of the Cuckoo is steady and straight forward. At times he may be seen perched upon a rail, branch, or eminence, swinging himself round with out-spread tail, and uttering his note the while in an odd and observable manner. On the ground they are but awkward, and out of their element, and at sea, so to speak. They sometimes perch lengthwise on a bough, after the manner of the Night-Hawk.

The food of these birds, generally procured in bushes or trees, but sometimes on the ground, consists of insects, spiders, and caterpillars, as also, I believe, minute shells; and White of Selborne says seeds, but they may have been accidentally swallowed with the insects. There seems some slight reason for supposing that the Cuckoo will eat the eggs of other birds, possibly those which she takes out to make room for her own; and one instance is mentioned by Bishop Stanley, in his 'Familiar History of British Birds,' in which a flock of Cuckoos, observed in the county of Down, devoured, or at least pulled in pieces the greater part of a late brood of young Blackbirds in the nest. The Cuckoo's food being insects, it is guided, one should say by instinct, but that its instinct is, as will appear, by no means unerring in this respect, to lay its egg generally in the nest of an insectivorous bird, for the most part in that of a Robin or a Dunnock. It does not, however, invariably do so, the egg having been found, as hereafter mentioned, in the nest of a Greenfinch, a Linnet, and a Chaffinch. It is, nevertheless on the other hand, very remarkable that such birds as these latter will very often, though not always, in such case, feed the young Cuckoo with insects; their own most natural food being grain, or rather seeds, and with which latter, when prepared in their craw, they feed their own young, as well as with the former. Even a Canary, in whose cage a young Cuckoo was lodged, fed it with caterpillars placed there for the purpose, instead of with the seed on which she herself was always accustomed to feed. At times, however, birds of the Finch tribe, at whose door these unwelcome foundlings have been dropped, supply them with young wheat, vetches, tender blades of grass, and seeds of different kinds.

The Cuckoo drinks frequently. They may often be seen pursued, or rather followed by small birds, especially by Titlarks, and this can hardly be wondered at after the facts here mentioned, which may also well leave it in doubt whether it be in hostility, or a kind of stupid and wondering admiration. Swifts join in the pursuit, though the Cuckoo does not lay her egg in their nests: their migration is too early for her young.

The food of the young Cuckoo consists of caterpillars, small snails, grasshoppers, flies, and beetles, but in either case, whether it be their natural, or rather their unnatural parents, or their foster-parents that purvey for them, they are insatiable in their cravings for food, and their continual cry, like Oliver Twist, is for 'more! more!' Equally earnest is the foster-parent in providing for their wants; one has been seen to alight on the back of the intruder who filled her nest, the better to supply it with food.

The note of the Cuckoo, uttered both when flying and perched in trees, is expressed by its name. It is often however, varied from the plain 'cuckoo,' to a quicker 'cuckoo; cuckoo; cuc-cuc-koo.' Both the male and female birds utter it, but the latter, it may be, only seldom; though I am inclined to think that it is equally common to both. They have besides another soft note, rendered by the syllables 'cule, cule,' uttered rapidly, and continually repeated several times; another exclamation of anger, and another more like the bark of a little dog: the young bird has a plaintive chirp. When making love in the spring, they give utterance to a small variety of curious croaking, chuckling, chucking notes. The female, as I imagine it to be, has also a very different note, which I can best liken, so at least I did most carefully some years ago, when I heard it, to the words 'witchet-witchet-watchet.' This note, preceded immediately by the ordinary 'cuckoo,' I heard myself most distinctly uttered from the throat of one and the same individual bird, flying only a few yards from me, over an open field, so that there could be no possibility of any mistake; and this undoubted fact may possibly suffice to set at rest the unfounded supposition that the female Cuckoo does not cry 'cuckoo;' for I have not yet heard it theorized that the male bird utters the note in question, which has been described as a 'harsh chatter.' The Italian proverb says, 'i fatti sono maschii, le parole femine'—'Facts are masculine, talk is feminine:' one is worth a hundred baseless fancies.

At this stage of the account of the Cuckoo its nidification should be described; but, as is so well known, there is none to describe. It deposits its parasitical eggs in the nest of some other small bird, for which they are not too large, being singularly small in proportion to its own size—just one quarter what they should be in proportion to those of small birds than which they are themselves four times larger: the provision of nature is obvious. If the Cuckoo's egg were larger than it is, it would require to be laid in a larger nest, with the natural possessors of which the young one, as Mr. Selby points out, would be, or might be, unable successfully to cope. And first, to mention the different species of birds with whose domestic arrangements it so unscrupulously makes free. The following have been already ascertained, and doubtless there are others to be added to the list, or even if not, there would be, did the parent Cuckoo stand in need of such, failing those about to be enumerated. These are the Dunnock, commonly called the Hedge-Sparrow, the Robin, the Titlark, the Pied Wagtail, the Redstart, the Whitethroat, the Willow Warbler, the Rock Lark, the Sky Lark, the Reed Warbler, the Reed Bunting, the Sedge Warbler, the Willow Wren, the Yellow-Hammer, the Blackbird, the Wren, the Throstle, the Whinchat, the Greenfinch, the Grasshopper Warbler, the Chaffinch, the Red-backed Shrike, and one writer, E. C. Taylor, Esq., in the 'Zoologist,' page 4477, says the Tree Pipit.

It is said that the Cuckoo deposits her egg before the other bird has laid hers, in some instances, and in others afterwards; but in the former, or indeed in either case the deceived little bird goes on to lay hers, in happy ignorance of the fate that awaits their embryo contents when or even before being hatched. It is, I think, quite an erroneous notion that the Cuckoo ever meets with any delay in finding a nest suitable for her to lay her egg in. At the time when she does lay, birds' nests of all the common species are abundant in every hedge, and there is no more difficulty in her finding one than another.

Cuckoo

Swift

It has been imagined that she lays her eggs later in the day than other birds; and this possibly may prove to be the case.

The eggs are not laid until the middle of May, and they require about a fortnight's incubation. Montagu found one so late as the 26th. of June; and Mr. Jesse records that a young Cuckoo which had only just left the nest of a Wagtail, was found in Hampton Court Park, on the 18th. of August, 1832. The young birds are not able to fly in less than five or six weeks.

Occasionally two Cuckoo's eggs are found in one and the same nest; but they are supposed to be those of different birds. It is thought, however, that the Cuckoo lays more than one egg in different nests, and probably more than two, at intervals, in the season—Bewick says from four to six; but I think this must have been a guess; Blumenbach also says six. Mr. M. Capper, of Shirley, informs me that he found on Shirley Common, in the nest of a Meadow Pipit, two Cuckoo's eggs, of dissimilar colouring and size, and therefore probably deposited by two different birds. Lighter-coloured varieties occur.

SWIFT.

MARTHIN DU, OF THE ANCIENT BRITISH.

COMMON SWIFT. SWIFT SWALLOW. BLACK MARTIN.
SCREECH. SCREECH MARTIN. SCREAMER.
CRAN. SQUEALER.

Hirundo apus,	LINNÆUS. PENNANT. MONTAGU.
Hirundo—A Swallow.	*Apus. Apous*—Without a foot.

The Swift is a native of the greater part, if not the whole, of the continent of Africa, as also of that of Europe.

It is met with in all parts of the United Kingdom; but it seems to be generally thought, and with some reason, that it is less frequent than it used to be. Why it is so, is entirely unknown, except so far as it may be accounted for by their wanton destruction by ignorant shooters.

The favourite haunts of Swifts are buildings in towns and villages, church-steeples, fortresses, and castles.

The Swift, migratory like all our Swallows, arrives among us later than the others, namely, not until the beginning of May, and leaves us in the beginning or middle of August. This is the rule; but exceptions to it, as a matter of course, have occurred, do occur, and will occur. Thus, the Rev. Gilbert White, in the year 1781, noticed that one pair of Swifts remained after all the others had, on or about the 1st. of August, taken their departure. In a few days but one bird remained, the female, as imagined; but there is nothing to shew that it was not the male. Whichever it was, it continued feeding its young, which were then discovered, until the 27th. of the month, when both parent and children disappeared. Mr. Yarrell imagines that the other parent forsook its family for its companions, but in the absence of proof of this, it will be a more charitable supposition, as far at least as the bird is concerned, and certainly very far from an impossible one, that some reckless shooter cut him or her off.

The arrival of Swifts is sudden and simultaneous, their departure the same, but they are more than ordinarily noisy for a few days previously. Cold or wet weather soon after their coming sometimes proves fatal to these birds; perhaps through lack of subsistence in consequence.

This bird, from the great length of its wings, and the extreme shortness of its legs, finds it difficult to rise from a level place, so that when it alights, it is almost always in some situation from which it can drop at once into the air. It may occasionally be seen adhering to the flat surface of a wall, 'the whole length of the toes being straitened by an action not practised by the generality of birds, so as to be opposed to each other in pairs; while the claws are bent beneath, with the points directed inward.' In the 'Magazine of Natural History,' volume v., page 736, Mr. Couch remarks, 'It is not long that Swifts have frequented stations convenient for my observation. At first there were about two pairs; but they have now increased to four or five; and it is singular that, according to my observation, there is always an odd bird.' Mr. Thompson, of Belfast, has remarked a like singularity for two successive years at Wolf Hill, near that place. Swifts are sociable and gregarious birds, joining in small troops of from half a dozen to a score, but restless, wild, and quarrelsome in the breeding season.

'Handsome is that handsome does,' says the proverb, and well and truly does the Swift deserve its name. Equalled in its powers of flight, it may be and is, by some other birds, and exceeded, doubtless, for the moment, by the impetuous dash of the Falcon, but in proportion to its size and the unceasing continuation of its evolutions, there must be few that can compete successfully with it. Wonderfully too, does it guide itself in all the mazes of its seemingly headlong course: one has, however, been known to be killed by being carried inadvertently against a wall. Like the rest of the Swallows, the Swift both drinks and bathes, or rather dashes while on the wing. It skims along the tranquil surface of the lake and river, and wings its way through the liquid air at a great height—the latter in clear and fine weather, the former when the atmosphere is damp and heavy. Rarely indeed do they take rest, except during the short summer night, or some say in the extreme of the 'noontide heat,' or in very stormy weather, when they are supposed to shelter in their holes, but Mr. Thompson points out that at such times they have only shifted their quarters to some more suitable hunting-place. They fly until the dusk of the evening, and have been noticed until after nine o'clock. In the morning again they are betimes on the wing.

They never seem to weary, nor do their wings once flag. They are indeed marvellously endowed in this respect, as when, says Bewick, they 'are seen in flocks describing an endless series of circles upon circles; sometimes in close ranks, pursuing the direction of a street, and sometimes wheeling round a large edifice, all screaming together; they often glide along without stirring their wings, and on a sudden they move them with frequent and quickly-repeated strokes.' In sweeping thus along, a distinct rushing sound is often made. Their speed has been conjectured to be at the rate of nearly one hundred and eighty miles an hour.

The food of the Swift consists entirely of insects of various kinds. Bishop Stanley relates, speaking of the quantity of insects destroyed by Swallows, that from the mouth of a Swift which had been shot, a table-spoonful were extracted. The indigestible part of the food is cast up in pellets.

The note is a harsh scream. Mr. Selby remarks upon the theory of White of Selborne respecting the note, that it is fanciful, and so it is; but the one he has suggested in lieu of it—that it is the consequence of 'irritability excited by the highly electrical state of the atmosphere at such times,' is certainly still more so; for it is uttered in the most opposite kinds of weather: I look upon it as a simple exclamation of enjoyment, 'particularly induced,' says Mr. Macgillivray, ' by fine weather and an abundance of food.'

The nest is generally placed in holes about steeples of churches and the old walls of lofty towers, as also under the eaves of cottages and barns, crevices under window-sills, and even in hollow trees; under the arches of bridges, in the sides of cliffs, and of chalk-pits. It is roughly formed of straws, wool, grasses, hair, feathers, and such like materials agglutinated together, picked up with great dexterity while the bird is on the wing, or purloined, so some say, from, or found in the nests of Sparrows, which they appropriate to themselves. It may be that no nest, or next to none is formed, unless the remains of a Sparrow's nest are used.

The ordinary number of the eggs is for the most part two, but sometimes three.

SWALLOW.

GWENNOL. GWENFOL, OF THE ANCIENT BRITISH.

CHIMNEY SWALLOW. COMMON SWALLOW. RED-FRONTED SWALLOW.

Hirundo rustica,   LINNÆUS. PENNANT.

Hirundo—A Swallow.   *Rustica*—Of or belonging to the country.

THE Swallows appear to be always considered as visitants to us, and are so spoken of accordingly: it seems to me, however, that this is an erroneous designation of them, for, although absent from us the greater part of the year, it is with us that they build and inhabit their dwellings, and here they rear their young: it is to other countries that they are visitants: ours is 'their own, their native land;' elsewhere they are but sojourners, unsettled excursionists, destitute of a 'local habitation.' No one who knows the meaning of the word 'Home' can doubt for a moment here!

The Swallow always makes friends among us; its useful and harmless life and social habits attract our notice, and its familiar approaches to our dwellings make it looked upon as half-domesticated; it lives among us, yet independent, requiring of us nothing but quiet possession of its accustomed nook or chimney. The Swallow is almost as much respected and cherished as the Redbreast himself, and shares with that favoured bird exemption even from the persecutions of village urchins.'

The Swallow attaches itself, for the most part, to the habitations of man, and frequents especially such as are in the neighbourhood of water, over which it delights to sweep in search of its food, which there abounds. The eye cannot fail to be attracted and pleased by its graceful flight, and when, in autumn, we first miss the favourite bird, we feel that a blank is made, and that the hey-day of that summer is gone. We are not, however, altogether taken by surprise, as, for some short time previously, we have seen the birds marshalling themselves in large companies for their approaching journey—collecting together at some selected place of rendezvous, flying to and fro, twittering and chirping, as if discussing their route and arranging all the preliminaries necessary for a lengthened voyage.

The Swallow so times its migration as to pass about half the year in this country. The period of its arrival is generally about the 10th. of April; but there is no fixed chronology. The time of departure is early in October, and so strong is the migratory instinct, that if the young of the second brood are not sufficiently advanced, they have been known to have been deserted. Some leave, or at least change their quarters, as soon as the middle of August; others about the middle or end of September, which is perhaps the chief time of their departure; and others not until the middle of October.

One would suppose, from their ceaseless flight while with us, that the Swallows would never know fatigue; but still they shew unmistakeable signs of being wearied, by alighting on the yards and rigging of ships when in their transit: nevertheless, and it is a most striking proof of the imperative impulse that guides them in their migration, they will not diverge from their pathway over the ocean, to rest on land that may be only a few miles on one side, but 'On, On,' is, like Marmion's, their motto, and from their bidden course nothing can induce them to swerve aside. They also, at such times, are said to refresh themselves by dropping on the sea, from which they rise with fresh invigoration. Audubon and other writers state this fact.

It was formerly imagined that Swallows passed the winter in a torpid state, submerging themselves in lakes for this purpose. The following is the scientific 'dictum' of Dr. Johnson:—'Swallows certainly do sleep all the winter. A number of them conglobulate together, by flying round and round, and then all in a heap throwing themselves under water, and lie in the bed of a river;' a very cold bed certainly. Alexander Mal Berger, also says, in a calendar kept at Upsal in 1755; 'August 4th.—Birds of passage, after having celebrated their nuptials, now prepare for departing;' and then 'September 17.—Swallows go under water.' The 'Kendal Mercury,' in 1837, detailed the circumstance of a person having observed several Swallows emerging from Grasmere Lake, in the spring of that year, in the form of 'bell-shaped bubbles,' from each of which a Swallow burst forth; and the editor added, 'we give the fact, well authenticated by the parties from whom we received it, in the hope that it may prove an acceptable addition to the data on which naturalists frame their hypotheses.' (!)

That the great body of them leave our wintry shores at the annual time of their migration for the 'sunny south' is unquestionable, but, nevertheless, it appears equally certain that some individuals, more or fewer in number, hybernate with us. Mr. J. B. Ellman records in the 'Zoologist,' page 2303, some instances of their having been dug out of hollows in banks in the winter, and Mr. Edward Brown Fitton, at page 2590, 'tells the tale as it was told to him' of 'immense quantities' having been taken out of the cleft of a rock in the cliff near Hastings.

'Who has not watched the Swallow on the wing,' says Linnæus Martin, 'who has not marked its rapid flight; now smoothly skimming along, now executing sudden turns and intricate evolutions with astonishing celerity? If the weather be warm, it dips in the water as it passes along, and emerges, shaking the spray from its burnished plumage, uninterrupted in its career.' The Swallow is, like all its compeers, indefatigable in its flight, and is not often seen to alight.

The food of the Swallow consists entirely of insects, and it is in pursuit of these that it is seen soaring far above in the settled days of summer, and, again, suiting itself to the changes in the weather, skimming close above the surface of the lake, or river, or meadow, along the side of a cliff, a hedge, a paling, or a sheltered avenue of trees. When feeding, it flies with the mouth more or less open, and the capture of an insect is indicated by an audible snap of the bill. It drinks and frequently laves itself while on the wing. The indigestible part of the food is cast up in pellets.

The utterance of the Swallow in the way of song, though neither powerful or varied, is cheerful and pleasant—a pretty warbling, which you like to stop in your walk and listen to.

In the month of May, about a month after the arrival of the bird, the nest is commenced, and, as imported by one of its trivial names, the inside of a chimney is a common selection, and some angle or corner a few feet down is taken advantage of for the support that it affords. The precise situation is frequently resorted to that had been made use of in previous seasons. The nest, which is open at the top, is formed of moist earth, which the bird collects bit by bit in its bill, from the side of a pond or stream, or the middle of a road, as may often be seen: it is moulded into shape, intermixed with straw and grass, and is finally lined with feathers, or such like soft materials.

Bell turrets are often built in, as also is the ledge under the roof of a barn, the inside of the arch of a bridge, the shaft of an old mine or well, an unused room or passage to which access can be gained, even such as a small orifice in a door affords; any projection of a spout, lintel, beam, or rafter that will serve as a buttress being built upon—a 'coign of vantage:' gateways, and outhouses of every kind are chosen.

In a natural state, or rather in a country where suitable structures are wanting, it is probable that rents and fissures in rocks and caves are always built in.

The eggs are usually from four to six in number, white, much speckled over with ash-colour and dark red, or brown and rufous.

Two broods are frequently hatched in the year, the first of which flies in June, and the second the middle or end of August. When the young are fledged, they may often be seen perched in a row

Swallow

Martin

on the edge of the chimney-top, pluming themselves, and waiting for, and watching their parents return with food for the supply of their wants. When they have advanced a step to some neighbouring bough or building, they still are dependant on them; and, even when they can fly, are still fed by them in the most dexterous, and almost imperceptible manner on the wing. The old birds supply them with food once in every three minutes, during the greater portion of the day. Think of this, and, in the words of the 'Wanderings,' applied to our present subject, 'Spare, O spare the unoffending' Swallow!

MARTIN.

MARTHIN, OF THE ANCIENT BRITISH.

HOUSE MARTIN.   MARTIN SWALLOW.   WINDOW MARTIN.

Hirundo urbica,   PENNANT. MONTAGU.

Hirundo—A Swallow.   *Urbica. Urbs*—A city.

The pretty chirruping of the Martin from its 'loved mansionry' over your window is the pleasantest alarum to wake you up to enjoy the 'dewy breath of incense-breathing morn,' and both the associations of earliest recollection and the adventitious aids of poetry combine to invest it with a never-failing charm. 'Where they most breed and haunt, I have observed the air is delicate.' So again, at night, when the parent bird has returned to her brood, for whom she has toiled all the day, and takes them under the shelter of her wings, what more pleasant sound is there in nature than the gentle twittering of the 'Happy Family'—the unmistakeable expression of the veriest and most complacent satisfaction!

The 'temple haunting martlet' is an attendant on civilization, and endeavours to establish itself about the habitations of man, but at the same time also it addicts itself, in some places, to natural eyries, such as are furnished by St. Abb's Head, the Bass Rock, and the hoary precipices of Sutherlandshire.

The trite remark of Cervantes, 'una golondrina no pace verano;' 'one Swallow does not make a summer,' is as true of this species as of all the rest. There is, in fact, hardly a month, nay, there is hardly a day in the winter half of the year, on which, upon one occasion or another, a Martin has not been seen, either an early arrival, or a late tarrying, or perhaps a sleeper roused up from the lethargic slumber of torpid hybernation, in which it would appear that, in some instances at least, these birds are wrapped. The average time of the arrival of the Martin is about the 21st. of April—a few days later than the Swallow, and on to the beginning of May; but, as already pointed out in the case of that species, after they have made their first appearance, they often disappear for weeks, and again shew themselves, and then remain through the summer. About the middle of October they generally depart in large flocks, having first congregated on house-tops, church-towers, and roofs, and even on trees. They are often, however, much later in leaving us; some the end of September, some most years not till the 6th. or 8th. of November.

Meyer gives the following correct account of their movements on these occasions:—'They fly, it is said, by night, and travel in flocks at a great height. These birds are remarked to congregate in large numbers together some days before they take their departure; and after settling on some raised object early in the morning, and basking in the sun, they start off repeatedly as if by a given signal, and return again and again with great clamouring; it almost seems as if they practice this mode of travelling, and train themselves for their journey.

The flight of the Martin is powerful and rapid, but often wavering and unsteady. They occasionally settle on the ground, especially when gathering materials for the construction of their nest, and, as every one knows, hold fast to the walls of houses, churches, barns, and other buildings.

Its food consists of insects.

Its note is a lively twitter, often elevated, especially early in the morning, into an extremely pleasing warble. Meyer renders it by 'skir,' 'screeb,' 'stræ,' and that of the young bird in the nest by 'brid,' which reminds one of the story in Herodotus about 'bekos' being the first word uttered by the child whom the king had kept till then, without hearing anything said, as an experiment to learn what was the original and natural language of mankind.

The Martin rears two broods in the year, and sometimes lays a third or even a fourth time, though the last brood cannot be attended to before they themselves leave. Dr. Jenner has recorded an instance of this extreme number in 1786, the last brood being hatched in the early part of October, but about the middle of that month they were forsaken by their parents. White of Selborne says that they are never without young ones in the nest as late as Michaelmas; for as soon as one brood is able to fly, the hen bird begins to lay again, but the latter clutch is smaller in number than the former one. Those which are unfortunately unable to fly when the 'moving power' seizes their parents, are left behind, speedily to perish, as has repeatedly been discovered. Dr. Stanley, Bishop of Norwich, writes, 'A pair of Martins which had deserted their family in the autumn, on returning in the spring, were observed to draw out the dead bodies of their nearly fledged nestlings. Another pair acted in a different manner: after vainly endeavouring to drag out the bodies, which had most probably formed a dried mass with the wool and feathers in the interior, they entirely closed up the opening of the nest with clay, and leaving them there entombed, proceeded to build another nursery.' When only two broods are produced, the first nest is commenced about the 25th. of May, and the young leave it about the 2nd. of August. The second nest is begun about the 11th. of August, and the second brood quit it about the 29th. of September. They build together often in parties of from twenty to one hundred, the nests frequently touching one another.

The same nest is resorted to from year to year. Thus the Rev. Gilbert White says:—'July 6th., 1783, some young Martins came out of the nest over the garden door. This nest was built in 1777, and has been used ever since.' The young birds of one year often add another the following to 'The Row' of nests which ornament the eaves where their parents have built, and sometimes the birds will form a continuous line of the mud they build with along the wall, without any apparent or discernible motive, for there it remains without any use being made of it. The mud they use in building is tempered and cemented in some way or other, for it will adhere firmly even to glass.

The nest, which is about six inches in width, and about half an inch thick above and an inch below, is generally built under the eaves of a house, or the corner of a window, or the arch of a bridge or gateway, but also frequently on the sides of cliffs. It is of an hemispheric form, closed all round except a small entrance usually on the most sheltered side, and just large enough for the master and mistress of the family in turn, and is lined inside with a little hay or grass and feathers. The interior is smooth, the outside rough.

The eggs are four or five in number, smooth and white, or pink white. Professor Thieneman figures one remarkable variety which is dotted over with small distinct pale yellowish red spots. They vary in size and shape. Incubation lasts twelve or thirteen days. At first the parent birds enter the nest each time to feed the young ones, but by and by the latter may be seen anticipating their arrival by thrusting out their heads at the door of their house, in expectation of the meal which they there receive; the old bird holding on to the nest outside, in the attitude depicted in the plate; when able to fly they are still fed on the wing.

PIED WAGTAIL.

BRITH Y FUCHES. TINSINGL Y GWYS, OF THE ANCIENT BRITISH.

WATER WAGTAIL. WHITE WAGTAIL. BLACK-AND-WHITE WAGTAIL. WINTER WAGTAIL. PEGGY-WASH-DISH. DISH-WASHER.

Motacilla Yarrellii,   GOULD. MACGILLIVRAY.

Motacilla—A Wagtail.   *Yarrellii*—Of Yarrell.

ONE is often led to wonder, and doubtless the same remark would apply to other lands, how the most trivial names of antiquity keep their place in the vocabulary of the country, while modern inventions last but for the day, or for the hour, and are then consigned for ever to the 'tomb of all the Capulets.' We may soon be lost in speculation as to the time when each of such old names was first assigned, and who it was that gave it; what combination of circumstances first procured for it the honour of the durability which bids fair to be perpetual; and through what succession of changes it has been maintained. These considerations make us smile at the vain conceits of some of our modern self-styled naturalists. Do they really think, dogmatically as they may lay down the law to their own entire satisfaction, that their whimsical combinations will ever be adopted by the people of the country—that the old will be displaced to make room for the new? They are fondly mistaken if they entertain the notion. The name of

Pied Wagtail

Meadow Pipit

the favourite and elegant little bird before us—no case of 'lucus a non lucendo' will ever remain one of the 'old standards:' no 'weak invention' will ever supersede it in the idiom of the nation. The Wagtail will always continue a Wagtail, not only in nature, but also in name.

The sides of rivers, and of lakes, of pools, streams, and mill-dams, water-meadows, and the shores of the sea, both among sand and pebbles, are the more natural haunts of the Pied Wagtail, but they are frequently to be seen deftly running about on the grass and walks in our gardens, coming up often to the kitchen door, and they also frequent ploughed fields and meadows. To the former watery situations they resort in numbers, when the early education of their family has been completed, and collect in small flocks previous to their autumnal departure.

In February these birds pair, and early in March begin their migratory movement: then they arrive from the continent: many at least of them, not all, for some have remained, and some still remain in the south, while others advance northwards, even to the extremest boreal shores of Scotland and Orkney. They leave the cold north for more southerly districts before the winter, and may be seen at that season in small flocks of from five or a dozen to fifteen or twenty, generally feeding by the side of streams or lands in their vicinity; and about the middle of August they again begin to move northwards to the sea coast. There, at the end of that month, or the beginning of September, they move in an easterly direction, and towards the middle of October many of them again wing their way elsewhere; but a considerable number remain. In severe weather these approach more nearly to houses, villages, and farmyards, and may then be seen quietly meandering along, flitting up, if disturbed, to the house tops, and occasionally, though but rarely, alighting on trees. Their movements appear to be rather uncertain, but after a periodical absence, those that had departed, again return—sometimes unexpected, but at all times welcome visitors.

The Pied Wagtail is a very elegant bird, and it is truly a pleasing sight to watch it dink and dainty nimbly running or lightly treading on the most treacherous sand in quest of its food, ever and anon flirting up its tail, which indeed is always rather elevated, as if to keep its neatness unsoiled. Occasionally you may see it wading ankle deep in the water, now perching on a little stone, now flying off on a sudden to join some neighbouring troop of its fellows, whose companionship it greets with a shrill though gentle twitter, now springing into the air to capture a fly, now threading its way among a herd of cattle, or a flock of sheep or domestic birds, still almost heedlessly awaiting your near approach. If disturbed, it springs up with a sharp but delicate note of alarm, and after a few aërial bounds frequently alights again, but sometimes goes right away.

The flight of this bird is light and undulated, but unsteady. It rises and falls alternately, renewing the motion of its wings at the pause of each descent. 'It runs with celerity, and is in continual motion in pursuit of the insects that fly near the surface, which it also catches by short turns of flight just above the ground, with singular dexterity.' It does not often, however, remain long on the wing.

Its food is chiefly composed of insects both of land and water, and their larvæ, and worms, minute fresh-water shells, and small grain and seeds, and these, as Mr. Macgillivray well describes, are sought in various diverse localities. One kept in confinement used to catch minnows in the most dexterous manner from a fountain in the middle of an aviary. Actively and dexterously the bird steps among rocks and stones, and then pitching on the top of one, instantly vibrates its tail, as if poising itself. Again, it makes a sally in the air, flutters about a little, seizes an insect or two, then glides over the ground, swerving to either side, and resumes its attitude of momentary pause. Now it essays an excursion over the water, one while darting forwards in a straight line, then hovering in the same spot, to seize some prey, and then, as if fatigued with the unwonted effort, it makes a sudden detour, and betakes itself to some offering place of rest.

The note is a sharp cheep, which it repeats frequently when alarmed, flying about in a wavering manner, as also when running on the ground, or as a prelude to the act of seizing its prey. It sometimes aspires to a pleasant modulation, which may almost be dignified with the name of a song. This often from the roof of a house, or the top of a wall.

The nest is commenced in the beginning or middle of April, according to the season. It is placed in situations of very opposite kinds, though never at any very great height, in a hole of a stone wall, the side of a bridge, in a hollow of a tree, on a heap of stones, the bank of a streamlet or river, the side of a stack of hay, peat, or wood, a stony or grassy bank. It is about five inches wide externally, by about three and a half internally, and is composed of stems of grass, leaves, small roots, twigs, and moss, lined with wool, hair, thistle down, the finer grasses, or feathers, or any other such soft substances, all somewhat rudely, or rather loosely put together. The same situation is resorted to, year after year, for a long time, the nest being placed either in, or very near to the same spot. Two broods are reared in the year.

The eggs, four, five, or six in number, and of an elongated oval form, are light grey, or greyish or bluish white, sometimes tinged with yellowish or greenish, spotted all over with grey and brown.

The young are hatched after an incubation of a fortnight; a second brood is generally reared in the year, the former one having been produced early.

MEADOW PIPIT.

COEG HEDYDD. COR HEDYDD, OF THE ANCIENT BRITISH.

TITLARK. PIPIT LARK. TITLING. MEADOW TITLING. MOSS CHEEPER. LING BIRD. GREY CHEEPER. MEADOW LARK.

Anthus pratensis, FLEMING. LATHAM. SELBY.

Anthus—Some small bird. *Pratensis*—Of, or pertaining to meadows.

Meadows and marshland, hill and dale, waste and wilderness, moorland and heath, plough and pasture land, all are the home of the sober-clad little bird before us, but especially the wilder districts. It is found on the summits of our highest mountains, and in the lowest depths of the plain below, on the stony summits of barren hills and the green pastures of fertile plains, in the grassy valleys of upland glens, the open downs that border on the sea, and the sedgy moors of the inland. I have observed them in hard weather to frequent much the neighbourhood of the sea, searching and finding among the heaps of sea-weed 'food convenient for them;' and indeed at all times the sandy places that are to be met with along the line of coast are a favourite resort of theirs, where they consort with other species. During snow they repair much to the edges of streams, lakes, and unfrozen marsh lands, and even the stackyards of the farmstead. They are frequently seen in small companies. On the coast they associate with the Rock Larks. Occasionally they may be seen in the streets of towns, driven thither by stress of weather.

The late Bishop Stanley, in his truly-named 'Familiar History of Birds,' mentions the fact of one of these little larks having alighted on board a vessel, in the midst of the Atlantic ocean, thirteen hundred miles from the nearest part of America, and about nine hundred from the wild and barren island of Georgia. They move in a southerly direction in the autumn, to avoid hard weather, and back again in the spring. In winter, as already spoken of, they affect the sides of upland streams and rills, retiring to lower grounds should the weather be severe.

This is one of the many different kinds of birds which feign being hurt or wounded, flying off in a cowering fluttering manner, in order to entice away apparent intruders from their young, in whose safety, and even in that of the nest and eggs, they display the greatest interest. The male is easily frightened, and will flutter about the interloper, uttering his shrill note, but the female sits very close, and will even sometimes allow herself to be taken on the nest. If alarmed, they either crouch or fly off, after repeating their ordinary note. At times they may be seen wading into the water, and washing themselves with much apparent satisfaction. They are alert and nimble in all their movements, 'watchful and wary,' but not particularly shy, though somewhat timid. They are easily tamed.

Their flight is but short, wavering and unequal, that of a very homely bird of passage: they have some more immediate object in view in their movements than to cross the ocean and visit a far distant clime. If, however, they do travel, they fly with speed in an undulating line. In the days of summer they hover occasionally in a desultory manner over or about their nest, singing the while, and now and then settle on a low bush or tree, wall, stone, rock, or may-be a rail, alighting with a sweep, or sometimes almost perpendicularly: this movement is often repeated several times during an hour, the song being begun when the bird is at the highest elevation, and as it descends afterwards 'with motionless wings and expanded tail, in a sloping, sometimes almost straight, direction to the earth or to the top of some bush;' but the mother earth is their more natural resort, and from thence 'their sober wishes seldom learn to stray.' They rest at night among dry grass, or under the shelter of tufts of heath, furze, or other low bushes. Akin to the Wagtails, this species frequently oscillates its tail when standing on some mound of earth, or stone, or other eminence, especially on first settling, and generally perches and roosts on the ground. Its motions there 'au pied' are agile and lively. They walk by short and quick alternate steps.

The food of the Titlark consists of small beetles, flies and other insects, caterpillars, chrysalides, worms, small slugs, and shells—of course with their contents, and also seeds. These it searches for on the ground, and will turn up small stones in quest of: a little gravel is also swallowed.

Its song, which is soft and musical, though with little variety, is uttered on the wing, frequently while, but more commonly after rising straight up into the air, falling slowly with outspread tail and extended wings, the descent accompanied with a curious quivering of the wings, when watching about its nest, and also occasionally when perched on a low bush, crag, stone, or even on the ground. It is commenced generally about the middle of April, but has been known earlier, not unfrequently in March, and on one occasion so soon as the 4th. of February; it lasts till the end of July. It is begun early in the morning, and after, for the most part, being discontinued during the heat of the day, is repeated again towards the cool of the evening, and in fine weather is continued even till long after dusk. The ordinary note is a gentle, weak, and rather shrill 'peep;' from whence probably the name of Pipit; and, when alarmed, a short double note, 'trit, trit.'

The nest, which is bulky, is placed either on or close to the ground, often in marshy places, among grass, near a tuft or hillock, and on or under the branch of a very low bush, a bank, or a wall of turf, and frequently much sunk in the ground, so as to escape the eye. It is neatly composed of grass, or sometimes fibrous roots, the finer portions constituting the lining, with occasionally a little moss and hair, and is often carefully concealed. One has been known to be built on the end of a plank, which formed part of a heap of timber; others in close proximity to farmhouses; one in a field of tares.

The eggs are from four to six in number, but commonly five, of a light reddish brown, or reddish white, pale grey, pale brown, dusky, or pale purple or blue colour, mottled over, especially near the larger end, with darker brown, or purple red spots and specks, sometimes quite covering the ground colour. They vary much in depth of colouring, some being much darker than others; hardly any two sets are exactly alike in this respect.

The eggs are laid about the middle of April, and the young are abroad by the end of May. A second brood is often produced about the middle of July.

SKY LARK.

HEDYDD. UCHEDYDD. EHEYDD, OF THE ANCIENT BRITISH.

LAVROCK. FIELD LARK.

Alauda arvensis,   PENNANT. MONTAGU.

Alauda—A Lark.   *Arvensis*—Of, or appertaining to fields.

The Lark is to be found in all situations, but particularly, in the winter half of the year, in ploughed or stubble fields, especially, in the latter case, when they are sown with clover seeds.

Larks are thoroughly terrestrial in their habits; it is but rarely that they alight on a tree, even a low bush, a wall, or a hedge, though I have several times seen them do so. They pass the day, except when soaring, and roost at night, upon the ground. They are sprightly in all their motions, and if anything like danger be observed or suspected, frequently stop to look round, raising themselves up, and elevating the feathers of the head as a crest, or else crouch down and hide themselves as much as they can, which the assimilation of their colour to that of the places they frequent, renders easy: ordinarily, on the ground, they move rather quickly about in a running manner, now faster and now more slow; they often lie very close till you almost walk up to them.

In the wild state, if on the nest, the hen bird will either crouch close, in the hope, very often realized, of escaping detection, or, if disturbed, will fly off to a short distance, in anxious distress, in a low cowering manner, or will hover about a little way overhead, uttering a note of alarm, which soon brings up the male. They will also attempt to deceive an intruder by remaining in one spot, as if to lead him to think that the nest is there, while it is in fact at some little distance. On the approach of danger they will often, as I have just said, lie close, even till a dog is within a yard of them. Larks are very good eating, and countless thousands are taken for the table, but still their numbers never seem to decrease.

As to the flight of the Lark, it is indeed, like the poet's, a 'lofty' one, continued upwards, higher and higher as the spring advances, and the sun, towards whom he soars, gets higher in the heavens; up, and up, into the very highest regions of the air, so that the eye is literally oftentimes unable to follow it; but if you watch long enough, as perhaps this equally long sentence will enable you to do with your mind's eye, you will again perceive the songster, and downwards in measured cadence, both of song and descent, but rather more rapidly than he went up, he will stoop, nearer and nearer he will come, until at last, suspended for a moment over the spot which contains his mate, for whose delight no doubt he has been warbling all the while his loudest and sweetest notes, and whom he has kept all along in his sight, slanting at the end for a greater or less distance, probably as danger may or may not appear to be nigh, he drops with half-closed and unmoved wings—and is at HOME:

'A charm from the skies seems to hallow us there,
Which, search where you will, you'll ne'er meet with elsewhere.'

This flight frequently occupies nearly ten minutes; sometimes, it is said, as much as an hour, during which time both throat and wings seem taxed to the utmost, but yet apparently without fatigue of either, even though the loftiest regions of the 'thin air' have been ascended to and traversed.

Their food consists of grain, grasses, and seeds, and also of insects, caterpillars, snails, and worms; and they may often be seen wading into little pools of water, probably in search of any insects that may happen to be there. In quest of these they have also been seen running along the top of a hedge. The Lark uses a quantity of sand and gravel with its food.

The note of the Sky Lark, so rich and clear, full and varied, is universally appreciated, so that one may surely say 'where is the man with soul so dead,' who, when on some clear bright day in early spring, when all nature is full of hope, and in the blue sky above scarce a cloud is to be seen, he for the first time that year hears the well-known carol, can help turning his eyes upwards to detect the utterer of it, and follow the happy bird, to trace, till he can no longer follow it, save faintly with his ear, in its aërial ascent, step by step, as it were, in the 'open firmament of Heaven,' this one of the 'fowls that may fly' there, by the permission given to them from the Great Creator when they were first called into existence? I think it is old Izaak Walton who says 'O GOD! what happiness must Thou have prepared for Thy saints in Heaven, when Thou hast provided bad men with such enjoyments on earth!' In descending, too, the same clear note is still heard, is sometimes continued again after the bird has alighted on the ground, and occasionally uttered by it when perched on a bush, and sometimes when hovering over a field at but a little height. I have more than once heard one myself warbling sweetly for some time from the top of a hedge, in the month of June. It has been heard long after sunset, even when the night had become quite dark, towards the 'witching hour' of midnight. If you have a Lark in a cage, give him his liberty, and make him happy.

And not only is the song of the Sky Lark thus beautiful, but it is abundantly bestowed upon us. It is to be heard throughout three quarters of the year, nay, one may almost say, in some degree, throughout the year, for in the beginning of January in the present year, I think I heard, as others have before, an attempt at it.

When 'April showers' begin to give promise of returning spring, or even earlier, in the beginning of March, as I have myself seen them, and in February, the Larks begin to separate from their companions of the winter months, with whom since the autumn they have associated in large straggling flocks, and form their 'reunions,' of a very different nature to those of the fashionable world. In the one there is that, of which in the other there is none; and this, as Aristotle says, makes 'not a little but the whole difference.' Two broods are frequently reared in the year, the first of which is fledged by the middle or end of June, or even the middle of May, the eggs being laid the end of April or beginning of May, and the second in August, the eggs being laid in June or July.

The nest is placed in a hollow scraped in the ground, with or without the fortuitous shelter of a clod of earth or tuft of herbage. It is placed in various situations, among others in a rut or track, and is rather carelessly made of grasses, and perhaps a few chance leaves, the coarser outside, the finer on the inner part. The male bird appears to bring the materials to the spot, where the female is engaged in arranging them. The young are hatched in about a fortnight: they do not quit the nest until fully fledged, but return to it to roost at night for some time after they have left it.

The eggs, three, four, or five in number, vary much both in form and colour; some are of a greyish white colour, with a tinge of purple or green, and freckled and mottled nearly all over with a darker shade of grey, greyish brown, or brown; others are of a deep sombre colour, and in some the chief part of the colour is concentrated at the larger end, either wholly, or only partially around it. They are usually placed in the nest with their smaller ends towards the centre.

YELLOW-HAMMER.

LLINOS FELEN. MELYNOG, OF THE ANCIENT BRITISH.

YELLOW BUNTING. YELLOW YOWLEY. YELLOW YELDRING.
YELLOW YOLDRING. YELLOW YITE. YELDROCK. YOLKRING. YOIT.
SKITE. GOLDFINCH. GOLDIE.

Emberiza citrinella,   PENNANT. MONTAGU.

Emberiza—..........?   *Citrinella. Citrus*—A citron or lemon tree, from
the colour of the bird?

THE Yellow-hammer is found throughout the European continent,
from Denmark, Norway, and Sweden, to the shores of the Mediterranean. It is, however, most plentiful in the midland parts—decreasing
in numbers towards the northern and southern extremities.

This is one of the most common birds that we have in this
country, and is more particularly observable in the summer time,
when there is not a hedge alongside of which you can walk without
seeing one after another flitting out before you, and then in again,
'here and there, and everywhere:' the nest is, or is to be, somewhere near, and hence the greater apparent frequency of the Yellow-
hammer at this season. In the winter they are more collected
together in flocks. They frequent, for the most part, the cultivated
districts, those that are destitute of wood being uncongenial to them,
but they are found on such wastes as are covered with gorse or
broom.

Yellow-hammers are gregarious birds, consorting in the winter months
with flocks of other species, as well as of their own. They roost
generally on the ground, and you may see them in the dusk of the
evening, when they are retiring to rest, flitting about in numbers on
the sides of banks, disturbed by your approach. In very cold weather
they are said to seek for the night the shelter of bushes, ivy, and
shrubs, as a protection against the 'cauld blast,' which the houseless
and homeless wanderer instinctively shrinks from encountering on the
wide heath, the solitary moor, or the lonely road, when it is a

'Winter's evening,
And fast falls down the snow.'

The male bird is carefully attentive to the female when engaged
during the period of incubation with her maternal duties, brings her
food, even placing it in her bill, and takes his turn in sitting upon
the eggs. They have a habit, when perched, of flirting the tail up
and down, when it is also slightly expanded. Both shew much
affection for their young, and in many cases, if not in all, the parent
birds keep in company throughout the winter, frequently with their
family also. Even when large flocks are collected together in hard
weather, it is very probable that the members of the different
families are still united to each other in some degree, and so continue
until in the following season they disperse to become the several
heads of families themselves. Like others of their tribe, these birds

Sky Lark

Yellow-Hammer

occasionally dust themselves in the roads, and at such times, and indeed frequently at others, may be approached quite closely. They are reckoned good eating, and great quantities are taken on the continent for the purpose.

Their flight is strong, quick, and undulated, and they alight suddenly and unexpectedly, displaying the feathers of the tail at the time. They move along the ground, when feeding, by a series of very short leaps, in a horizontal position, with the breast nearly touching the ground. When perched, the tail is much deflected, hanging down as if the bird were listless, and this attitude is often continued for some time.

Their food consists of grain and other seeds, and occasionally, but rarely, of insects and worms. They consume a considerable quantity of corn in the farm-yard, clinging on to the outside of the stack, and frequently pulling out the long straws, winnowing the ears, and devouring the grain either on the spot, or at some little distance to which they have flown with it.

The note, which may be heard so early as February, consists usually of two or more chirps, followed by a harsher one in a lower key, 'chit, chit, chirr,' and these at rather lengthened intervals. The bird generally utters it when perched on the outer or topmost spray or bough of a hedge or a tree. When a large flock is disturbed in winter from a farm-yard, and alight in a body on any neighbouring trees, a great clamour is sometimes raised, and the twittering continued for a considerable time, as if all the individuals were holding a 'conversazioné' together, and each wished to have his say on the subject, which, however interesting to them it may be, is a puzzle to the ornithologist even to guess the purport of: all on a sudden a few, first one and then another, glide down again from the trees, followed presently by the whole party; the conversation is over, the forage recommenced, the association in the mind of the listener which recalled some long since 'by-gone hour,' is dispelled, and conjecture as to the meaning of the language just heard is left in its previous uncertainty. Meyer relates of a tame Yellow-hammer which he had, that it displayed considerable powers of ventriloquism. The male bird not unfrequently sings while sitting on the nest in the middle of the day.

Towards the beginning of April, the associations of winter are broken up, and those of summer are made.

The nest, which is rather bulky, is usually placed either on or very near to the ground, on a bank, or sheltered by some bush, among the twigs, or in a clump of grass, or tuft of other herbage. It is formed of moss, small roots, small sticks and hair, tolerably well compacted together; the finer parts of the materials being of course inside. The late William Thompson, Esq., of Belfast, knew one in the middle of a field; he also relates that in the garden of a friend of his near that town, a pair of these birds built at the edge of a gravel walk, and brought out four young, three of which being destroyed, the nest was removed with the fourth one for greater safety to a bank a few feet distant, and the old birds still kept to it, and completed the education of their last nestling. Mr. Blackwall mentions in the first volume of the 'Zoological Journal,' his having known an instance in which, in the month of June, the female laid her eggs upon the bare ground, sat upon and hatched them; and Mr. Salmon, of Thetford, mentions in the second volume of the 'Naturalist,' old series, page 274, his having on one occasion, on the 29th. of May,

1834, found the nest at the height of seven feet from the ground, in a broom tree. Mr. Hewitson too, found one at the height of six feet from the ground in a spruce fir; and Mr. M. C. Cooke has informed me of one found near Swanscombe, in a bush, at a height of twelve feet.

The eggs, from three to four or five, and occasionally six in number, are of a pale purple white colour, streaked and speckled with dark reddish brown; the streaks frequently ending in spots of the same colour. Some have been known of a red hue, with reddish brown streaks and lines, others quite white, some entirely of a stone-colour, and others again of a like ground marbled in the usual way. In a nest in which was one egg of the ordinary size, there were two others of the Lilliputian dimensions of those of the Golden-crested Wren. The young are seldom able to fly before the second week in June, being about a fortnight after they have been hatched; they keep together at night for a short time before they finally separate. Two broods are occasionally reared in the year.

CHAFFINCH.

BRONRHUDDYN, OF THE ANCIENT BRITISH.

SHILFA. SCOBBY. SHELLY. SKELLY. SHELL-APPLE. BEECH-FINCH. TWINK. SPINK. PINK. TWEET. HORSE-FINCH.

Fringilla cælebs, PENNANT. MONTAGU. BEWICK.

Fringilla, also *Frigilla*—A Chaffinch.   *Cælebs*—A Bachelor.

The Chaffinch is with us in some degree migratory, and is remarkable for the separation, in some parts of the country, of the males and females, during the winter months, and their collection at that season into separate flocks. Mr. Selby, speaking of this singular habit says, that in the county of Northumberland, and in Scotland, their separation takes place about the month of November, and that from that period till the return of spring, few females are to be seen, and those few always in distinct societies. The males remain, and are met with, during the winter, in immense flocks, feeding with other granivorous birds in the stubble land as long as the weather continues mild and the ground free from snow, resorting, upon the approach of winter, to farm-yards and other places of refuge and supply. He adds that it has been noticed by several authors that the arrival of the males, in a number of our summer visitants, precedes that of the females by many days; a fact from which we might infer that in such species a similar separation exists between the males and the females before their migration. When at school, at Bromsgrove, in Worcestershire, I noticed this fact, I mean as regards the Chaffinch, myself. There the hen birds used to be met with in large flocks in the winter months, and also, I am nearly certain, the male birds likewise in flocks by themselves. I am inclined to think that this is most the case in severe winters.

The Rev. Gilbert White, in his 'Natural History of Selborne,'

Hampshire, remarked the same thing, the large flocks to be met with in hard weather being almost, but not quite, exclusively composed of females. Linnæus, in his 'Fauna of Sweden,' records his observation of the like circumstance there, and says that the female Chaffinches migrate from that country in the winter, but that the males do not. Hence the assignment by him to this species of its specific Latin name, equivalent to our word Bachelor.

With the advance of spring, however, our bird becomes 'Cælebs in search of a wife;' nor does he seek in vain, for in every lane in the country that is lined with trees, a 'happy pair' are to be seen; the absurdities of Malthus and Miss Martineau—to whom I wish no worse than that she may remain to the end of her days in 'Single Blessedness'—weighing not a feather in the scale with them against the Divine Edict which Nature publishes to them, 'Encrease and multiply.'

In autumn these birds become gregarious, frequenting hedgerows and stubble fields, where they unite with companions of various other species, whose similar pursuits lead them to the like localities. Still later on in the year they assemble in stack-yards, and are to be met with in every direction, searching for food in orchards, gardens, and fields, by hedgerow sides, along open roads, in copses and woods, and near houses. Towards the end of March the flocks break up, and in April preparations for an addition of family are made.

The Chaffinch is considered to act the useful part of a sentinel for other birds, by uttering a note of alarm, and so giving them timely notice of approaching danger. No bird is also more ready to join with others in mobbing any unwelcome intruder, whether in the shape of cat or weasel, owl or cuckoo; nor is any more neat in personal characteristics. Even in the depth of winter, when the pools are covered with ice, he may be seen washing in some place that affords a lavatory to him, and then he flies off to some neighbouring branch, where he preens and dries his feathers. It is a sprightly species, and confident in behaviour, allowing often the very near advance of observers or passers by, without exhibiting much alarm. The male bird, when not at rest, usually raises the feathers of the head to a trifling extent in the way of a crest.

Their flight, which on occasion is protracted, is rather rapid and somewhat undulated, being performed by quickly-repeated flappings, with short intervals of cessation. Their movement from the ground to a tree, when disturbed by your too near approach, is singularly quick —an upward dart, executed with scarce any apparent effort.

The food of the Chaffinch consists of grain, seeds, and the tender leaves of young plants, as also of caterpillars, aphides, and other insects; and these latter it may sometimes, especially in the early months of the spring, be seen hawking after for a little way, somewhat after the manner of the Flycatcher. They feed their young with caterpillars at the rate of about thirty-five times an hour, for five or six times together, at intervals of from eight to ten minutes.

There is something very cheerful in the common note of the Chaffinch, and, as harbinging the return of spring, it is always hailed with welcome by the observer of the sights and sounds of the country. It is heard so soon as the beginning of February, or even the end of January, ordinarily resembling the monosyllables 'twink, twink,' and afterwards 'tweet, tweet, tweet, tweet.'

Chaffinch

Sparrow

Two broods are hatched in the year. The first is usually abroad by the beginning or middle of May; the second by the end of July.

The nest of the Chaffinch is built on fruit or other trees in orchards and gardens, in the fields and hedges, and in the latter themselves also; occasionally, against a wall. The late Mr. Thompson, of Belfast, has recorded one which was placed in a whin bush, and another, which came under the observation of Mr. J. R. Garrett, which was built against the stem of a pine tree, and rested on one of the branches, to which it was bound with a piece of fine whip-cord: this was taken once round the branch, and its ends were firmly interwoven in the materials of the nest. It is commonly placed from six to twelve feet from the ground—sometimes higher; it is rarely completed before the end of April. While it is being fabricated, the birds shew great disquietude at the approach of any one, by continued notes of alarm, and actions depictive of uneasiness. The nest of one pair has been known to have been built in a bean rick. The male bird assists in the work of incubation. The hen bird, when sitting, is strongly tenacious of her place, and is not easily frightened from it; sometimes allowing herself to be captured sooner than forsake her charge; in one instance she has been found frozen to death at her post.

The nest is truly a beautiful piece of workmanship, compact and neat in the highest degree. It is usually so well adapted to the colour of the place where it is built, as to elude detection from any chance passer by—close scrutiny is required to discover it. It is therefore variously made, according to the nature of the elements of construction at hand. Some are built of grasses, stalks of plants, and small roots, compacted with the scales of bark and wool, and lined with hair, with perhaps a few feathers; the outside being entirely covered with tree moss and lichens, taken from the tree itself in which it is placed, the assimilation being thus rendered complete. Others are without any wool, its place being supplied by thistle-down and spider-cots.

The eggs are four or five in number, of a short oval form, and of a dull bluish green colour, clouded with dull red, often blended together into one tint. They are slightly streaked and somewhat spotted irregularly over their whole surface with dark dull well-defined red spots.

SPARROW.

ADERYN Y TO. GOLFAN, OF THE ANCIENT BRITISH.

HOUSE SPARROW. COMMON SPARROW.

Passer domesticus,   SELBY.

Passer—A Sparrow. *Domesticus*—Domestic—of, or pertaining to houses.

THE geographical range of this well-known bird is very extensive. Everywhere he is the same, at least under the same circumstances, except indeed in appearance; for, 'unlike, O how unlike,' is the smoke-begrimed Sparrow of the town, to the handsomely-plumaged bird of the country! Everywhere he makes himself at home, and 'æquo pulsat pede pauperumque tabernas, regumque turres.' The 'cloud-clapt towers' and the 'Poor Law Union,' the 'lowly thatched cottage' and the splendid Gothic mansion, nay, the very palace of the Queen of England herself, one and all bear testimony to the universality of the dispersion of the Sparrow, and the self-accommodating nature of his domiciliary visitations.

For a considerable portion of the year, Sparrows are occupied in pairs in bringing out their several broods of young, and when the last of these is able to fly, the old and young ones together repair to the fields, where, during the time that the corn is ripe, they are to be seen in large flocks, gathering in their own harvest; but when the crops are carried, and the gleaning is over, they soon repair to their former quarters, and renew their familiarity with the habitations of men. They may indeed at all times be considered as gregarious birds in some degree; at all events they are generally brought together in greater or less numbers, so that the 'Sparrow that sitteth alone upon the house-top' has been well selected by the Psalmist as an emblem of forlorn melancholy. They shew considerable affection to each other, and anxiety for their young, and are spirited, courageous, energetic, cautious, cunning, and voracious birds. They are said to be trained in Persia to hunt butterflies, such being one of the royal sports there. In the spring of the year contests among themselves are frequently to be witnessed. Two at first begin; a third comes up and joins in the fray, when he is presently attacked by a fourth. Others stand still and look on, and behold the war,—

'Suave mari magno turbantibus æquora ventis;'

the din and clamour increase until some think it time to retreat, and this probably has the effect of breaking up the party, and so the 'emeute' is quieted. As in the cases of the modern 'duello,' no danger is done to either life or limb—the 'honour' of the parties is easily satisfied without; a hostile 'meeting' and a 'sham fight' are quite sufficient, without ulterior result.

Sparrows are very fond of bathing, and also of dusting themselves in the roads, at all seasons of the year, as well as of sunning themselves, lying on one side in some warm and sheltered place, such as a gravel walk, the roof of a house, or even against the wall of one. When not engaged in feeding, they perch on trees, bushes, and hedges, the tops of stacks and houses, walls, and wood. At night they repose under the eaves of houses, about chimneys, in holes and crevices of buildings, in bushes, the sides of straw stacks, and among ivy, or other evergreen plants with which walls are covered. They often live in their nests in the cold weather, repairing them with straw and feathers, either for their own warmth, or providing thus early for their future family.

'It is often remarked what impudent birds are London Sparrows, and not without reason. Born and bred in the bustle of the town, they must either live and jostle with the crowd, or look down from the house-tops and die of hunger. Naturally enough, they prefer the former; and all our London readers will, we are sure, testify to the cool intrepidity with which this familiar bird will pounce upon a bit of bread, or some other tempting morsel which happens to catch its eye upon the pavement, and with what triumph and exultation it bears it off to its mate, seated on some window-sill or coping-stone above, or followed, perhaps, by three or four disappointed companions, who were a moment too late in siezing the spoil.'

The flight of the Sparrow is undulated and rather rapid, but if only made for a short distance, nearly direct with a continued fluttering motion. On the ground it advances by hops and leaps, both long and short.

The food of the well-known bird before us consists of insects, grain, and seeds, as also indeed of almost anything eatable that comes in its way; I have seen the seeds of the privet eaten with great contentment. Sometimes it pursues a butterfly or other insect on the wing, but it is not very expert as a fly-catcher: nevertheless, from what I have myself noticed, I would rather not be a fly pursued by a Sparrow on the wing. It may be seen in menageries fearlessly feeding among birds and beasts of all possible descriptions. It feeds its young for a time with soft fruits, young vegetables, and insects, particularly caterpillars. It is itself good eating.

The note is a monotonous chirp, known to every one, and in addition to it a curious buzzing noise has been observed by one or two persons to have been uttered by this bird, but whether produced by the motion of the tail, which was kept fluttering all the time, or whether it proceeded from the throat, they seem to have been unable correctly to ascertain.

The nest, which is large in size, and very loosely compacted, is usually placed under the eaves of the tiles of houses or other buildings, or in any hole or cavity that will supply the Sparrow with a convenient receptacle for its brood. It is compiled of hay, straw, wool, moss, or twigs, and a profusion of feathers, which the birds are sometimes seen conveying to their holes even in winter. It often measures as much as six inches in diameter, and sometimes even much more, if the situation requires it. The materials just mentioned, as also any others that may meet the requirements of the bird, are variously disposed and arranged together, according to circumstances. Dove-cotes and pigeon-houses are frequently built in, and the same situation is continued to be resorted to, and this even when the young have been exposed to misfortune from rain. It would appear that trees are built in more from necessity than choice, namely by yearling birds which commence nidification late, by which time convenient places in walls have been pre-occupied, or by individuals which from some cause or other, had been obliged to give up the latter localities. Fewer broods in the year are produced therefore in the case of nests in trees, both from their being commenced later in the season, and from their requiring naturally more time in the construction: they are accordingly better made. Mr. Meyer describes one which was handsomely built of moss, grass, and lichens, and neatly lined with hair. The entrance in these cases is by the side, and the interior is profusely lined with feathers.

The Sparrow pairs early in the season, and two or three broods are reared each year. A pair built a nest, and laid several eggs, at Markle, near East Linton, about the 15th. of December, 1842; a nest was found at Darley Abbey, near Derby, on the 20th. of December in the same year, containing four eggs; and on the 22nd. of the following February one was observed building its nest in the spout of the school-room at the same place, by Robert John Bell, Esq., of Mickleover House, near Derby. Sometimes, and not very rarely,

I believe even four broods have been known to be produced in the same year. The young birds often come abroad before they are well able to provide by effective flight for their security, and thus individuals are frequently either pushed accidentally from the nests, or lose their footing and totter over, falling to the ground. Almost as soon as they are partially able to take care of themselves, they are attended by the male alone, and the female prepares again for a new family. As soon as the nest is ready, the first brood are left to themselves, but they still remain about the premises, roosting at night with other individuals either older or younger. The male birds, while the hen is sitting, roost somewhere in the neighbourhood. When the young are abroad and fed by the old ones, the latter carry themselves in an erect manner, with a sort of pride in their deportment, and the former testify their wishes by a quivering of the wings and a constant chirping.

The first set of eggs generally consists of five or six. They are dull light grey, or greyish white, much spotted and streaked all over with ash-colour and dusky brown, varying greatly in appearance, though preserving for the most part, a general resemblance. They also differ very frequently and very much in size and shape.

The plate is from a capital drawing by my friend the Rev. R. P. Alington, Rector of Swinhope, Lincolnshire.

GREENFINCH.

LLINOS WERDD. Y GEGID, OF THE ANCIENT BRITISH.

GREEN GROSBEAK. GREEN LINNET.

Coccothraustes chloris,   FLEMING. JARDINE.

Coccothraustes. *Coccos*—A berry. *Thrauö*—To break. *Chloris.* *Chloros*—
Light green; properly, the colour of young grass.

THE geographical range of the Greenfinch is extensive throughout Europe and Asia. It is found from Sweden and Norway to Belgium, Crete, and the countries bordering on the Mediterranean; in Asia Minor and other parts.

It is a plentiful species throughout the year in all the cultivated parts of England. The same remark applies to Scotland, excepting the northern and western islands. In Ireland it is common, and resident in suitable localities. Also in Guernsey and Sark. It is a winter visitant in Shetland and Orkney, frequently appearing during that season with flights of Linnets, Larks, Snow Buntings, and other birds.

They frequent open fields, shrubberies, plantations, orchards and gardens.

About the middle of March, or earlier, they begin to move, and disperse over the length and breadth of the land: by the middle of April they disappear from their winter haunts.

Towards the end of autumn Greenfinches collect into flocks, frequently of considerable amount, attendant chiefly on the farm-stead or its neighbourhood. They by no means isolate themselves from the company of other birds, especially those of their own 'order'—Chaffinches, Yellowhammers, and others, but though not exclusive in their habits, they in general keep by themselves in straggling parties; even in summer small flocks have been seen: as many as thirty have been noticed together the last week in June. They are rather timid, though not particularly shy birds, but are easily caught, and kept in confinement.

In the spring time combats between them are frequently witnessed; at this season, too, they fly and wheel about, mostly in the morning in a curious frolicsome manner, rising and fluttering, and then returning to the same bough many times in succession. They then resort still more nearly to the vicinity of human habitations, principally no doubt on account of the earlier shelter which plantations of evergreens, such as yew trees, holly bushes, and fir trees, afford them for building their nests: to these also in winter they mostly repair at night for harbour, returning to the same spot. They are fond of washing themselves. The old birds pay great attention to their young, and Meyer points out how, on a sudden, as I have observed myself in the case of the Rook, on a signal note being given by the former that danger is apprehended, the latter will instantly cease their clamour, though even for food.

Their flight is quick, strong, and undulated, performed by two or three rapid flaps of the wings, which are then closed, and a sweep follows, down, and then up. 'Previous to retiring to rest, quitting the company of their extraneous associates, they make many circular flights in a compact body round their sleeping station, before they settle for the night.' They sometimes wheel about for some little time before alighting, but often settle down abruptly, and set to work in search of food. If alarmed, they fly up to the highest parts of any trees that may be near, from-whence they drop again when the danger appears to be removed. They associate, as before observed, in autumn and winter with other birds.

Their food consists of wheat, barley, and other grain, and seeds, those of the hawthorn occasionally, and green weeds, such as the turnip, charlock, dandelion, groundsel, and chickweed; and in the spring the buds of trees are picked off, and the larvæ of different insects also consumed: all these, as well as insects themselves, form their 'bill of fare:' with the latter the young are fed. Various mineral substances are swallowed to assist the process of digestion. The husks of corn are ground off before being swallowed.

Their note, which Meyer likens to the word 'tway,' is at first rather harsh, but becomes, as the year advances, tolerably full and mellow, and is uttered in summer from the topmost spray of a hedge, or some tree a little higher than others, as well as on the wing, but there is not any approach to a song until the spring, generally about the middle of April, but earlier or later according to the season, and only to a trifling extent even then, but they are able to learn the notes of other birds.

Nidification begins generally in April, or even earlier; the work has been known to have been completed by the 26th. of March.

The nest is pretty well compacted, and much more so in some instances than in others. It is composed of small roots, twigs, moss, and straws, and lined with finer materials of the same kinds, mingled, as the case may be, with thistle-down, feathers, and hair: one was built last year in the trellis-work near the drawing-room of Nafferton Vicarage, a few yards from that of the Spotted Flycatcher, but though undisturbed, it was not resorted to again this year, as was that of its near neighbour. It is placed in various situations—a low bush, or an evergreen, a hedge, the ivy against a wall, or between the branches of a tree. Many nests are often found in propinquity to each other in the same shrubbery, more than one sometimes even in the same bush.

The eggs, from four to six, or even seven in number, are of a bluish or purple reddish or orange white, spotted with darker purple, grey, light brown, and blackish brown, streaked also in general more or less with black. They differ much in size, shape, and colour; sometimes the whole surface is mottled over, and again there have been known no markings at all: the smaller end is rather pointed.

Two broods are frequently reared in the season, the nest for the latter one being fitted at the end of May or beginning of June. A nest with full-fledged young ones was found in a barley-rick at Gusbery, in Dorsetshire, in October, 1863. The young, if fledged, fly off in a body from the nest, if approached. The young of the Spotted Flycatcher I have seen do the same, though they had never flown before, on my going to the nest to place a young orphan Greenfinch in it, with a view to its being fed with them as a foster-brother.

GOLDFINCH.

GWAS Y FIERRI. PENEURIN, OF THE ANCIENT BRITISH.

GOLDSPINK. THISTLE-FINCH. GOLDIE. KING HARRY. RED-CAP. PROUD-TAIL.

Carduelis elegans,   MACGILLIVRAY.

Carduelis—A bird that feeds on thistles. *Elegans*— Elegant.

THIS lovely bird is one one of the most beautifully-plumaged of our native species; its form at the same time is neat and graceful, and its gay exterior is accompanied by gentleness of nature, docility of habit, and sweetness of song. It need therefore hardly be added that it is a deserved favourite, and one only regrets to see it ever otherwise than in the cheerful enjoyment of its natural liberty. Individuals have been known to live ten years in captivity, continuing in song the greater part of each year, and some even sixteen and eighteen. Willughby mentions one which lived in confinement for twenty-three years.

In this country it is found in sufficient plenty throughout England and Wales, as also in the south of Scotland, but is certainly not so numerous as formerly. Whomever else 'Free trade' may be beneficial to, it is not so to the Goldfinch; for 'Agricultural improvement,' necessitated thereby, cuts off with the tops of the thistles, so ready otherwise to run to seed, the harvest which the bird would fain reap in the autumn and the winter. Those tracts, therefore, which still remain in their original and uncultivated state, and furnish accordingly the greater quantity of wild seed-bearing plants, are their most natural resort—the uncultivated common, the now almost extirpated warren, the chase, the moorland, and the wild waste of the mountain side, and, as next best to them, large pasture fields and the borders of waste lands.

They abide with us throughout the year, but roam about the country, and appear to be observed in the greatest numbers together in the spring. A partial migration seems to take place—in the middle of the autumn and again in April. The flocks generally consist of not more than from fifteen to twenty or thirty, and often only five or six.

In procuring its food, the Goldfinch often permits your near approach, seeming regardless of it, intent upon its one main object. It is very pleasant to watch them fluttering over the stems of the thistle, hanging on in various attitudes about them, and scattering about the down in picking out the seeds. On a sudden the little flock, probably the family of the summer, flit off, twittering their lively notes.

They are easily tamed, and have been taught by those who might employ their time much more profitably, to perform various tricks, such as to feign themselves dead, let off fireworks, pushing down the lid of a little box to get at their food, and such like. They are sometimes seen in large, and sometimes in very small, but generally, as just mentioned, in moderate-sized flocks, and they also associate occasionally with Linnets. Severe winters prove fatal to many. In summer they frequently repair to gardens, shrubberies, and pleasure-grounds, to build. In their wild state two instances have been known of the female pairing with the Greenfinch, and rearing the young, and so also in confinement with the Siskin and very commonly with the Canary. They roost in trees. They are fond of washing. In the spring violent conflicts frequently take place between the cock birds.

The late William Thompson, Esq., of Belfast, records that Randal Burrough, Esq., of the county of Clare, had two tame Goldfinches which were allowed not only to fly about the room, but also through the open window. The winter was beginning to be severe, and the food suitable for small birds consequently scarce, when one day the two birds brought with them a stranger of their own species, who made bold to go into the two cages that were always left open, and regale himself on the hospitality of his new friends, and then took his departure. He returned again, and brought others with him, so that in a few days half a dozen were enjoying the food provided for them. The window was now kept up, and the open cages, with plenty of seed, were placed on a table close to it, instead of on the sill as before. The birds soon learned to come into the room without fear, and as their numbers had continued gradually to increase, there was soon a flock of not less than twenty visiting the apartment daily, and perfectly undisturbed by the presence of the members of the family. As the inclemency of the winter decreased, the number of the birds gradually diminished, until at length, when the severe weather had quite passed away, there remained none except the original pair.

Their food consists of the seeds of the teazel, the plantain, knapweed, chickweed, groundsel, ragwort, hemp, the thistle, the horseknot, the burdock, the dandelion, the hawthorn, corn, fir-cones, grasses, and

Greenfinch

Goldfinch

various herbaceous plants: occasionally also beetles and other insects, which are triturated with small gravel. The young birds are fed for a time with caterpillars and insects.

The note, as is well known, is very sweet and varied. It is commenced about the end of March, and is continued without much interruption till July. The bird has a habit, while singing, of turning itself quickly from side to side.

The nest, which is a beautifully-wrought structure, is placed in orchard and other trees, especially those which are evergreen, in bushes, and in some instances in hedges, and at times as much as thirty feet from the ground in gardens and plantations: it is composed externally of grass, moss, lichens, small twigs, and roots, or any other appropriate substances which different places may differently furnish, thistle-down, willow catkins, the seeds of groundsel, and so forth. Inside it is elaborately interwoven with wool and hair, lined with the down of willows and various plants, and sometimes a few or more leaves or feathers. It is, as above stated, very neatly finished, and Bolton says is completed in three days. It is often placed in frequented situations, without much regard to passers by. The same place is resorted to in successive years. A pair built and reared their young in the aviary of Mr. Thomas Walker, of Rosebank, near Tunbridge Wells. W. K. Bridger, Esq. has favoured me with a specimen for the use of my work.

The eggs, four or five in number, are bluish white, or pale greyish blue, sometimes tinged with brown, and are slightly spotted with greyish purple and brown or orange brown, mostly towards the larger end, with occasionally a dark streak or two.

SISKIN.

Y DDREINIOG, OF THE ANCIENT BRITISH.

ABERDEVINE.

Carduelis spinus,   MACGILLIVRAY.

Carduelis—A bird that feeds on thistles.
Spinus—A bird so called by the Greeks, whence our 'Spink,'—(used in Aristophanes.)

THOUGH inferior to the Goldfinch in beauty of plumage, the Siskin is its equal in pleasing neatness—the one, as it were, embodying the striking beauty of the fruit of the orange tree, and the other the more chastened and sober hue of the lemon, in the general tone of its colour.

In this country it is but locally distributed, and therefore an uncommon bird, though found in tolerable plenty where, or rather when, it occurs. In Yorkshire it is tolerably common in some winters near Sheffield,

Halifax, where it was very plentiful in the winter of 1835-6; Doncaster, a large flock was seen in Sandal Beat, in April, 1837; Barnsley, Hebden-Bridge, and York, as also in the neighbourhood of Bridlington; one was found dead at Beverley, by my sister, Miss Joanna H. Morris, in the very severe snow-storm of March, 1853. It has also been met with near Barnsley by Mr. J. Lister. When at school, at Bromsgrove, in Worcestershire, I and my schoolfellows used to shoot several of these birds out of pretty considerable flocks, which occasionally frequented the gardens near that town, and more generally the alder trees by the side of Charford brook. I just missed seeing them in April in the year 1852, in the same neighbourhood, namely, at Stoke Prior, lower down the said stream, where my friend the Rev. Harcourt Aldham, vicar of that parish, had seen a flock several times just before I visited him.

The Siskin, with us, migrates from the north to the south in the autumn, leaving in September, October, and November, and returning in April. A few have been known to breed in the latter-named portion of the island, and more in the former. Mr. Yarrell mentions two such instances near London, and Mr. Meyer two others, both in Coombe wood, in the same neighbourhood. Near Lancaster, several pairs remained and bred in the summer of 1836.

They are companionable birds with each other, going in flocks, generally of from twelve to twenty, in association also not unfrequently with others of their 'country cousins,' the Linnets of the smaller and the larger species. In confinement they shew great affection for their mates, and pair with the Canary. One has been kept for ten years. They are easily taught various tricks.

They are almost constantly in motion, both in their wild and confined state, and sometimes use the bill in climbing. They are by no means shy, and are gay, lively, and active.

They fly in a light and bounding manner.

Their food consists of the seeds of the alder, the willow, the fir, the birch, the elm, the maple, the sycamore, the beech, the broom, the thistle, the dandelion, the ragwort, chickweed, groundsel, and those of other plants and trees.

Their song, though short and low, is sweet, and much esteemed; and pleasant it is to hear this 'Bonnie wee thing' twittering its small note, as it hangs in every variety of attitude on the alder, or flits from bough to bough, and tree to tree, in search of its accustomed food. It has been heard singing in the winter, and utters a twitter while flying.

The nest is placed in trees, at only a short or moderate height from the ground, or near the top of a spruce fir, and is composed of stalks of grass, and small roots and fibres, moss and lichens, lined with hair, rabbit's fur, thistle-down, wool, or a few feathers. It has been known more than once placed in a furze bush within three feet of the ground.

The eggs are pale greenish white, spotted around the thicker end with purple, and a few brown dots. W. F. W. Bird, Esq. has kindly sent me a drawing of the egg from one in the collection of the Right Honourable Lord Garvagh.

Incubation lasts fourteen days; the young are fledged in fifteen more, and are able to leave the nest at the end of the third week.

LINNET.

LLINOS BEN-GOCH FWYAF, OF THE ANCIENT BRITISH.

BROWN LINNET. COMMON LINNET. GREATER LINNET.
RED-BREASTED LINNET. GREY LINNET. ROSE LINNET. WHIN LINNET.
LINTIE. GREY LINTIE.

Linaria cannabina,   MACGILLIVRAY.

Linaria. Linum—Flax.   *Cannabina*—Belonging to canes or reeds.

In this country it is generally distributed throughout the year in
England, Scotland, Ireland, Guernsey and Sark, Orkney, and Zetland.
The Linnet is easily reared from the nest.

Towards the end of autumn individuals collect together in flocks,
and these again, as winter advances, further unite, often to their own
destruction, a too dense crowding together proving fatal to them as
well as to their superiors in the scale of creation. I remember picking up nine which I once shot in Berkshire; and I saw in the
newspaper a few years since, that, 'si rite recordor,' upwards of a
hundred and forty were killed at one fell discharge. In Yorkshire
they are frequent in most districts, especially the moorlands. Sometimes they join with other birds of the Finch tribe, but generally
keep to themselves. Partial migrations or movements take place.
In spring the flocks break up, and leave for the most part the
cultivated districts of the country, to which they had betaken themselves,
for the more hilly and mountainous regions of the north, commons,
moors, furze covers, and wastes, rejoicing in the wild heather, the
gorse, the broom, and the sloe. The Linnet occasionally makes its
nest in gardens. A few build in the south, but not farther than
Thetford, Barham, and Calford, Norfolk, so far as I am aware, where
Alfred Newton, Esq., has found the nests. William Robson, Esq.,
since I wrote the above, has forwarded me the eggs taken in Mid
Kent, where he is informed they build plentifully. In winter they
may often be seen on the sea shore, as well as in the stubble fields
and ploughed lands.

The Rev. J. Pemberton Bartlett, curate of Fordingbridge, Hampshire,
has sent me the following anecdote of a Linnet; the locality is not
mentioned. He says, 'In passing a low furze bush, my attention
was attracted to a bird which fluttered and fell a few feet before me,
as if in a fit. My first impulse was to step quickly forward and pick
it up, the former of which I did, but when within about two feet of
it, it rose and fluttered on a few yards further. Thinking it was
wounded I again attempted to pick it up, when it again appeared to
receive a fresh amount of strength, and made another intoxicated sort
of progress for a few yards. This it did several times, and I began
to doubt if I should catch it after all, when at last, to my great
surprise, just as I was near enough to 'put some salt on its tail,' it
rose up and flew away, twittering, (laughing at me as I found
afterwards,) like the pertest and strongest Linnet in the world. At
first I was puzzled to account for its very eccentric behavior, but it

Siskin

Linnet

struck me that possibly, like the Partridge, it might have performed the antics described to decoy me from its nest. I therefore returned, and searched the furze bush, where, sure enough, I found it with five eggs, which were still warm from the heat of that body which the faithful little bird had exposed for their preservation, for had I been so disposed, I could, with my stick, without difficulty, have knocked her down. This trait in the character of the Linnet was new to me, and delighted me much.' They will, when engaged with their young, drop sometimes into the bushes about them for concealment, contrary to their usual practice, which is to fly off when approached.

The flight of this bird is quick and undulated—a series of curves performed by the alternate flapping and cessation of the motion of the wings. In flocks they glide and wheel about in a manner which, to the ornithologist, is pleasing to behold. On the ground, too, they are quick and sprightly in their movements, advancing by short leaps. They stand upright when perched. They roost in hedgerows, whin-covers, low evergreen plantations, and bushes.

Its food consists of the seeds of various plants—the dandelion, the sow-thistle, the thistle, rape, flax, chickweed, of which it also eats the leaves, and such like. In winter they make a meal of hips and haws, and the berries of the ivy, holly, and mountain ash. They feed much upon the ground, especially in this season.

The note is soft and mellow, varied, and sweet, so that it is valued, unfortunately for it, as a cage bird, possessing, as it also does, the power to imitate the notes of others, even of the Nightingale; nay, to utter distinct sounds and articulate words. A fine voice has proved the ruin of many, and not only of birds. Meyer suggests that its name of 'Linnet' is derived from its ordinary call. 'If we approach a company of Linnets, who are amusing themselves, without seeming to be conscious of what is passing around, a twitter is first heard from one or other of the flock, and, on the slightest further advance, all within hearing become so much alarmed as to fly off to a quieter station,' but otherwise, 'if undisturbed on a fine and serene evening, the flock will assemble on some tree or more elevated bush, pluming themselves, and rehearsing, as it were, their songs for the coming spring. The song is taken up by the whole flock, each warbling his own strain, and this, when the air is still, may be heard at a considerable distance.'—So Sir William Jardine.

The nest, of rather large size, is commonly placed in heath, grass, furze, or gorse, and is neatly constructed inside, but the outside rather roughly, being formed of small twigs, roots, straws, fibres, and stalks of grass, thistle-down, or willow catkins, intermixed with moss and wool, and lined with hair and sometimes feathers. It is occasionally placed in a gorse, thorn, or other bush or tree, and has been known at a height of ten or twelve feet, but is usually about four, from the ground; also in hedges; one on the top of a gate-post; often in trees trained against a wall, particularly the pear, as affording the most concealment; one high up in a white thorn. A pair of Linnets have built and reared their young in the aviary of Mr. Thomas Walker, of Rosebank, near Tunbridge Wells.

The eggs are from four to six in number, of a bluish white colour, spotted, most so at the larger end, with purple grey and reddish brown; some are of a reddish black colour without spots, others with only a few spots of reddish black colour, others again are only speckled around the zone with rufous brown, and some, exceptional ones, have been known pure white.

The young are usually able to fly by the end of May, and there are mostly two broods in the season.

CROSSBILL.

COMMON CROSSBILL.   EUROPEAN CROSSBILL.   SHEL-APPLE.

Loxia curvirostra,   LINNÆUS. LATHAM.

Loxia. Loxos—Curved, oblique.   *Curvirostra. Curvus*—Curved.
Rostra—The beaks of birds.

IT has been abundantly and conclusively demonstrated that the curious beak of the Crossbill, so far from being, as described by Buffon, 'an error and defect in nature, and a useless deformity,' is most peculiarly and admirably adapted to the mode of life of its owner for which it was created.

On the European continent these singular birds are met with in Russia, Denmark, Norway, Lapland, Sweden, Bavaria, Poland, Germany, Silesia, Bohemia, Prussia, Holland, France, Switzerland, Italy, and Spain. In and towards the north they are the most abundant, and less migratory. In Asia also, in Siberia, and even to remote Japan; as also in North America in various parts.

In every or almost every county of England they have at one time or other been met with. In Cornwall, however, they are very rare. One was shot in the Orchard, Grove Hill, Woodlane; and three at Carclew, in April, 1850; it also has occurred at Enys, the seat of Mr. Enys.

In the month of June, and the latter end of the year 1821 and the beginning of 1822, Crossbills were very numerous in many parts of the country, especially in Scotland; so they were also in 1828, 1829, 1830, 1833, 1834, 1836, 1837, 1838, 1839, as likewise in 1806, 1791, when hundreds were taken near Bath, and 1593, of which the following account is given in an old manuscript, quoted by Mr. Yarrell:—'That the yeere 1593 was a greate and exceeding yeere of apples; and there were greate plenty of strang birds, that shewed themselves at the time the apples were full rype, who fedde uppon the kernells onely of those apples, and haveinge a bill with one beake wrythinge over the other, which would presently bore a great hole in the apple, and make way to the kernells; they were of the bignesse of a Bullfinch, the henne right like the henne of the Bullfinch in coulour; the cocke a very glorious bird, in a manner al redde or yellowe on the brest, backe, and head. The oldest man living never heard or reade of any such like bird; and the thinge most to bee noted was, that it seemed they came out of some country not inhabited; for that they at the first would abide shooting at them, either with pellet, bowe or other engine, and not remove till they were stricken downe; moreover, they would abide the throweing at them, in so much as diverse were stricken downe and killed with often throweing at them with apples. They came when the apples were rype, and went away when the apples were cleane fallen. They were very good meate.'

So also in Childrey's 'Britannia Baconica:'—'In Queen Elizabeth's time a flock of birds came into Cornwall, about harvest, a little bigger than a Sparrow, which had bils thwarted crosswise at the end, and with these they would cut an apple in two at one snap, eating onely the kernels; and they made a great spoil among the apples.' They had also been noticed so early as the year 1254.

These birds are by no means shy, and are very easily tamed: in one instance, namely, in the aviary of Lord Braybrooke, at Audley End, near Saffron Waldon, Essex, they have been known to build and lay. Even in the wild state they may be approached, or themselves approach very nearly. Of those mentioned before as having occurred in 1791 many were taken with a noose on the end of a fishing-rod. In confinement they shew their connexion with the Parrots by climbing about their cage in all directions, both with beak and claws; even when dead they still cling on, with the tenacity of life, to the bough which has afforded them a resting-place—'the ruling passion strong in death.' They are reckoned very good eating on the continent, and are sold for the purpose in considerable numbers.

Their flight is undulated, and at the same time quick and rapid. In moving to any distance they fly in a strong but rather undulated manner.

Their food consists of the seeds of the various species of fir trees, as also at times those of the apple, the pear, the mountain ash, the alder, the hawthorn, and others, if need be even those of the thistle; sand and small fragments of stone are also swallowed. In extracting the seeds from the smaller cones of the larch, spruce, fir, and others of the pines, they frequently, having first cut one off from the tree with their bill, hold it firmly against a branch between the claws of one or both feet, after having flitted with it to some neighbouring bough, or removed to the nearest convenient part of the one they are on. The sound of the cracking of the cones arrests attention. These are 'split up one or both sides longitudinally, and are so torn in search for the seeds as to be easily perceived, and mark the progress of the flock, while the ground beneath is strewed with numbers which have been unable to withstand their attacks on the branch.' On the larger ones they perch, and make them at once their dining-table and their dinner—'mensas consumimus:' sometimes the cone falls down—an unfortunate turning of the tables for the poor bird. They occasionally descend to drink.

In spring, the note, though low, is pleasing and agreeable; at other times while feeding they keep up a constant chatter—a 'chip, chip,' and 'soc, soc,' accompanied by a movement of the body, and in flying from one place to another emit a sharp tone. On warm sunny days, they sometimes indulge in a sudden flight, and after disporting themselves about for a short time in full chorus, alight on the tops of the trees, continuing for a time a gentle warbling: both the male and female sing.

Nidification commences very early in foreign countries, even in January or February, the young having been found fledged in March. According to Temminck, these birds nestle at all seasons of the year.

The nest is placed in the angle of the junction of the branches

Crossbill

of the tree, low down and also high up, and is loosely compacted of small twigs, grass, small straws, and moss or lichens, according with the colour of the tree it is placed on, lined on the inside with the dry leaves of the fir tree, and also with hair, wool, or feathers. They have been known only about ten feet from the ground. The edges of the nest extend from three to five inches beyond the middle part.

The eggs, four or five in number, are white or greyish white, sometimes tinged with blue or green, and spotted, chiefly at the thicker end, with red brown, reddish, bluish red, purple, or brown.

These birds vary very greatly in size, as they also do in colour, exhibiting a diversity of shades, according to age or season, of yellow, orange, red, scarlet, green, and olive. They are of a thick-set make.

STARLING.

DRUDWEN. DRUDWY. Y DRYDWS, OF THE ANCIENT BRITISH.

STARE. COMMON STARLING.
COMMON STARE. SOLITARY THRUSH, (THE YOUNG.)

Sturnus vulgaris,   PENNANT. MONTAGU.

Sturnus—...........?   *Vulgaris—*Common.

Starlings are common even in London; many couples constantly breed in Gray's Inn Gardens, where they may be seen daily. They are quite numerous in Kensington Gardens and Hyde Park; so my friend W. F. W. Bird, Esq. informs me.

They are partially migratory, or rather moveable, in some places at some seasons.

So early as the latter end of the month of June, as soon, in fact, as their young have been sufficiently educated, which has been known to be the case by Dr. Stanley as early as the 6th. of that month, Starlings begin to collect together in flocks of twenty or thirty, and, as the season advances, each of these is severally added to by re-cruits from other families, who join them in their flights, and thus the original party 'crescit eundo' until in the end a vast mass is congregrated. In the evening they collect in troops of thousands in the reed-beds which adjoin a river, the marsh, the mere, the loch, or lake, and especially in the fen districts of Lincolnshire, Nottingham-shire, Essex, Cambridgeshire, and Huntingdonshire, and their harsh cry may be heard at a great distance, sounding almost like the noise of a steam saw-mill; so they also gather in numbers towards the end of the summer even in gardens and on houses, and only after a great chattering retire to rest. Their habits, therefore, are social at these portions of the year, and even in the breeding-season many pairs will frequent the same locality, if it presents a sufficiency of favourable situations. They are very assiduous in their care of their young. They frequently may be seen in company with different other species, such as Redwings, Fieldfares, Wood Pigeons, Jackdaws, Plovers, and especially Rooks, a common purpose bringing them together on neutral ground. They are occasionally a little quarrelsome over some mutual 'bone of contention,' but in general live peaceably together, nor do they molest other birds. In barren districts they roost at night all the year round in the holes and crevices where they have built, but in other parts of the country, where a choice of shelter is afforded, they repair to different places for the purpose. They will at times remain for hours together perched in the same tree, sentinels being appointed to keep a look out, and on a note of alarm being given, they at once betake themselves to flight. They are good enough to eat, but rather tough, and slightly bitter.

Their flight is straight, strong, vigorous, and rapid, performed with regularly-timed beatings of the wings: on the ground they walk with alternate steps. They alight in an abrupt manner on the open pasture, and immediately disperse, running nimbly along in earnest search of food, which if discovered underground is uprooted from thence. 'During their search they are seldom altogether silent, some individuals commonly keeping up a chattering noise, and occasionally uttering a low scream when interfered with by others. This scream prolonged and heightened is the intimation of alarm, and when heard from one or more of the flock, they immediately cease their search, look up, and if they should judge it necessary, fly off with speed to another generally distant part.'

In winter they consort, as already stated, with Rooks, Jackdaws, and Pigeons, and sometimes join flights of other birds in the air, such as Lapwings, and seem to keep in the van, and lead and guide the others backwards and forwards. It is a beautiful sight to watch a cloud of these birds, dividing in a moment into various detachments, and again as suddenly reuniting with as much harmony as the ranks of the best disciplined army. They assume in these flights all manner of shapes, even that of a balloon, and if threatened by a Hawk, present a dense and compact mass, resistant on every side.

When sweeping down to settle to rest for the night, some would appear to alight at each descent, while the bulk of the flock fly round and round, sometimes for half an hour, until the whole conclude their manœuvres, and join the first settlers in their roosting-place. Where the reeds are made use of, much damage is caused by the breaking them down.

Their food consists of insects, caterpillars, grashoppers, worms, snails, grain, fruits, and seeds, and in search of each severally of these they may be seen now sweeping off from their secure retreats in the grey old church tower, or the 'cool grot' of the lonely cliff that overhangs the pebbled beach of the glorious ocean, and hurrying to the ploughed field or the farm-yard, the quiet cow-fold and the pasturing herd, now perching on an adjoining wall, and now on the back of a familiar sheep, and now whistling their quaint ditty from the house-top or a neighbouring tree. In the winter, in very hard weather, they frequent the sea-shore, turning over, with a sudden opening and twirling of the bill, the stones which hide the marine insects. They also swallow a little gravel to aid the digestion of their food.

On sunny days, even in winter, they may be heard gurgling a low and not unpleasing note, which, when the result of the 'concerted music' of a flock, forms a body of sound to which you like to listen. In the early spring there are several modulations and intonations of this voice, uttered from the top of a tree, church roof, or other building, accompanied by a curious shuffle of the wings sideways. It is no doubt the language of courtship.

Nidification commences about the end of March or the beginning or middle of April. They build in church-steeples and in holes of the walls of houses, castles, spires, towers, or ruins, as also in those of trees, as well as in cliffs and rocky and precipitous places; at times in dove-cotes and pigeon-houses, as also in caverns and under rocks, and even have been known to occupy the holes deserted by rats, more or less fashioned for themselves. Where any or all of these are awanting, the abutment of a bridge, or any suitably high building, is put up with.

The nest is large, and fabricated of straws, roots, portions of plants, and dry grass, or hay, with a rude lining of feathers and hair. The birds will sometimes resort most pertinaciously to the same building-place, in spite of every opposition, discouragement, and blockade. In one instance the eggs have been said to have been found in the nest of a Magpie. One pair, having with much difficulty forced their way into one of the balls used by being raised or let down to act as a signal on a railway, there built their nest, and though the ball was elevated and lowered to within a few feet of the ground fourteen times a day, this did not interfere with their proceedings, and in due time four eggs were laid with every prospect of being duly hatched. This near Kilwinning, on the Androssan line, in 1853, and the circumstance was recorded in the 'Dumfries Courier.'

The eggs, four or five to six in number, are of a delicate pale blue or blue green colour: some have a few black dots. G. Warren, Esq., of Witnesham Vicarage, near Abingdon, found a nest, with the eggs all but pure white, and forwarded me two of them as specimens.

Incubation lasts about sixteen days: both birds feed the young. Two or three broods may be raised in the year.

THRUSH.

CEILIOG BRONFRAITH, OF THE ANCIENT BRITISH.

THROSTLE. SONG THRUSH. COMMON THRUSH. MAVIS.

Turdus musicus,   PENNANT. MONTAGU.

Turdus—A Thrush.   *Musicus*—Musical.

THIS favourite bird is a native of Europe generally, being common, during summer, in Denmark, Norway, Sweden, and Russia, from whence it extends over Germany, France, Italy, and Greece. In Asia Minor it is also to be seen.

The Thrush is a tameable bird, and, if encouraged, in hard weather will come close to the window for food. He is, however, not deficient in cunning, and will often baffle a pursuer by lying close

Starling

Thrush

in the bottom of a hedge, until the danger has past, when he will fly off in the opposite direction, with a loud chattering noise. They are not, strictly speaking, gregarious, but often in the winter are met with in considerable numbers, along with the Fieldfares and Redwings. Thrushes are good birds to eat, and are often sold in the markets with their kindred species. They have not unfrequently been known to take refuge in houses, when pursued by Hawks.

Their flight, which is capable of being prolonged to a great distance, is rapid, performed in moderate curves, with quick flaps, intermitted at intervals, often at a considerable elevation, but generally rather low. On the ground, in quest of food, they droop the wings a little, and with the tail nearly horizontal, raise the head askance; if anything in the shape of food is descried, they move quickly to it, their general mode of progression being by a series of leaps. If in a listless mood, the tail and wings are drooped, the neck drawn in, and the feathers ruffled out: in this attitude they may often be seen perched on a stone, or branch of a tree or hedge. They settle very suddenly, but run along a few paces after alighting, and the same before taking wing.

Their food consists of snails, insects, worms, caterpillars, and fruits, and in winter the berries of the mountain ash and other trees and shrubs, whelks and other shell-fish; slugs, in winter, and seeds of different kinds contribute to their sustenance. The former they break the hard shells of by hammering them with their bills against some accustomed stone, as on a Druidical cromlech, deriving, as they do, their origin from the ancient British times, before the treacherous Saxons or the Norman adventurers had touched the soil. If a stone be not at hand, any other hard substance is made to answer the purpose. A heap of broken shells often marks the place, their resort perhaps one year after another. In summer they do some damage in gardens by eating the soft fruits, such as gooseberries, currants, and raspberries. A dry season, by depriving them of sufficient plenty of more suitable fare, renders them unusually destructive, and they also pluck up many plants in search of insects concealed about the roots.

As for the note, that man can have no music in his soul, who does not love the song of the Throstle. Who would not stand still to listen to it in the tranquil summer evening, and look for the place of the songster? Presently you will discover the delightful bird pouring forth his lay from the top of some neighbouring tree; you will see his throat swelling with his love song, and hear it you may, if you choose to linger, till sable night casts her dark mantle on all around, and wraps the face of nature in the shroud. Begun with the dawn of day, the Mavis has continued his clear and liquid notes at intervals, ceasing only at midday, till now that evening has come, when he must chant his evening hymn, and remind you of your own orisons to the Great CREATOR. The calm eventide is the hour at which he most delights to sing, and rich and eloquent then, as always, are his strains. Uninterruptedly he warbles the full and harmonious sounds, which now rise in strength, and now fall in measured cadence, filling your ear with the ravishing melody, and now die away so soft and low, that they are scarcely audible. If you alarm him, you break the charm; he will suddenly cease, and silently drop into the underwood beneath.

The Thrush begins to sing so early as from one to two o'clock in the long midsummer mornings, and may be heard at night till long after dusk. It may be taught to whistle many tunes and waltzes with great precision. It sometimes sings while sitting on the nest, and I have seen and heard one which had been singing on a tree continue the notes in flying from it. When perched upon a tree, whether it be a high or a low one, it is almost always at or near the top that the strain is uttered.

Nidification commences the latter end of March, and the eggs are deposited earlier or later in April, though sometimes not until May, according to the season. Nests have been known to have been begun even so early as the middle of February, but frost caused them to be deserted. The young are correspondingly able to fly from the latter end of April to the middle of June, and have been known to have been hatched even on the last day of March. Mrs. Murchison, of Bicester Priory, has forwarded me intelligence of a nest with four eggs, which was found at that place on the 6th. of January, 1853. A second brood is generally reared in the season, and if one set of eggs is destroyed, a second is produced in a fortnight, or even a third if need be. The female is extremely attentive to her charge, and will sit on the nest until quite closely approached, and will sometimes suffer herself to be taken sooner than forsake it. In frequented places she soon becomes familiarized to persons passing and repassing. If you disturb and alarm her, she will testify her anxiety by flying round you with ruffled feathers and out-spread tail, uttering a note of alarm, and violently snapping the bill.

The nest is composed of moss, small twigs, straws, leaves, roots, stems of plants, and grass, compacted together with some tenacious substance with tolerable ingenuity, and is lined with a congeries of clay and decayed wood, and in some instances reeds and thistle-down. 'It is smoothed by the action of the bird turning round in the inside, evidently for the purpose, a similar action being employed by many other birds to lay close the down or hair, or other material selected for the lining of the nest. Its diameter is usually about three inches and a half or four inches inside, and about seven outside, its depth from two and a half to four. It is placed in a hedge, evergreen, low tree, hazel, black-thorn, white-thorn, or thick bush of any kind, at a small height from the ground, and likewise at times on a rough bank among roots, moss, brambles, or shrubs, as also, where the country is unwooded, under the shelter of some projecting stone or crag, in the crevice of a rock, or in a tuft of heath; sometimes on the stump or against the side of a tree, especially if covered with ivy: at Nunburnholme Rectory we found one in a yew tree at a height of twelve feet from the ground.

The eggs, usually four or five in number, very seldom six, are of a beautiful clear greenish blue colour, with more or fewer distinct black spots and dots, principally over the larger end. The youngest of my three boys, Marmaduke Charles Frederick Morris, has one entirely plain, with the exception of a single dot. N. Rowe, Esq., of Worcester College, Oxford, has also taken the eggs of a uniform blue without any spots or specks, and J. R. Wise, Esq., of Lincoln College, Oxford, has another of the same variety. James Dalton, Esq., of Worcester College, Oxford, has forwarded me another: they seem to be not very uncommon. They vary considerably in size: some are very small.

BLACKBIRD.

YR ADERYN DU. CEILIOG MWYALCH, OF THE ANCIENT BRITISH.

Turdus merula,   PENNANT. MONTAGU.

Turdus—A Thrush.   *Merula*—A Blackbird.

THOUGH sober and unpretending in plumage, yet, as thoroughly associated with every sylvan scene, the Blackbird must always be, as doubtless he always has been, one of our most favourite songsters. When the ground is covered with snow, that of the day as white, as Aristotle says, as that which has lain congealed for a thousand years, then is our bird seen to the greatest advantage, a sable beauty indeed, black as ebony itself, the dazzling white contrasting well with his dark garb, and each in turn setting off and heightening the appearance of the other.

It frequents gardens, both walled and others, groves and shrubberries, hedgerows and copses, moist places in woods, marshy grounds, tangled brakes, the sides of walls, the margins of streams, especially if bordered by wood, in more or less abundance.

In its habits it is restless, shy, and vigilant, and if alarmed or disturbed, either lies close till the danger is past, or suddenly takes wing with a vociferous chattering cry; if in the breeding-season, its partner soon shares its flight. It is most seen in the morning and evening, following its avocations in a more retired manner in the middle of the day. It is rather of a pugnacious disposition, and especially jealous in the spring of the approach of others to the spot selected for its nest. They are very good birds to eat.

Its flight is quick and hurried, hasty and precipitate, as if, for some reason or other, it were conscious that concealment suited it best: when suddenly alarmed, it generally only flits along for a little distance, and then turns in again to its cover. If its flight be at all extended, it is even and steady, but its short flittings are, as just mentioned, fitful, undulated, and capricious, and in the season of incubation a series of starts, a single flap of the wings, and a consequent bound. When perched on a branch, it bends forward, raises or lowers its tail, now and then flaps its wings, then perhaps sings, and then flies to another tree or a wall, there to perform the like postures and evolutions. Often, if it thinks that it shall be passed by without notice, it skulks about under cover, with the stealthy tread of a kinsmanlike Blackfeet or Crow Indian, but the dry and fallen autumnal leaves betray the presence of the cautious bird in the coppice or wood through which you pass, and the rustling sound of its footfall almost startles you in your lonely walk, perhaps many a mile yet from home, as you return from some outlying village or distant solitary house.

In the spring, summer, and autumn, the Blackbird feeds on moths, beetles, and other insects and their larvæ, worms, snails, fruits, and seeds, such as cherries, currants, blackberries, gooseberries, peas, and

Blackbird

Dunnock

pears, the place of the latter being supplied in winter by wheat, oats, and other grain and seeds, the berries of the hawthorn, the mountain ash, the holly, and others. It sometimes does a little damage by pulling up plants, in search of insects. The shells of snails it breaks against a stone or any hard spot, in the same way that the Thrush does. In the autumn it much frequents, as before said, turnip-fields in search of insect food. Doubtless, as in so many other similar cases of supposed injury, the evil that it may do is counterbalanced by a proportionate amount of good. It begins its pilfering as soon as it is light, and has a habit when searching for food, of frequently raising and depressing the tail, expanding at the same time the tail feathers: it hops or leaps very quickly along. It swallows a little gravel at times to aid the digestion of its food. It is a hardy species, and is able to bear the severity of most of our winters, but very inclement weather compels many from their comparative retirement to the farm-yard, and sometimes they will approach quite close to the house door, to feed on berries growing against the wall, or to pick up any crumbs placed there for them; one has been known to eat out of the hand while sitting on the nest.

With regard to the song of the Blackbird, it has long been my opinion that he is neither more nor less than a mocking-bird, and that all his best notes are borrowed from those of the Thrush, to which, as is the case with most imitations of an original, they are much inferior; they are more remarkable for power, and in some degree for tone, than for compass or variety.

A chatter, somewhat resembling that of the Magpie, is frequently uttered, especially in the spring season, the wings being fluttered and the body bent forward at the same time, as if overbalanced; an advance is made, and the posture and the note repeated, particularly if the bird be alarmed or excited: he has also a 'chink, chink.' One has successfully imitated the song of the Nightingale; another the cawing of a Crow; one again the crowing of a Cock; and another attempted the chuckling of a Hen. One, which was kept tame in a house without being confined in a cage, has been known, when irritated, not only to peck with its bill, but to rise and strike with its claws, after the manner of a Cock. The Blackbird may be taught to whistle a variety of tunes, and to imitate the human voice.

The Blackbird's warble is one that attracts attention, and you will see him perched on one of the top twigs of the tree, from whence he carols his glad notes. He begins his song in the middle of summer with the earliest dawn, and continues it at intervals throughout the day, even until the twilight and his own black plumage begin to fade together into night. His first morning ditty is but harsh and unmusical, but when the sun advances up towards the horizon, and the red rays of 'Fair Aurora' gild the sky, he hails the glorious sight with a louder and more joyous strain. In dull, cloudy, and ungenial weather he is much later in commencing, and is, on the other hand, heard to the greatest advantage when some refreshing summer rain falls upon the thirsty earth, even though the thunder should utterly for the moment drown his voice, and while the lightning flashes its most vivid gleams. On the approach of danger the Blackbird utters, as do several other birds, a peculiar note, which, as indicative of alarm, is at once noticed by even an ordinary observer.

This species pairs in February or March, but occasionally much earlier.

The nest is placed in a variety of situations, and is frequently found in a heap of sticks, even though placed in an outhouse, but most commonly in a bush; sometimes in a tree against a wall, or in a tree or wall covered with ivy, also against the side of a summer-house in the garden of Nunburnholme Rectory. The female sits for thirteen days.

The eggs are commonly five in number, sometimes four, and sometimes, though but rarely, six; they are of a dull light blue or greenish brown colour, mottled and spotted with pale reddish brown, the markings being closer at the larger end, where they sometimes form an obscure ring.

DUNNOCK.

LLWYD Y GWRYCH, OF THE ANCIENT BRITISH.

SHUFFLE-WING. HEDGE-SPARROW. HEDGE-WARBLER. CUDDY. WINTER FAUVETTE.

Accentor modularis,   JENYNS.

Accentor—A chanter, (a factitious word.)   *Modularis. Modulor*—To sing—to warble—to trill.

UNOBTRUSIVE, quiet, and retiring, without being shy, humble and homely in its deportment and habits, sober and unpretending in its dress, while still neat and graceful, the Dunnock exhibits a pattern which many of a higher grade might imitate, with advantage to themselves, and benefit to others through an improved example.

Hardy in its habits, it needs not to migrate, but remains in its 'local habitation' throughout the year. In the depth of winter indeed, it approaches more nearly to houses, which again it leaves with the change of season for the hedgeside, the garden, the orchard, the plantation, or the pleasure-ground, and there, or among bushes, it passes its summer, seldom advancing into open ground, or frequenting trees of larger size.

Even in the depth of the severest winter, when, as in February, 1853, the ground is everywhere covered with snow a foot deep, and you would think that all emotion must be chilled in the breast of the very hardiest bird that is exposed to the damaging attacks of the two 'weird sisters' cold and hunger, by night and by day, you will see the Dunnock flirting about some low bush in the splendid sunshine that succeeds the bitter blasts which have come and gone, and warbling its unpretending little lay, as if to shew that an even and quiet temper is that which will best sustain under the most adverse circumstances of life. Now it has come down upon the snow, and its tiny feet move nimbly over the crystal surface, its tail quickly moved up and down the while; now it stops for a few moments, and now hops on again, and now is gone, in company with its mate, pursuing or pursued. Or, half-hopping, half-walking, its usual gait, it approaches the door, in search of a few chance crumbs, which, if you are charitably disposed, you will have placed there for any feathered pensioners whom the inclemency of the season may compel to a more intimate acquaintance than they otherwise would have chosen. 'Never turn thy face from any poor man,' says the Holy Word.

These birds never under any circumstances, or at all events very rarely indeed, enter into houses by the open door or window, as some others do through stress of weather, though so devoid of shyness in their approaches to them. The neighbourhood of the hedge is their favourite haunt, from whence they venture but a little way into the field, or the road. Sometimes however, they are seen in towns, in such places as squares, where trees and shrubs are planted.

They are by no means gregarious, though three or four may sometimes be observed at no great distance from each other. They are seldom seen among or on the upper branches even of a bush or hedge, and as Mr. Macgillivray remarks, it is very rare to see two flying in the same direction, although they are generally observed in pairs. In dry sunny weather in summer, they may be seen sometimes basking in the sun. They are inoffensive towards other birds, and friendly also with one another

Their flight is straight, and generally very short, as also low.

The food of this species consists of small seeds, particularly those of the grasses, grain, and insects, minute snails, chrysalides and larvæ, in addition to which small fragments of stone are swallowed, and in search of such, or any other minute eatables, too small even for you to observe at all what they are, you will see it quietly, peaceably, and industriously searching about, advancing with that gentle raising and shuffling of the wings, most exhibited in the breeding season, from whence one of its vernacular names. It also frequently moves the tail up and down with a somewhat similar motion, and in the spring floats in the air in a manner foreign to its usual habit. Even though you may approach within a few yards of it, it moves or flits but a little way off, or hops into the nearest covert until you have passed by. The young are fed with insects.

The song of this gentle, modest, and retiring little bird, which is heard even in winter, and continued until the end of May, and in fact for nearly the whole of the year, is, as might be expected, of a quiet and subdued tone. It is, however, particularly mellow and pleasing, making up in soft richness what it wants in compass and power: I have heard it on the 19th. of February, which is about the period that it is usually commenced. It frequently utters it in fair weather, from the middle or top of a bush, hedge, or low tree, though sometimes from the ground, or on a wall, repeating it eight or nine times in succession; but should the temperature change, and a storm of the 'bitter piercing air' of the north succeed a comparatively milder time, it chills the heart of the little warbler, and his strains are in consequence curtailed.

The nest is generally placed in hedges, low furze or other bushes, or shrubs, a few feet from the ground, but also, in lack of these, in holes of walls, stacks of wood, in the ivy against a wall, and other similar places.

It is deep and well rounded, and from four and a half to five inches in diameter on the outside, and nearly two inches deep. It is made of small twigs and grass, lined with moss, and then with hair, grass, wool, down, or any appropriate substances at hand.

The eggs, which are sometimes seen so early as the beginning of April, are four or five, rarely six, though sometimes, it is said, seven in number, and of a very elegant greenish blue colour, with a rather glossy surface.

REDBREAST.

YR HOBI GOCH. BRON GOCH, OF THE ANCIENT BRITISH.

ROBIN. ROBIN REDBREAST. RUDDOCK. ROBINET.

Sylvia rubecula,	PENNANT. FLEMING.
Sylvia. Sylva—A wood.	*Rubecula. Ruber*—Red—ruddy.

THE thoughts of our earliest days are those, each one of which, 'ære perennius,' abides with us through life, while those of later years pass away, oftentimes like a shadow without recall. Who then is there in whose oldest memory the legendary tale of the 'Babes in the Wood' does not for ever dwell; and who is there in remembrance of it that with the Robin's so-called faults will not 'love him still?' Faults he certainly has, or at least dispositions which would be such in us, but he fulfils to the letter the mission of his nature, and that is what 'no man living' can say of himself.

An inhabitant of the wildest wood and the gayest garden, the most frequented road, and the most retired lane, the hedge of the pasture field, and the neighbourhood of every country-house, the Robin is an acquaintance of both old and young, and to each and all he seems like an old friend.

As you walk along the hedgerow side at almost any season of the year, it may be 'nescio quid meditans nugarum,' your wandering thought is for a moment arrested by the sight of a red breast perched on one of the topmost sprays, or by the sound of the pretty note that its owner warbles before you: you cannot help but stop a moment and speak a word to the well-known bird, as if to an old companion, and you almost fancy from his winsome attitude, the attention he seems to pay, and the quietness with which he remains, that he understands, if not your language, yet the purport of it, and is aware that you are a friend who will not hurt or harm him.

The Redbreast remains with us throughout the year, unless indeed it be a contradiction of this statement, that some are supposed to migrate hither from more northern parts in the winter: they are believed to perform their migrations singly. In summer they for the most part, but by no means universally, remove from that more close propinquity to human habitations, which in winter they had sought, to a greater distance, where retirement is to be better gained.

As one proof, 'unum e multis,' of the pugnacious disposition of the Robin, for which he is indeed noted, Mr. George B. Clarke has sent me the following anecdote, since recorded in 'The Naturalist,' volume i., page 45:—'I.thought I would try it with one of its own species stuffed, of which I have a very fine one. I first of all placed it inside the window, so that the Robin in the garden could see it, and he immediately flew to the window and commenced pecking at the glass; but not succeeding in getting at the stuffed one, he flew away for about a minute, and.then returned and commenced pecking again at the glass, through which he could see the bird. I then placed the stuffed Robin outside, on the window-sill, and went and hid myself, so that I could see what the Robin would do now that he could get at it; he very soon returned, and commenced pecking at the stuffed bird most furiously. At last he knocked it off the sill of the window; he followed it as it fell down, and seemed to be quite pleased at being victorious, and continued pecking at and pulling feathers out of it, while it was lying on the ground. I then came out of my hiding-place, and frightened him away, or else he would soon have spoiled my bird.'

An exactly similar circumstance has also been related to me by Dr. Henry Moses, of Appleby, since the above was registered. He had placed a recently-stuffed Robin in the garden to dry; some Sparrows and a Dunnock soon began to eye him curiously, and with evident signs of hostility; they did not, however, seem to like his look—a piece of wire which had been left projecting from his head giving him a rather fearful appearance—and sheered off. No sooner, however, had they been gone than a Robin made a most furious attack upon his supposed rival, dashed at him with the greatest violence, buffeted him with his wings, knocked out one of his eyes, and so miserably mauled and distorted him that he was rendered totally useless as a specimen of the art of taxidermy. It must be acknowledged that the Robin is of a very masterful temper and disposition. You are looking out of your window, watching perhaps a Dunnock, a Tomtit, or even a Sparrow in the tree in front of it: on a sudden the bird is flown, vanished as if by the wave of the wand of a magician; but the next moment the cause appears, and, in the place of the quiet Shuffle-wing or lively Titmouse, the necromancer, a pert Redbreast stands, whose only object in appearing there seems to have been to dislodge those, who would have remained with a Sparrow or a Thrush, undisturbing and undisturbed. He is even unsociable with those of his own kind; in winter so many as two are scarcely seen together, and as for other species he rarely mingles at all with them.

The Robin, when accustomed to be undisturbed, will frequently approach very near to those who are working in gardens, to pick up any insects which they may happen to disturb; and will sometimes even alight on the edge of the basket of a fruit-gatherer. The Misses Gilchrist, at Sunbury, had a tame Robin, which spent all its life with them, using the house as a spaniel would; rarely absent from the breakfast-table, accompanying them in their walks, and perching on the hand at call. It died, an old bird, on the night of Murphy's Frost, which it was extremely unwilling to face, instead of the warm fireside.

The flight of this bird is usually rather quick and straight, mostly performed near the ground, and for only a short distance—from one neighbouring resting-place to another. It progresses by a few hops at a time, when it suddenly halts, tosses up its head or looks askance, and after a brief pause advances again.

The Robin feeds on various fruits, seeds, and berries, such as elderberries and black-berries, as also on flies, beetles, and other insects, earwigs and worms, the larger are frequently held in one claw, and so picked: occasionally it will capture insects on the wing, sallying out at them time after time, quite after the manner of a Flycatcher. The hard parts of any are cast up, as is done by the Hawks. One has been seen to attack the formidable stag beetle on the wing, when both fell together to the ground; what the result would have been been was not ascertained, for the former flew away on the observer coming up. In the winter this bird frequently visits the sea-shore, searching among the sea-weed for small marine insects. In summer he eats not a few currants and other small fruits, with which the young are sometimes fed; but insects are his chief food. Its manner of feeding is not an assiduous pecking about, but it hops on for a few steps, and then halts, and then hops on again with a diligence of observation to which we for the moment are blind, though we presently are almost sure to see its successful result, as it darts upon its prey with a shuffle of the wings.

There is something peculiarly touching in the soft, sweet, and plaintive note of the Redbreast, especially when first re-heard again at the close of summer, when the leaves begin to fade and fall, and autumn gives presage of the storms and cold of returning winter. So likewise when winter has again in its turn passed away, and the first signs, though ever so faint, of long-wished-for spring begin to dawn, then is the well-known note a pleasant sound to the ear that loves the country for the country's sake. The Robin in fact sings throughout the year, except while too much engaged with his family in the nest. And as for his annual, so also for his diurnal habit; retiring late to roost, his voice is heard in every lane and garden, while any glimmer of twilight remains, but then it ceases, and up he is betimes again after daybreak, before the sun, and his 'Good Morning' is a pleasant welcome to the early riser on the following day.

'In speaking of the Robin,' says Mr. Jesse, 'I may observe that when they sing late in the autumn, it appears to be from rivalship, and that there are always two singing at the same time. If one of them is silenced, the other immediately ceases its song. I observe also that they always sing while they are preparing to fight with each other. The Redbreast is indeed a very pugnacious bird: I lately observed two of them, after giving the usual challenge, fight with so much animosity, that I could easily have caught them both, as they reeled close to my feet on a gravel walk. After some time one of them had the advantage, and would have killed his opponent, had they not been separated. Indeed these birds will frequently fight till one has lost his life. It has been asserted that the female Robin sings, and I am much inclined to be of this opinion, having heard two Robins sing at the same time in a situation where I had every reason to believe there was only a pair.'

Nidification commences very early in the spring, and the eggs are usually laid about the beginning of April.

The nest of the Robin, which is built of fine stalks, moss, dried leaves, and grass, and lined with hair and wool, with sometimes a few feathers, is generally placed on a bank under the shelter of a bush, or sometimes in a bush itself, or even a tree, such as a yew, at a low height from the ground, and occasionally in a hole in a wall covered with ivy, a crevice in a rock, among fern and tangled roots —the entrance perhaps being through some very narrow aperture, or an ivy-clad tree. I have found one in a hollow apparently made by the bird, in a heap of grass, and have seen another on the level ground at the foot of a tree. I have heard of one built in a hedge at a height of about three feet from the ground. It measures about five inches and three quarters across, and two and a half in internal diameter. It is concealed with great care and success.

His late Majesty King William the Fourth had a part of the mizen-mast of the Victory, against which Lord Nelson was standing when he was mortally wounded, placed in a building in the grounds of Bushy Park when he resided there. A large shot had passed through this part of the mast, and in the hole it had left, a pair of Robins built their nest and reared their young. The relic was afterwards removed to the dining-room of the house, and is now in the armoury of Windsor Castle. 'VICTORIA pacem!'

The eggs, generally five or six in number, are of a delicate pale reddish white, faintly freckled with rather darker red, most so at the larger end, where a zone or belt is sometimes formed. Some are entirely white. N. Rowe, Esq., of Worcester College, Oxford, has written me word of five eggs found in the elegant gardens of that, my own, college, whose 'classic shades' I so well remember, and which, the eggs I mean, were quite white and spotless.

The attitude of the figure in the plate is partly taken from one designed by the Rev. R. P. Alington, if we may call that designed, in the artistical sense of the word, which is copied exactly from nature, but the 'Better half' of Cock Robin, which formed one side of the original picture, has been obliged to be left out for want of space.

STONECHAT.

CLOCHDER Y CERRIG, OF THE ANCIENT BRITISH.

STONECHATTER. STONECLINK. STONE SMITH. MOOR TITLING. BLACK CAP.

Sylvia rubicola,   PENNANT.

Sylvia. Sylva—A wood.   *Rubus*—A bramble.   *Colo*—To inhabit.

THIS species is extensively distributed, being found throughout Europe in Holland, Germany, Switzerland, France, and Italy, as also, it is said, in some parts of Russia.

In England, though nowhere abundant, it is not uncommon in suitable localities in all parts of the island, Yorkshire, Dorsetshire, Devonshire, Cornwall, Suffolk, Norfolk, Northumberland, and other counties, but the most numerous in the south; in Ireland also; Wales; Guernsey and Sark; Scotland, in East Lothian and so far north as Sutherlandshire and Caithnesshire; and in the Hebrides.

It frequents uncultivated places, the sides of cliffs by the sea, open

Redbreast

Stonechat

moors and heaths, warrens and chases, commons and downs, at least those parts of such where low brushwood, the wild broom, and the gorse with its golden blossoms, so deservedly the admiration of Linnæus when in this country he for the first time saw it, the bramble, the juniper, and the sloe, afford it alike a shelter and a home. Such lonely spots it enlivens with its gay and handsome appearance, its varied and conspicuous plumage presenting an attractive object, to which, if otherwise unobservant of it, its singular note will probably draw your attention.

It is of a restless and noisy habit, and seldom remains long in one spot, perching on the topmost part of a bush or stone, or hanging on some twig that bends with its weight, and flying down from thence to pick up something from the ground; on the latter, however, it but seldom stops for any lengthened space.

The Stonechat is a hardy bird, and remains with us throughout the year, but would appear to make a partial home migration in the autumn, leaving the wilder for more sheltered and warmer situations: the young birds at all events seem to quit their place, if the parents remain behind. About the end of March they return again to their haunts.

They are found singly or in pairs, though several individuals may frequently be seen near together in the same immediate neighbourhood. In very severe winters they come into gardens, and approach quite close to cottages and houses. They, too, like others of their class, have a frequent movement of the body and the tail. They are very anxious for their young, if danger approaches, and keep flying about in evident alarm as long as it appears to threaten, shewing great anxiety to draw any strangers from the nest. They often seem to vanish suddenly from sight, dropping, as it were, from where they stood, and then after flying close to the ground for some way, rise up again to some other resting-place. They are not shy in their habits, though rather wary.

The flight of this species, which is rather quick, is, for the most part, a succession of short flits or starts. Their favourite perching place is the uppermost spray of a bush. They roost upon the ground, and are sometimes taken by bird-catchers in their nets.

Their food is made up of insects, larvæ, and worms; the former they frequently take on the wing, making short sallies from their stand on the top of a branch.

The ordinary note of this bird, which is somewhat of a melancholy cast, is a 'chat,' 'chat, chat,' resembling the sound produced by striking two stones together; hence the name of the bird, unless it be derived from its supposed habit of frequenting stony places, which however is not the case, farther than that barren districts, which are its favourite resort, are for the most part stony, not having come under the hand of the cultivator—these are the two roots of the name, and 'utrum horum mavis accipe.' Buffon likens the note to the word 'ouistrata;' and Gmelin to that which he has assigned in consequence as its specific name.

The song of the Stonechat is of little power, but soft, low, and sweet. It is uttered either from the top of some bush, or when hovering for a short space at a low elevation above it. It is seldom heard before the beginning of April or after the middle of June, but sometimes so early as the middle of February.

These birds pair in March, and commence building towards the end of that month.

The nest, which is large and loosely put together, and composed of moss, dry grass, and fibrous roots, or heath, lined with hair and feathers, and sometimes with wool, is placed among grass and low herbage, at the bottom of a furze, or other bush, or in the bush itself, as also in heather, and even, occasionally, in some neighbouring hedge adjoining the open ground which the. bird frequents. It is exceedingly difficult to find, on account of its situation in the middle of a cluster of whin bushes—such not admitting of the most easy access—the female also sitting very close, and, when off the nest, being very watchful of all your movements, hopping quickly from bush to bush, and disappearing suddenly by retreat into the cover.

The eggs, generally five or six in number, rarely seven, are of a pale greyish or greenish blue colour, the larger end minutely speckled with dull reddish brown. They are laid the middle or latter end of April, sometimes in the earlier part of that month; and have been known so late as the 12th. of July—perhaps a second brood.

The young are usually hatched about the middle of May, and are abroad by the end of that month, or the beginning of June. They have been seen coming out from under a bush to be fed by the old ones, and then immediately retiring to their concealment.

SEDGE WARBLER.

SEDGE BIRD. SEDGE WREN. REED FAUVETTE.

Sylvia salicaria,   LATHAM.

Sylvia. Sylva—A wood.   *Salicaria*—Of or pertaining to willows.
                     Salix—A willow.

THE Sedge Bird is generally spread over Europe, its range extending even to the Arctic Circle; in the middle parts of the continent, it is however the more numerous. In Holland it is very abundant; and is found also in France and Germany, Norway, Russia, Italy and Sweden. In Asia, it has been noticed by my friend Mr. Hugh Edwin Strickland, in Asia Minor; it belongs also to Siberia.

Throughout England it is more or less abundant, according to the nature of the locality. In Yorkshire this bird is very common in the Driffield neighbourhood, and also near Thirsk, Doncaster, Barnsley, Sheffield, Hob-moor, York, Swillington, and Brotherton, in fact in most parts; near Halifax and Huddersfield it is less numerous. It is plentiful also in Essex, Suffolk, Hampshire, Dorsetshire, Devonshire, Norfolk, Lincolnshire, Northumberland, and Lancashire. In Cornwall it seems to be not uncommon.

In Scotland it is no where abundant, but is most met with in the southern and middle divisions. In Sutherlandshire it is constantly to be heard at night, about reedy lochs and swamps, and is to be met with even to the northernmost extremity; also in East Lothian. The

Sedge Warbler, as its name imports, is for the most part found in the neighbourhood of water, but such is not exclusively the case, for it often resorts to thick hedges, lanes, and other cover at some distance from it. In Wales it is common near Llandudno.

It migrates to us the latter part of April, or sometimes later with the season, seldom arriving in Scotland before the beginning of May. The males are believed to arrive before the females. They come in small parties of from two to five or six each. They are late in leaving, some being seen till the middle of October, even in the north of England; one has been observed near High Wycombe, in Buckinghamshire, in winter.

This is another species of hidling, though not exactly of shy habits, and is most frequently seen if disturbed, for otherwise it keeps to its haunt in the middle of the thick hedge, tall sedge, reeds, or other aquatic plants among which it harbours. This very day on which I am writing, I watched one for some time playing at hide and seek with me, in some large hawthorn bushes which covered the steep bank of a stream, overhanging it almost down to the water's edge: beyond all doubt the nest was there. Now it would fly a few yards off; now, if thinking itself unobserved, slyly return to its place; now sing lustily from some hidden covert, and on a sudden emerge and shew itself; then again descend to the recesses of the thick brake, and so quickly re-appear at a little distance that it would almost seem as if it had flown straight without hindrance through the tangled underwood; once more it would set up its ringing note, a watchman springing his rattle to alarm his household, for the sound of such in its small way it closely resembles, and finally disappear from view and from hearing together, unless again disturbed. The hen bird sits close on her nest, and you may often pass close by without her leaving it. If alarmed for her young she evinces great anxiety, moving in and out of the neighbouring cover. These birds are able to be kept in confinement.

They feed on insects of various kinds, some of which are captured on the wing, and others snatched from the surface of the water; also on worms and small slugs.

The note, which is heard from the midst of 'The Bush,' or when perched on the top of a small branch or spray, as also while flying for some short distance to the next cover, is. very powerful for so small a throat, and they sing sometimes in a most violent chiding sort of manner, as if in defiance of approach. The common note is a small shrill cheep, but their song, though somewhat of a chatter, is very lively, and not without a mellow modulation. It is heard at night as late as twelve o'clock on the fine still summer evenings, with little intermission, and even still on 'till morning comes again.' Any sudden alarm brings forth its rattle with renewed vigour. It is correctly said by some to imitate the notes of other birds; I have heard it myself closely take off the chirping of the Sparrow. Mr. James R. Garrett says Mr. Thompson has known it repeat the cricket-like note of the Grasshopper Warbler, and suddenly burst out into the song of the Swallow or some other bird. So also Mr. Stewart narrates, as quoted in the same work, that he has heard it mimic the clear warble of the Thrush, and the hoarse twitter of the Sparrow; to which Mr. Selby adds the notes of the Lark and the Linnet.

Sedge Warbler

N. Rowe, Esq., of Worcester College, Oxford, has taken the nest in a Syringa tree. It is usually placed at about two, and never at a greater height than three or four feet from the ground, on a stump of a willow or alder tree, but generally among the tall grass or flags that grow along the side of the river or pool. G. B. Clarke, Esq., of Woburn, has been kind enough to forward me specimens of the nest and eggs: so has also James Dalton, Esq., of Worcester College, Oxford. The nest is made of stalks of grass, and other smaller plants, lined with finer parts of the same and hair: it is rather large and but loosely put together. Selby says that moss is sometimes used. The young leave the nest very soon.

The eggs, four, or generally five, Sir William Jardine says six or seven, in number, are of a pale yellowish brown colour, marked with light brown and dull grey. They are usually closely freckled all over. Mr. Heysham mentions a nest which contained three quite white. Sometimes they are uniform dull yellow: they are laid early in May.

NIGHTINGALE.

EOS, OF THE ANCIENT BRITISH.

Sylvia luscinia,	PENNANT. TEMMINCK.
Sylvia. Sylva—A wood.	*Luscinia*—A Nightingale.

THE Nightingale is found in Europe, in Russia even and Sweden, Holland, Denmark, Germany, France, Spain, Italy, and the islands of Greece. It is known also in Asia—in the more temperate parts of Siberia, and in Asia Minor and Syria; also in Africa.

Woods, groves, plantations, and copses are its favourite resort, but it is also found in gardens, even in the neighbourhood of London, and also among thick hedges in shady and sheltered situations.

Insects of various sorts, spiders and earwigs furnish them with food. The young are fed principally with caterpillars.

The Nightingale favours us with its company about the middle or end of April, sometimes it is said not until May, the males arriving about a week or ten days before the females. It has been known to arrive on the Suffolk coast as early as the 7th. of the former month. It departs again in August or September. It would appear that its migration is made in an almost due south and north direction, few being found in Devonshire, and none in Cornwall, Wales, or Ireland, nor any, it is said, in Brittany, or in the Channel Islands. Many have been introduced into the western parts, and others into Scotland by Sir John Sinclair, but they have never returned the following year: the birth-place possesses an overpowering attraction for some, but the Nightingale takes a still higher ground, and will pine in any place but that in which it ought to have been born. They seem to travel by night, and to arrive singly, one by one. The older birds too are thought to arrive before the younger ones.

In its habits it is not shy, and, as is but too well known, may be kept in confinement: unfortunately they are easily captured. Bechstein has known one which thus lived for twenty-five years. Those taken on their first arrival are said to do better than those taken afterwards —slavery is somewhat the same in birds as in the human species: the right-minded man and the right-minded ornithologist will reprobate both. These birds return to their native haunt, and each one appears to exercise proprietorship over its own more peculiar domain.

Its flight is swift, light, smooth, and even, though not extended far. On the ground it stands very erect. When alighting on a branch the wings are slightly shaken or quivered.

It takes its prey just in the same way that the Thrush does, flying to the ground, hopping quickly along in search of any, then suddenly seizing it, and after a sidelong glance returning to its post, often the very spot from which it had descended. It also searches for insects along the branches and under leaves. It is fond of the eggs of ants, and of the larvæ of wasps, hornets, and bees. The young are said to be fed with caterpillars.

It is a fancy of Viellot, and the idea, though fanciful, is a pretty one, that the Nightingale loves a neighbourhood where there is an echo, as if aware of and admiring its own music. Certainly the echo of such sounds, for most beautiful they are, are well worth listening to, and the softened strain may be mistaken by the enamoured bird for the answering note of his partner, and so may have a heightened enchantment to his ear.

The name of Nightingale is derived, as Pennant remarks, from the word night, and the Saxon word galan—to sing; and 'oft in the stilly night,' when you are far away from every worldly association, and there is nothing but the voice of the Nightingale to break the 'charmed air' and the repose in which all nature is hushed, your soul may well be raised to happy and holy contemplation, and you will be able to enter into the spirit of the Old Hundredth Psalm, and 'Praise GOD from whom all blessings flow.'

When the young are hatched the song ceases in great measure, though it is in fact continued in some degree to within a few days of their departure. They do not sing on their very first arrival; it is not till the females have come that the serenade begins; then 'Buona notte, Buona notte, amato bene' is the nightly strain for about a fortnight, until the arrival of a family busies it too much with sublunary cares. If the female be accidentally destroyed, the male then resumes his song until he finds another partner, which, curious to say, as in the case of other species, he generally meets with, but where or how is 'passing strange.' A warning note is excited by the approach of danger, or a snapping of the bill uttered against it, and a short 'tack,' heard also at other times. The Nightingale begins its morning song from half-past three to four o'clock. Sometimes, indeed, especially if the moon be shining, it sings throughout the night, and its song, attended however by its peculiar objurgatory note, instead of being checked, is only excited the more by any casual disturbance. The sound of music or other noise will arouse their attention, and at times their rivalry. An anecdote is on record of one which entered into competition with the instrument of a performer, and fell at his feet exhausted with the struggle to outvie him. Pliny, too, says 'They emulate one another, and the contention is plainly an animated one. The conquered often ends its life, its spirit failing sooner than its song.' It has been known to imitate the human voice.

The nest of the Nightingale, which is almost always placed on the ground, in some natural hollow, amongst the roots of a tree, on a bank, or at the foot of a hedgerow, though sometimes two or three feet from the surface, is very loosely put together, and is formed of various materials, such as dried stalks of grasses and leaves, small fibrous roots, and bits of bark, lined with a few hairs and the finer portions of the grass. It is about five inches and a half in external diameter, by about three internally, and about three and a half deep.

Here again let me 'enter a plaint' in behalf of the bird and her nest. He who takes a Nightingale's nest, robs his neighbour, as well as the owner of it, and is guilty at once of burglary and petty larceny. Mr. Meyer observes, 'The attachment of this species to its young, and its grief at their loss, have been noticed by many writers, ancient and modern. Our friend, the Rev. E. J. Moor, sends us, on this subject, a memorandum from his journal: 'one evening while I was at College,' he says, 'happening to drink tea with the late Rev. J. Lambert, fellow of Trinity College, he told me the following fact, illustrative of Virgil's extreme accuracy in describing natural objects. We had been speaking of those well-known lovely lines in the fourth Georgic on the Nightingale's lamentation for the loss of her young, when Mr. Lambert told me that riding once through one of the toll-gates near Cambridge, he observed the keeper of the gate and his wife, who were aged persons, apparently much dejected. Upon inquiring into the cause of their uneasiness, the man assured Mr. Lambert that he and his wife had both been made very unhappy by a Nightingale, which had built in their garden, and had the day before been robbed of its young. This loss she had been deploring in such a melancholy strain all the night, as not only to deprive him and his wife of sleep, but also to leave them in the morning full of sorrow; from which they had evidently not recovered when Mr. Lambert saw them.'

The eggs, of a regular oval form, are of a uniform glossy dull olive brown colour.

BLACKCAP.

PENDDUR BRWYN, OF THE ANCIENT BRITISH.

BLACKCAP WARBLER.   MOCK NIGHTINGALE.

Sylvia atricapilla,   PENNANT. JENYNS.

Sylvia. Sylva—A wood.   *Atricapilla. Ater*—Black.
Capillus—The hair of the head.

THE Blackcap is more cosmopolite in its character than any other of the British Warblers. It frequents the whole of the temperate parts of Europe, from Sicily, Spain and Portugal to Germany, Switzerland, Italy, Lapland, Norway, Denmark, and Sweden. In Africa it is found from the northern parts to the Cape of Good

Nightingale

Blackcap

Hope, and midway in Senegal, as likewise in Madeira and the Azores. In Asia also it is known, in Persia, Java, and Japan.

Throughout England it is met with in all quarters of the country, but mostly in the south, from Sussex to Devonshire and the Land's End, and from Suffolk and Norfolk to Derbyshire and Wales.

In Ireland it seems to be a regular summer visitant to certain districts, but must be considered very local.

In Scotland it is sparingly distributed throughout the southern parts. Mr. T. Edward has heard them sing near Banff, at Mayen and Rothiemary, and in the grounds of Duff House. It is not uncommon in the Valley of the Clyde, especially about Hamilton. They occur also near Paisley, in Renfrewshire, and Stevenston, in Ayrshire, and have been met with in Perthshire, Forfarshire, East Lothian, and Edinburgh.

In Orkney one was shot in Sanday, in the summer of 1846.

It haunts thick hedges and brakes, woods, groves, and plantations, shrubberies, lanes, orchards, copses, and thickets, and addicts itself especially to dense brushwood.

It migrates hither, in uncertain numbers, the middle of April, or earlier with the season, and leaves again in September. I have seen it at Nunburnholme Rectory, East Yorkshire, on the 1st. of October, 1866. In late seasons it does not arrive till the beginning of May, and has been observed on the other hand on the 9th. of April; sometimes, on the eastern coast, even as early as the 28th. of March. The males do not travel quite 'pari passu' with the females, but arrive some days before them. It appears however to be certain, from the many instances already adduced, that some must stay with us every winter, and especially it would seem in Ireland.

It is a bird of rather shy and timid habits, and at the same time lively and restless in its movements, quickly retiring, on being observed, into the denser parts of its cover. It is also of a solitary nature, more than two individuals being seldom seen in company. The cultivated parts of the country are its resort. It is capable of being kept in confinement. In the 'Zoologist,' page 356, Vivian Walmesley, Esq. relates a curious circumstance of a Blackcap attacking a rabbit which he had shot, and appearing to triumph at its death.

It seldom takes a long flight, but flits from bush to bush.

The Blackcap feeds on insects, caterpillars, chrysalides, berries, those of the ivy, the rowans of the mountain ash, and others, and fruits, such as strawberries, raspberries, blackberries, dewberries, elderberries, cherries, pears, and currants. The first-named are sometimes captured when flying, but chiefly found among buds, blossoms, and leaves, and in various parts of the trees or bushes which the bird frequents, and in pursuit, or rather in search of them, it creeps among the dense foliage, or threads its way through the tangled underwood with the most graceful nimbleness and minute investigation. It occasionally descends to the ground for the like purpose.

A very beautiful roundelay is that of the Blackcap, inferior only in the estimation of many to that of the Nightingale. It is usually first heard in the middle of April, but in very mild seasons has been noticed so soon as the 29th. of March. It will sometimes be continued until August, if there should be a second brood. Its tones, though desultory, are very rich, deep, full, loud, varied, sweetly wild and witching. It is generally given forth from some of the higher branches or twigs of the bush or hedge. The notes of other birds are also imitated—those of the Nightingale, Blackbird, Robin, Thrush, and Garden Warbler. The throat is much distended in a somewhat curious manner, and the crest set up while the bird is singing. When the young are hatched, 'the song becomes broken, the melody gradually ceases, and we hear only the usual call notes. Either are easily interrupted; and a slight noise, or the intrusion of a stranger, will induce silence, and the bird will remove itself gradually and quietly to the closer parts of the thicket; or having gained the edge of a more limited shrubbery, it will silently flit to some more extensive and secure retreat.' They have also a note of alarm like the syllable 'tack.'

The nest, built about the end of April to the end of May or the beginning of June, is commonly placed in a bramble or other bush, sometimes in a honeysuckle, a raspberry, or currant tree, about two or three feet or rather more from the ground; sometimes among nettles. It is made of dry grass and small fibrous roots, with occasionally a little moss and hair—the latter as a lining, and the outer parts cemented together with spiders' webs and wool. It is strong and tolerably compact, though slight. Anything like meddling with it, or intruding upon it, is jealously watched, and the smallest disturbance causes the nest to be forsaken. Several in fact are frequently abandoned, either from apprehension or caprice, before they have been finished.

The eggs, usually four or five in number, sometimes six, are of a pale greenish or reddish white colour, mottled with light brown and grey, with a few spots and streaks of olive, dusky, and dark brown. They vary a good deal both in size and shape.

Both birds sit on the eggs, but the female naturally the most. The male frequently sings while so engaged. The female, when sitting, is occasionally fed by her partner. The young are said to leave the nest rather soon, roosting with their parents on the adjoining boughs.

CHIFF CHAFF.

LESSER PETTYCHAPS. LEAST WILLOW WREN.

Sylvia rufa,   TEMMINCK.

Sylvia. Sylva—A wood.

THIS diminutive bird extends in its European range as far as Norway in the summer, remaining through the winter in some of the southern parts of the continent.

It inhabits groves, woods, coppices, beds of reeds, gardens, the sides of small streams where trees grow, such as, in the latter situations, the alder and the aspen, and in the former the oak, the fir, and the birch. Among these it may be seen in the early vernal season, in sheltered places, searching among the boughs and branches for its food, and emitting at intervals its shrill note.

This is one of the earliest of our summer, or rather of our spring visitants, arriving here the end of March, or the beginning of April. Some have been seen, by Montagu, so early as the 12th. and the 14th. of the former month, and several by the 20th. He also once saw one about Christmas, in 1802: near Swansea it has been heard on the 30th. of January. In Devonshire one was shot near Torquay on the 10th. of January, 1851; another on March 21st., in 1848 on March 23rd., and in 1849 on March 18th., and commonly is seen or heard from the 25th. to the 29th. In Kent it has been known on the 24th., in the year 1851, and in Bedfordshire, by George B. Clarke, Esq., on the 22nd. of that month, in 1852. In Oxfordshire on the 25th., by the Revs. A. and H. Matthews, and in Yorkshire, on the banks of the Don, near Sprotborough, the seat of Sir Joseph Copley, Bart., by Peter Inchbald, Esq. It leaves also late, not till the beginning of October, giving us a longer stay than most others; some few however have been found in the southern counties at all seasons of the year, and Mr. Macgillivray had one, killed near Newhaven, in January, 1836. It is somewhat uncertain in its appearance, many appearing in one year, while not an individual is to be seen the next. It is very possible that those individuals which have been noticed at so early a date in the year, have remained in this country through the winter. In Ireland its earliest recorded arrival is the 3rd. of April, and on the 7th. of that month it was seen in 1838 and 1844, and not till the 15th. in 1847, a year in which the vernal migrants were very late in making their appearance. One was heard on the 8th. of September.

In the spring these birds keep for the most part in the same haunt. They are lively, active, and restless in their movements, often frequenting trees of lofty growth, especially in situations where they are surrounded with tangled vegetation. They display much anxiety for the safety of their young; if the latter be taken out of the nest, it is said that the old birds will hover about, and even come and stand beside and flutter around them. They are easily captured, and soon become tame in confinement. Mr. Sweet mentions one which used to perch on the hand without shewing the least symptom of fear, and it also would fly up to the ceiling, and bring down a fly in its beak every time.

Their food consists of small caterpillars, aphides, small moths, and flies; the latter they sometimes catch on the wing: the young are fed with caterpillars, flies, and other insects.

The song, frequently heard overhead from the upper part of some tall tree, and on one occasion so early as the 5th. of February, is melodious and varied. The ordinary bitone note is a mere 'cheep, cheep, cheep, chee,' likened by some to the syllables 'chiff-chaff,' whence the name, and a 'chiff, cheff, chaff,' repeated in a quick, and as if agitated, manner, almost a 'vox et præterea nihil,' but it comes from the tops of the trees with a ringing sound, reminding one of the faint chime of the distant village church bell; it is continued even till late in September. The alarm cry Meyer represents by the word 'hoo-id;' the note is also frequently repeated on the wing.

The nest, which is arched over, is skilfully constructed of various indiscriminate materials, according to the situations it is placed in, fern, moss, leaves, grasses, the bark of the birch tree, the shells of chrysalides, wool, and the down of flowers, with sometimes feathers

Chiff Chaff

Wren

and a few hairs for lining for the whole of the interior; it is covered over more than half-way, the other portion of the upper half being left open by the side; if the roofing be removed, even three or four times, the patient little architect will renew it. It is placed on the ground, generally, but not always, in the immediate neighbourhood of trees, or on a hedge bank, or near a brook, or on the moss-clad stump of a tree, as also beneath the shelter of the trailing boughs of some bramble, furze, or other bush, or clod of earth. Mr. Henry Doubleday has found one at a height of two feet from the ground, in some fern; and Mr. Hewitson mentions another, which was built in some ivy against a garden wall, at a like elevation. Occasionally the nest is placed in a row of peas, or a bed of ground-growing wild plants.

The eggs, usually seven in number, are more than ordinarily rounded at the larger end, and pointed at the smaller. They are hatched in thirteen days: they do not vary much, and are of a white ground colour, with very small dots and spots of blackish red or purple brown, chiefly at the thicker end, which they sometimes surround in the way of a zone or belt. Mr. Neville Wood saw a nest which contained five eggs of the usual colour, and the sixth pure white. The shell is very thin, and but little polished. The eggs are laid towards the middle or end of May, and the young birds are fledged about the middle of June: they quit the nest early.

Incubation lasts thirteen days, and the male occasionally relieves the female at her post. Two broods are sometimes reared in the season.

WREN.

DRYW, OF THE ANCIENT BRITISH.

COMMON WREN. KITTY WREN. JIMPO.

Sylvia troglodytes,   PENNANT.

Sylvia. Sylva—A wood.   *Troglodytes*—The name of an ancient race of people, said to live in holes and caves.

RICHARD DOWDEN, ESQ., Mayor of Cork in the year 1845, will doubtless be rather surprised at seeing, if, which is perhaps rather problematical, he ever should see, his name at the head of an article in this 'History of British Birds,' but I place it there to do him all due honour for having issued a proclamation during his mayoralty, to forbid, on the score of cruelty, the hunting of this little bird on St. Stephen's Day by all the idle fellows of the country. There are different traditions as to the origin of this absurd custom,—one dating from the time of the incursions of the Danes, when it is said that a Wren perched on a drum, and there sang so loud as to awaken the enemy, who would otherwise have been slaughtered in their sleep; and the other from such a recent date as the reign of William III., when it is said that the noise of Wrens picking up the crumbs on a drum-head, in like manner saved his army from being cut off early in the morning by James II.; the result being to make these birds ever since objects of detestation to the Jacobites, and of favour with the Orangemen. It is however manifest that these traditions cannot both be true, and I shall therefore take the liberty of not believing either of them. Suffice it to say that on the Saint's Day in question, the 'Wren Boys' go about the hedges pelting the unfortunate victim with sticks and stones, and carry it about when caught, on the top of a pole in the midst of holly or ivy, singing some doggrel verses, which begin with

'The Wren, the Wren, the king of all birds,
St. Stephen's day was caught in the furze;
We hunted him up, we hunted him down,
We hunted him all about the town,' etc., etc.

The whole being an excuse for begging, and its consequent debauchery.

The Wren is found in Europe as far north as Sweden, the Ferroe Islands, Iceland, and 'Greenland's icy mountains,' as also in the other direction in Spain and Italy.

In England it is a universal favourite, and plentiful in most districts. In Yorkshire it is said to be less common near Halifax than in other parts. It is known likewise throughout Ireland, Scotland, Shetland, and most parts of Orkney; as also in Jersey, Guernsey, and Sark.

It remains with us throughout the year, braving the rigour of the northern winter, and generally without harm.

The Wren is one of our best known and most familiar birds, frequenting not only lanes and hedges, but gardens close to houses, and sheltering itself in the neighbouring and often ivy-clad outbuildings, several at times roosting together, and frequently in the old nest, for warmth's sake, in such places, or among heaps of stones, or the hollows in the roots of old and decayed trees, in the cold and frosty winter nights. They make, says William Ogilby, Esq., a prodigious chattering and bustle before finally settling down for the night, as if contending which shall get into the warmest and most comfortable place, and frequently come to the mouth of the hole to see that they are unobserved.

They often suffer a near approach, but nevertheless are easily alarmed, and then quickly steal back into the concealment which is most congenial to them, or fly away to some short distance, They are somewhat pugnacious, and have been observed fighting together with much animosity. In the daytime they may be seen with erect tail, now here, now there, creeping like a mouse among the branches. They are fond of seclusion, and are of solitary habits, being never seen in flocks, and seldom but in the spring in pairs, choosing also sombre, quiet, and lonely places for their tenantship.

Their flight, usually short and near the ground, is performed in a straight line, with repeated fluttering of the wings.

The young are assiduously attended to by the parent birds, and fed with insects and their larvæ and worms, the same that they themselves feed on; these, however, are not their exclusive food, for they make free with currants in the season.

The note, which is heard throughout the greater part of the year, but is not so powerful in the winter months, is very lively, clear, and cheerful, and while uttering it, the whole body vibrates with the effort, the bill is raised and opened wide, the throat swelled out, and the wings drooped. It is generally given forth from the upper branch of a hedge or bush, and when it is ended the singer descends from her place in the orchestra quite 'à la mode.' I was sitting in my breakfast-room one morning, when I heard a loud, clear, ringing note in the garden, whose authorship I could not divine, nor, on going out to endeavour to do so, detect. The following morning I heard it again, and this time was more fortunate. It was that of a Wren! There he or she the 'cantatrice' stood, pouring forth a volume of song enough almost to make the very welkin echo it. I was never more astonished at anything of the kind; it was so utterly disproportionate to the size of the tiny bird.

The nest, very large in size in proportion to the bird, and ordinarily of a spherical shape, domed over, but flattened on the side next the substance against which it is placed, varies much both in form and substance according to the nature of the locality which furnishes the materials and a 'locus standi' for it. It is commenced early in the spring, even so soon as the end of the month of March, the birds pairing in February. One found by my second son, Reginald Frank Morris, in autumn, in the beautiful grounds of Mulgrave Castle, near Whitby, the seat of Lord Normanby, was placed against the trunk of a large tree, about eight or ten feet from the ground, and was chiefly composed externally of dry leaves. Others are variously made of fern and moss, grass, small roots, twigs, and hay, closely resembling in most cases the immediate situation in which they are placed; some are lined with hair or feathers, and others not. The nest is firmly put together, especially about and below the orifice, which is strengthened with small twigs or moss, and is in the upper half and nearly closed by the feathers inside. It is in thickness from one inch to two inches, and about three inches wide within by about four in depth, and outside about five wide by six deep. At times they are found on the ground, and also in banks, as well as against trees, even so high up as twenty feet; so, too, under the eaves of the thatch of a building, in holes in walls, rocks, the sides of stacks, among piles of wood or faggots, or the bare roots of trees, and under the projection at the top of the bank of a river; one has been known to be placed in an old bonnet fixed up among some peas to frighten the birds, and another close to a constant thoroughfare.

The late Mr. Thompson, of Belfast, records one adapted from a Swallow's nest of the preceding year, built against a rafter supporting a floor; another which did not present any appearance of a dome and was placed in the hole of a wall inside a house, the only entrance being through a broken pane of the window; and another constructed in a bunch of herbs hung up to a beam against the top of an outhouse, almost the entire nest being formed of the herbs, and the whole bunch very little larger than the nest itself. The door of this house was generally kept locked, the only mode of entrance at such times being beneath it, where there was barely room for the birds to pass through; —in all these instances the broods were reared in safety. He also mentions the circumstance of a Wren having been detected in the act of purloining materials from a Thrush's nest, which was built in a bush adjoining its own tenement, then in course of erection, the thefts being committed during the temporary absence of the owner in search of food for its young. Mr. R. Davis, Jun., of Clonmel, also communicated to him the curious fact of a family of young Wrens, which, having left their own nest, and being probably in want of shelter, took possession of that of a Spotted Flycatcher, having apparently broken or thrown out all the eggs but one.

Ten days or a fortnight are occupied in the construction of the tenement, a few small stems of grass supported on the rugged bark or any rough part of the tree, if placed against one, indicating its commencement, and this is subsequently built on to, till all is completed.

The eggs are usually from seven to eight in number, but generally not more than eight, though as many as a dozen or even fourteen have been found, of a pale reddish white colour, the former tint being transient; some are dusky white. This ground colour is sprinkled all over with small spots of dark crimson red, and these most numerous at the obtuse end; some are quite white: the shell is very thin and polished. The male feeds the female white sitting. Two broods are produced in the season. The least disturbance will cause the nest to be forsaken, and a new one built, and this again and again, if so required, until the eggs are laid; even then, if they or the young be once handled, the bird will sometimes desert them. This, or some interruption of the ordinary course of laying, may be the cause of tenantless nests of the Wren being so frequently found; it is, however, said that a forsaken nest will sometimes be again returned to. Thus several nests of the same year are often found near together, the work of one and the same pair of birds, and other nests, in the making of which both birds assist, are not very unfrequently put together in the autumn, and in these the birds shelter themselves in the winter, possibly as being of the newest, and therefore the best, construction, and made too late in the year for a further brood; these nests seldom, if ever, contain any feathers. The young are said to return to lodge in the nest for some time after being fledged.

WOOD PIGEON.

YSGUTHAN, OF THE ANCIENT BRITISH.

RING DOVE.   CUSHAT.   QUEEST.

Columba palumbus,   PENNANT.   MONTAGU.

Columba—A Pigeon.   *Palumbus*—A Wood Pigeon.

THIS bird is a universal favourite, an emblem, as it is always considered, of peace, innocence, and conjugal fidelity. 'It was a Dove, ever since sacred to peace,' says Booth, 'that brought the olive branch to the ark of Noah, for which she has her place among constellations; and the Christian world still personate the HOLY SPIRIT under the mystic emblem of a Dove.'

It is with us a stationary inhabitant, but in the winter many are said to come over from the continent, and a departure again is accordingly supposed to take place in the spring. Of the enormous flocks which congregate in the winter, some do not separate till late in the spring, while others, in parliamentary phrase, 'pair for the session' by the beginning of March. In hard weather they sometimes make limited migrations, but such are not often called for—their food, unless covered with snow, being almost everywhere to be met with.

The Wood Pigeon is very good eating, except when in the winter it feeds on turnip tops, and then a disagreeable flavour is imparted to it. When they come home to roost in their accustomed trees in fir plantations, or tall oaks, ash, or other trees in woods, by lying in wait below they are easily to be procured, but in the open day they are shy, and with difficulty approached, unless it may be when engaged with their young. They are capable of being tamed if brought up from the nest, and have even been known to shew some personal attachment, perching on the head or shoulders of their friend, and eating out of the hand.

It is well known that few birds are wilder and more distrustful than the Ring Dove in autumn and winter; but that at the approach of spring they throw off much of their wildness, and become comparatively familiar and confiding.

In a Scotch paper for February 13th., 1838, it is stated, 'A circumstance, perhaps unprecedented in the annals of freezing, was discovered here last week. A person found in this neighbourhood, (Crieff,) a Wild Pigeon literally frozen to the branch of a tree, and so intense was the freeze, that the individual cut the branch, and carried the Pigeon home in that state alive.'

'If the habits,' says Meyer, 'of the Wood Pigeon are accurately observed, it will be seen that it leads a very regular life, and that it divides the day after the following manner:—From six to nine in the morning the time is occupied in searching for food. About ten o'clock the whole party returns home, and may be heard calling their 'hoo, hoo, coo, coo, hoo.' At eleven the calling ceases, and the party is again off in search of drink, and probably also to bathe, as we know them particularly to delight in the latter exercise. From twelve to two is again set apart as a season for resting, after which they go to feed until five; then return to their wood; where they repeat their concert until seven, when, after having taken some more water, they retire to roost.' This, however, cannot apply to the winter portion of the year.

Wood Pigeons are often seen in vast flocks, as well as in smaller ones, and some will occasionally intermingle with tame Pigeons in the field. Several pairs frequently build near each other, as if in this respect of gregarious habits, but single nests shew also that it is not the universal rule. The young birds, no doubt 'in terrorem' both active and passive, swell out their necks if approached, and utter a puffing sort of sound. This in one instance was known to alarm and frighten away a foster tame Pigeon, under whom the eggs had been placed; she was possibly as strange to them as their unknown language was to her.

Its flight, though rather slow at times, is on occasion strong, swift, straight, and powerful, the pinions sounding as they cut the air, the result of repeated strong and regular flappings, and generally at a considerable height in the air, unless the wind be very high.

'At first she flutters, but at length she springs
To smoother flight, and sports upon her wings.'
DRYDEN.

On the ground it moves in an easy and graceful manner, now walking more erect, and nodding the head at every step, now in a lower position,

Wood Pigeon

Peewit

and now peering about in suspicion of any approach of danger. It roosts near the tops of the tallest trees it can resort to, and comes home for that purpose about sunset, leaving them again at sunrise for the fields. Before settling they usually wheel about the spot where they desire to alight, and if disturbed from it, fly off to a short distance and then return, but if more frequently alarmed move away. 'In fine weather they bask in the sun on dry banks, or in the open fields, rubbing themselves, and, as it were, burrowing in the sand or soil, and throwing it up with their wings, as if washing in water, which they often do, like most birds. In drinking they immerse the bill to the base, and take a long draught.'

On arriving at a feeding place, they alight suddenly, and generally stand for a short time to reconnoitre. While searching for food the body is depressed, and they walk quickly along, moving the head backwards and forwards. The flock disperse about, but keep out of the way of danger.

The Wood Pigeon feeds on grain in all its stages—wheat, barley, and oats, peas, beans, vetches, and acorns, beech-mast, the seed of fir cones and wild mustard, charlock, ragweed, and other seeds, green clover, grasses, small esculent roots, ivy and other berries, and in the winter on turnip leaves, and their roots in hard weather—the first-named, even the larger ones, are all swallowed whole. It may safely be said that any damage it does, and some, it must be confessed, is done by it among seed tares and in pea fields, is abundantly compensated by the good that it effects in the destruction of the seeds of injurious plants.

The well-known note of the Cushat—its soft 'coo, coo-coo, coo-coo, coo,' begun sometimes towards the latter end of February, and continued till October, always harmonizes well with every quiet rural scene, and pleasant it is to listen to the plaintive 'melancholy music' as you 'walk in the fields to meditate,' or lie on some grassy bank in the settled summer time, when all nature has thrown off the mantle that cold had wrapped around her, and again comes forth in her renewed beauty, courting scrutiny in the full blaze of the sun, 'shining in his strength.' 'You may look, and look, and look again,' and in every insect that hovers about you, every overhanging flower, every passing cloud, every murmuring breeze, and the note of every bird, see what you cannot see, and hear what you cannot hear, the hand and the voice of God.

Early in the spring, at sunrise, the Ring Dove cooes to his mate, perched on the same or some neighbouring bough, then mounts in the air, and floats or sails to the top of the nearest tree, or, cooing all the while, will continue rising and falling several times, with a peculiar sort of flight, and when at its greatest elevation flapping the wings together backwards with a distinct sound, audible at some distance on a still day.

The nest, wide and shallow, placed usually at a height of from sixteen to twenty feet from the ground, is little more than a rude platform of a few crossed sticks and twigs, the largest as the foundation, so thinly laid together that the eggs or young may sometimes be discovered from below. It is often built in woods and plantations, but not unfrequently also in single trees, even those that are close to houses, roads, and lanes, the oak and the beech, the fir or any other suitable one, or, too, in ivy against a wall, rock, or tree, or in a thick bush or shrub in a garden, or an isolated thorn, even in the thick part, so that in flying out in a hurry, if alarmed, many of the loosely-attached feathers are pulled out.

The eggs, which are delicious eating, are two in number, pure white, and of a rounded oval form; two and sometimes three broods are produced in the season, but the third may possibly be only the consequence of a previous one having been destroyed or prevented: the eggs are hatched in sixteen or seventeen days. The young are fed from the bills of the parent birds with the food previously swallowed, reduced to a sort of milk. The male and female both take their turns in hatching the eggs and in feeding the young, the former sitting from six to eight hours—from nine or ten in the morning to about three or four in the afternoon.

PEEWIT.

CWTIAID YR AUR, OF THE ANCIENT BRITISH.

PE-WIT. TE-WIT. LAPWING. COMMON LAPWING. CRESTED LAPWING. GREEN LAPWING. GREEN PLOVER. LAPWING SANDPIPER. FRENCH PIGEON.

Vanellus cristatus,   FLEMING. SELBY.

Vanellus—Quære from *Vannus—*A fan, from the fanning motion of the wings?   *Cristatus—*Crested.

THIS very beautiful bird seems to be spread over the whole of the European continent.

It occurs throughout the whole of this country, but least plentifully in the midland and south-western parts.

They frequent open places, heaths, commons, marshy grounds, the sides of drains, fallow and other fields, especially those which have not been drained. Hitherto the low districts of Essex, Kent, Norfolk, Cambridgeshire, and Lincolnshire, have furnished the largest supplies of their eggs for the London market; but even the last-named county, once so proverbial for watery wastes, is now fast becoming altogether drained, and its agriculture has long since been second to none, so that in time different tenants will, beyond doubt, occupy the soil to the exclusion of other of a lower class.

They collect into large flocks in the autumn, the component parts thereof resolving themselves into their respective individualities in the spring.

Lapwings can hardly be called migratory birds, as some are to be seen nearly throughout the year, but at the end of February or the beginning of March they arrive, first in small and then in greater numbers, on the downs and other open places, frequenting the same haunts annually. They then pair and separate, and so spread themselves over the face of the country. In November, or later if the weather has been till then open, they retire southwards. They are extremely good birds to eat in the autumn and winter, but indifferent in the summer.

They are often kept in gardens, where they are very serviceable in devouring insects, and at the same time ornamental. One has been known to have lived in this half-domesticated state for fourteen years. Bewick gives an account of one thus kept by the Rev. J. Carlyle, vicar of Newcastle; when 'winter deprived it of its usual supply, necessity soon compelled it to draw nearer the house, by which it gradually became familiarized to occasional interruptions from the family. At length a servant, when she had occasion to go into the back kitchen with a light, observed that the Lapwing always uttered his cry, 'pee-wit,' to obtain admittance. He soon grew more familiar; as the winter advanced he approached as far as the kitchen, but with much caution, as that part of the house was generally in-habited by a dog and a cat whose friendship the Lapwing at length conciliated so entirely, that it was his regular custom to resort to the fireside as soon as it grew dark, and spend the evening and night with his two associates, sitting close by them, and partaking of the comforts of a warm fireside. As soon as spring appeared he left off coming to the house, and betook himself to the garden, but on the approach of winter, he had recourse to his old shelter and his old friends, who received him very cordially. Security was productive of insolence; what was at first obtained with caution was afterwards taken without reserve; he frequently amused himself with washing in the bowl which was set for the dog to drink out of, and while he was thus employed he showed marks of the greatest indignation if either of his companions presumed to interrupt him.' They are restless, watchful, and shy birds, and rarely approach houses, or even the vicinity of trees, preferring wide and open places. Even when roosting in the middle of the day, some sentinels are on the look out to give timely notice to the flock of any approaching danger.

'The Lapwing,' says Mr. Conway, 'will fly round and round, tumbling and tossing in the air, and at the same time making the country resound with the echoes of its endless 'pee-wit!' and thus lead the intruder farther and farther from its nest.' Its gyrations on these occasions are such as must strike the most inattentive passer-by, and the thoughtful mind will watch them with pleasing admiration. It is the male bird that is most clamorous: the female on being disturbed runs first from the eggs or young, and then flies a little way, near the ground and in silence.

The flight of the Lapwing is indicated by this, one of its vernacular names derived from it, a rather slow flapping of the wings. It seems at one and the same time both laboured and light, and is seen to advantage when the bird is chasing some prowling crow who has come too near. In dashing and whirling about in the air, when you by chance approach the spot where its young or egg are located, it frequently makes a rushing sound with its wings, which really at times bears a striking resemblance to the puffing of the engine of a railway-train, heard at some distance, or against the wind. Before taking wing it stretches the head out, and previous to alighting skims along the ground.

They feed on worms, slugs, caterpillars, and insects, and this chiefly during twilight or clear nights. Bishop Stanley says that one which a friend of his had, used to stand on one leg and beat the ground regularly with the other, in order to frighten the worms out of their holes. I should have thought that it would have had a contrary effect, but his Lordship gives the following as the theory on the subject:—'Their great enemy being the mole, no sooner do they per-ceive a vibration or shaking motion in the earth, than they make the best of their way to the surface, and thus fall into a greater and more certain peril.' Dr. Latham says the same.

The well-known note of the Peewit, from whence it derives its name, composed namely of these two syllables, the latter uttered 'crescendo,' 'pe-wit, pewit, pe-wit,' 'pees-wit, pees-wit,' or 'pees-weep, pees-weep,' is one that cannot fail to attract the ear, whether heard for the first or the thousandth time. The French, in like manner, call the bird Dixhuit. It has also a note of alarm or 'quasi' alarm, which after listening to to-day, I can best describe as a sort of whining sound.

The young are often hatched so soon as April, and begin to run about almost immediately after being hatched.

The nest is that which 'Mother Earth' supplies by a small and slight depression in the soil, with the addition sometimes of a few bits of grass, heath, or rushes, and this, perhaps, answering to the geographical description of an island, 'entirely surrounded by water,' on the marshy ground. To avoid, however, the evils attendant on this contingency, a mole-hill or other slight eminence is often chosen for a cradle. The young are not capable of flying till nearly full-grown.

The eggs, which are, like those of most if not of all small birds, very delicate eating, and sold in immense numbers for the purpose, are four in number, and so disposed in their narrow bed as to take up the smallest amount of room, the narrow ends pointed inwards, like the radii of a circle, to 'one common centre.' They vary to an extraordinary degree, though generally very much alike; some are blotted nearly all over with deep shades of brown. A fine series will be found described in my 'Natural History of the Nests and Eggs of British Birds.' In general they are of a deep green colour, blotted and irregularly marked with brownish black. They are wide at one end and taper at the other, as is the case with the birds of this class. They are hatched in fifteen or sixteen days.

TURNSTONE.

HUTTAN Y MOR, OF THE ANCIENT BRITISH.

COMMON TURNSTONE.   HEBRIDAL SANDPIPER.

Strepsilas interpres,   FLEMING. SELBY.

Strepsilas.   Strepho—To turn.   *Laas*—A stone.
Interpres—An interpreter. I conjecture from the bird's habit of careful investigation, and turning over, as a translator does in the case of the words of a book.

THE geographical range of this species is wide, extending to all the four great divisions of the globe.

This is another of our winter visitants, arriving the end of August, and departing in March, April, or May; in the one case in anticipation of the production of a family, and in the other after that event. The young, when full grown, quit, in most localities, the place of their birth, and, in company with their parents, move southwards along the coast. These, for the most part, compose the small flocks of Turnstones that are seen.

They are birds of sociable habits, both among themselves, and towards different kinds, but are shy otherwise of approach. They may, however, easily be tamed, and kept in confinement: one has been known to eat out of the hand. They appear to be fond of bathing. The parents exhibit great attachment to their young, but, as is the case with another species, their too great fondness is sometimes the ruin of their offspring, their cries of distress at the approach of an intruder directing attention to them. The like cause produces great pugnacity in them towards other larger sea-fowl, and especially towards the predatory Gulls, who have a natural inclination for the eggs of other kinds.

A curious circumstance is mentioned in the 'Zoologist,' page 2652, by Mr. James C. Garth, of one of these birds having been shot out of a flock of pigeons, and also quite inland, namely, near Knaresborough, in the West Riding, in October, 1849; it was a young one. The following much more extraordinary occurrence is narrated by Mr. Edward, in the same magazine, pages 3077-8-9:—

'Passing along the sea-shore on the West of Banff, I observed on the sands, at a considerable distance before me, two birds beside a large looking object. Knowing by their appearance that they did not belong to the species which are usually met with in this quarter, I left the beach, and proceeded along the adjoining links, an eminence of shingle intervening, until I concluded that I was about opposite to the spot where the objects of my search were employed. Stooping down with my gun upon my back, prepared for action, I managed to crawl through the bents and across the shingle for a considerable way, when I at length came in sight of the two little workers, who were busily endeavouring to turn over a dead fish, which was fully six times their size. I immediately recognised them as Turnstones. Not wishing to disturb them, anxious at the same time to witness their operations, and observing that a few paces nearer them there was a deep hollow amongst the shingle, I contrived to creep into it unobserved.

I was now distant from them but about ten yards; and had a distinct and unobserved view of all their movements. In these there was envinced that extraordinary degree of sagacity and perseverance, which comes under the notice only of those who watch the habits of the lower creation with patience and assiduity, and which, when fully and accurately related, are not unfrequently discredited by individuals, who, although fond of Natural History, seem inclined to believe that anything in regard to animals must necessarily be false, or at least the result of ignorance, unless it has been recorded in books which are considered as of authority on the subject. But to return: having got fairly settled down in my pebbly observatory, I turned my undivided attention to the birds before me. They were boldly pushing at the fish with their bills and then with their breasts: their endeavours, however, were in vain—the object remained immovable. On this they both went round to the opposite side, and began to scrape away the sand from close beneath the fish. After removing a considerable quantity, they again came back to the spot which they had left, and went once more to work with their bills and breasts, but with as little apparent success as formerly. Nothing daunted, however, they ran round a second time to the other side, and recommenced their trenching operations, with a seeming determination not to be baffled in their object, which evidently was to undermine the dead animal before them, in order that it might be the more easily overturned.

While they were thus employed, and after they had laboured in this manner, at both sides alternately, for nearly half an hour, they were joined by another of their own species, which came flying with rapidity from the neighbouring rocks. Its timely arrival was hailed with evident signs of joy. I was led to this conclusion from the gestures which they exhibited, and from a low but pleasant murmuring noise to which they gave utterance as soon as the new comer made his appearance: of their feelings he seemed to be perfectly aware, and he made his reply to them in a similar strain. Their mutual congratulations being over, they all three fell to work, and after labouring vigorously for a few minutes in removing the sand, they came round to the other side, and putting their breasts simultaneously to the fish, they succeeded in raising it some inches from the sand, but were unable to turn it over: it went down again to its sandy bed, to the manifest disappointment of the three. Resting however, for a space, and without moving from their respective positions, which were a little apart the one from the other, they resolved, it appears, to give the matter another trial. Lowering themselves with their breasts close to the sand, they managed to push their bills underneath the fish, which they made to rise to about the same height as before; afterwards, withdrawing their bills, but without losing the advantage they had gained, they applied their breasts to the object. This they did with such force, and to such purpose, that at length it went over, and rolled several yards down a slight declivity. It was followed to some distance by the birds themselves, before they could recover their bearing. They returned eagerly to the spot from whence they had dislodged the obstacle which had so long opposed them; and they gave unmistaken proof, by their rapid and continued movements, that they were enjoying an ample repast as the reward of their industrious and praiseworthy labour.

I was so pleased and even delighted with the sagacity and perseverance which they had shown, that I should have considered myself as guilty of a crime had I endeavoured on the occasion to take away life from these interesting beings at the very moment when they were exercising, in a manner so happy for themselves, the wonderful instincts implanted in them by their great and ever merciful Creator. When they appeared to have done and to be satisfied, I arose from my place of concealment. On examining the fish, I found it to be a specimen of the common cod; it was nearly three feet and a half long, and it had been imbedded in the sand to about the depth of two inches.'

Meyer observes, 'The general appearance of the Turnstone is very handsome, owing as much to its figure as to its gay apparel; its motions on the ground are graceful and dexterous, it runs much like the Lapwing, every now and then stopping short to rest or pick up food, especially when it has reached any elevation, either large or small; it is able to run very fast, and does so when pursued before it takes wing. Its flight is elegant and quick, performed generally with half extended wings that are considerably curved; its evolutions are very dexterous, skimming either close over the water or the ground, and rising high in the air it seems to depart, when, on a sudden, it returns again to the spot.'

Their food consists of marine insects and their larvæ, beetles, and small crustacea, and these are obtained, either among the sea-weed, or the rocks left dry at low water, by turning over stones on the beach with the beak—whence the name of the bird. During the time of high water, too, they resort to the lands that border on the shore, and there pick about in search of beetles, worms, and other such.

The note, uttered frequently when flying, is a clear twittering or whistling cry.

The time of breeding is about the middle of June.

They lay their eggs on sandy and rocky coasts, both where a stunted vegetation obtains, and where sterility alone is characteristic of the scene. They appear to have no tie to any previously tenanted situation, but choose a new summer residence, like other tribes, if so it suit them, year after year. The nest is sometimes placed under the shelter of a stone, rock, plant, or other break in the surface, and at other times on the mere rock, sand, or shingle. It is but some trifling hollow, natural or scraped out for the purpose, lined, perhaps, with a few dry blades of grass, or leaves.

The eggs, four in number, vary much in colour and markings, some being of a green olive ground, and others of a brown olive colour; some much and others only a little spotted, principally about the obtuse end, with dark grey, olive brown, and black, or reddish brown of two shades. They are cleverly concealed.

OYSTER-CATCHER.

PIOGEN Y MOR, OF THE ANCIENT BRITISH.

PIED OYSTER-CATCHER. SEA PIE. OLIVE.

Hæmatopus ostralegus,	PENNANT. MONTAGU.
Hæmatopus. *(H)aima*—Blood.	*Pous*—A foot. *Ostralegus.*
Ostræa—An Oyster.	*Lego*—To collect.

THIS fine and handsome bird is well known on the coast in many parts of England and Ireland, from the Scilly Islands to the extreme north.

They are seldom seen inland, though that is the case sometimes, but are principally to be noticed on the rocky shores of inlets, the sand banks of bays and creeks, and mud-covered flats, where scant Oases of vegetation and moist patches are interspersed.

In winter they unite in small flocks, which again in spring divide into pairs, but several of these resort to the same breeding-places. In the winter myriads are seen along the eastern coast. The male bird keeps watch while the hen is sitting, and gives notice by a loud shrill whistle of the supposed approach of any danger. The hen, if need be, silently quits the nest, and after making a circuit to deceive as to its situation, joins her partner, and both unite together in endeavouring to decoy away the supposed enemy with loud cries, flying round and round him, often very near. Any such, however, that are winged, as, for instance, a Crow, Rook, or Skua-Gull, they are quick to give notice

Turnstone

Oyster-Catcher

of the approach of, and attack and drive away from the neighbourhood with blows from their powerful bills. They are tameable birds, and will associate with domestic poultry. In their wild state, too, they play about in a lively manner with their own and other species, and at times enter into contests, attacking fearlessly even such as are larger than themselves. They are watchful and shy in their habits, avoiding betimes any suspicious intruders.

They run about in an easy manner, and also, if necessary, with great rapidity, and both swim and dive, the former not unfrequently, for short distances, when seeking for food; but the latter, for the most part, only if alarmed. The young too evince the same habits, and run about almost immediately after being hatched. They fly strongly in regular lines like an army, battalion after battalion, and sail for some short distance before pitching down. When the sky is dark they look like a long white streak, and in like manner when it is bright, like a dark one. If the wind is high they invariably settle with their heads to windward, and if they come down the wind to the place on which they intend to stop, they fly past it, and then face the breeze again and alight with their heads in that direction.

They feed in the mornings and evenings, and at night, on various shell-fish—muscles, limpets, winkles, and other crustacea, worms, and marine insects. For dislodging and penetrating the former their strong and wedge-shaped bill is admirably adapted. Dr. Stanley says that in thus trying oysters they have sometimes been caught by the bill —'the biter bit.' They roost during the day, standing either on one or both legs on a stone, rock, or bank. While the tide covers their feeding-places they repair to the neighbouring corn and other fields, which they again quit for their more natural resorts as soon as per-mitted.

They are extremely noisy during the time that they have young, screaming loudly, or scolding in their defence. Meyer says, 'the call-note of the bird in question sounds most like the word 'quip' or 'whip,' uttered in a very high tone, and repeated several times when on the wing; the concert is generally begun by one bird in a moderate 'tempo,' which increases to 'allegro,' and finally 'presto, presto,' being joined by an increased number of voices until all unite in the chorus.'

The nest is placed among gravel or stones, or among grass near the sea bank, in situations above high-water mark, where these materials of building are at hand, and the bird seems to be especially partial to a mixture of broken shells, which it carefully collects together and places in a slight hollow in the ground, using considerable care in their disposition. Several nests appear to be made, sometimes, before the architect can fashion one to give perfect satisfaction; many nests are also placed in contiguity to each other, intermixed too, it may be, with those of other aquatic birds. Some have been met with on the top of isolated rocks, at a height of from ten to fifteen feet from the ground. In lieu of shells small pieces of stone or gravel are selected, and the whiter they are the better the seem to please. In-cubation lasts about three weeks.

The eggs are four in number, and of a yellowish stone-colour, spotted with grey, brown, and brownish black. They have been found variously in April, May, June, and July, so that it would appear that two broods are reared in the year. The eggs are disposed with their small ends inwards.

The young birds run soon after they are hatched, and are very active. If pursued they hide their heads in the first hole they come to, as if thinking, like the Ostrich, that if they cannot see you, you cannot see them.

The plate is taken from a design by the Rev. R. P. Alington.

HERON.

CRYR GLAS. CRYHYR CAM. CRYR COPPOG, OF THE ANCIENT BRITISH.

HERN. HERONSHAW. HERONSEWGH. COMMON HERON.
CRESTED HERON.

Ardea cinerea,   LATHAM. SHAW.

Ardea—A Heron.   *Cinerea*—Ash-coloured—grey.

The almost total discontinuance of hawking, and the consequent dispersion of the great Heronries of the olden time, carefully then preserved for the purpose, have naturally led to the establishment of smaller settlements in various other places, and even of single pairs from time to time. The changes that the lapse of ages introduces into the human colony, work corresponding effects in an infinite variety of ways, among the natural creation.

Heronries are inhabited from spring to the latter end of summer, and are occasionally returned to by individual birds in the winter months from time to time. They are clung to with great tenacity by their occupants.

They are shy and solitary birds, and make off at once if approached, when standing in ever so apparently listless a manner by the side of the pool, or the margin of the stream. Clear water is preferred, on account of the better view it affords of their prey. I remember well one fine summer evening, when a boy, seeing one 'light at a bend in a small river, where I thought I could manage to get him within range, and after running home for a gun, and stealing close to the ground till near him, when he at last perceived his danger and rose suddenly to escape it, bringing him down dead by a shot through the neck. It was a young bird, and the only one, I am glad to say, that I ever killed, or, I believe, ever fired at —alas! 'tempus fugit.'

If not cut off, they are said to be long-lived. They are formidable if attacked at close quarters, defending themselves, so to speak, both with tooth and nail. They are always objects of interest, and comport well with the retired unfrequented scenes to which, and to which only, they seem naturally to belong. There you may see the Heronshaw for hours together standing on one leg, on the ground or the branch of a tree, the neck retracted and the bill resting on the breast, 'chewing the cud of sweet or bitter reflection,' according as he has been comparatively satisfied, or is waiting for a further supply of food. One might almost fancy that he was musing in pensive melancholy over the altered times which have changed protection into proscription, and foreshadow, to look on the dark side of things, the future extirpation of the English branch of his race. Royal game in the times of falconry, and prized also for the table, now-a-days he is the object of all but universal hostility, and his conspicuous appearance marks him out as a victim.

Seen for the most part at other times of the year in the singular or the dual number, these birds become gregarious in the building-season. An island in a lake is then a favourite resort.

The flight of the Heron, in which the wings are much arched, and the neck doubled back, is slow and heavy, and the long legs are carried straight out, projecting behind as if a tail: the legs are drooped before alighting. They are able to swim, but perform the operation slowly. Though generally speaking of an awkward and ungainly appearance, yet the different curvatures assumed by this bird in its positions give it a line of beauty which the ornithologist at all events can appreciate and admire.

Herons are very voracious birds, and always seem hungry. Their usual food consists of trout, flounders, eels, carp, and other fish, which they swallow head foremost; water-lizards, snakes, toads, frogs, rats, both land and water, and mice; the young of other birds, beetles and various insects, shell-fish, shrimps, and the roots and blossoms of plants: a trout has been seen taken about four pounds in weight.

The hair, feathers, and bones of their prey are cast up in pellets, after the manner of the Owls. 'It is perhaps worth remarking, that when the Herons drop any of the food which they bring to their young among the trees of the Heronry, they make no attempt to recover it, but, probably from a consciousness of their inability to rise from the ground in a confined space, allow it to remain where it falls.' The result is often beneficial to the neighbours, and a good pannier of fish may in such cases be collected under a large Heronry. The prey is brought from a distance, it may be, of two miles or more to the young, and much ado with snapping and chuckling the latter make on the bringing home of each fresh supply.

They feed ordinarily in the mornings and evenings, but when they have a young family to provide for, are obliged to forage through-out the days. Standing motionless in the shallow edge of the river or lake, the head, as before remarked, drawn back in the attitude of expectation, you may see them watching, with the patience for which all other anglers ought to be equally proverbial, for a 'bite.' True waders, their food is mostly taken in the water, but none is refused that occurs elsewhere. If dropped from the bill, it will be picked up again more than once at the place of capture. It is very rarely indeed that the Heron misses its mark. It strikes with the most unerring precision, and transfixes the quarry with the strong blow that it gives.

Their note is a harsh, wild cry, uttered on the wing, and frequently repeated, 'the word 'craigh' uttered in a lengthened manner, with cracked and high-pitched voices,' as the bird heavily wends its way to any accustomed haunt by the bank of some river, reedy lake, or rushy pond, the margin of some muddy estuary or creek, or the

Heron

Curlew

edge of some stagnant swamp or quaggy morass. It is also heard while on migration.

The Heron builds, according to circumstances, either on the ground, in which situation Montagu saw several, or on trees of any sort; also, it is said, on cliffs, preferring situations in the vicinity of water. Many nests are often placed on such together—as many as eighty have been counted in one tree. Preparations for nidification are made about the month of April. The nest is placed on the very summit of the tree, or as close to it as the case will admit of, and also, near the extremity of the branch, the size of the bird not allowing of a ready passage inwards. The nest, flat in shape, is rather small for the size of the tenants that have to inhabit it, but in some cases is much larger than in others, probably from an old one being built on. It is made of sticks and twigs, and has a lining of wool or hair, rushes, dry grasses, water-flags, straws, or any soft materials.

Two broods are reared in the season, and both parents assist in the work of providing the young with food: the male also feeds the female while sitting. If alarmed for their young, they soar about aloft over the nests.

The eggs are generally three in number, sometimes, it is said, four or five, and of a green colour. They vary in shape, some being pointed at both ends, and others only at the lower end. They are hatched in about three weeks, and it is five or six more before the young birds are able to quit the nest.

The finest specimen of this bird that I think I ever saw, is preserved in the hall of the Rectory at Swinhope, the residence of my friend, the Rev. R. P. Alington. It was shot in the parish of Thoresway, Lincolnshire, February 21st., 1853.

The plate is from a design by the Rev. R. P. Alington. I will thank any one to shew me a better.

CURLEW.

GYLFINHIR, OF THE ANCIENT BRITISH.

COMMON CURLEW. WHAAP. WHAUP. WHITTERICK.

Numenius arquata,   PENNANT.

Numenius. Numenia—The New Moon, from the crescented shape of the bill.
Arquata—Arched.

THIS fine bird well comports in its native demeanour with the wild places which it usually frequents, both upland and lowland, and more especially as regards the former.

Early in April they begin to leave their haunts by the sea, and to seek the far distant interior, in which for the summer months they will abide. Small flocks, of from five to ten, are generally seen thus passing through inward districts, and larger numbers along the coast, the union of different flights which have come one after another.

The Curlew breeds in the most retired situations, and for the most part in hilly regions, on the lone wild heath, the solitary moor, the open down, and the barren sheep-walk, especially near places that are wet and marshy. It also frequents the sea-shores, the mud-banks and sand-flats of rivers, and the edges of lochs, both maritime and in the mainland. At times it perches on high trees. It walks well, and wades deep, and is able to swim with ease. It is a very difficult bird to approach, but may be enticed by a skilful imitation of its whistle. It is exceedingly good eating. It soon becomes tame in confinement, whether captured young or old, and will follow the person about that is accustomed to feed it. In the wild state they are very timid and shy, except when engaged with their nest, and are only to be circumvented by stratagem. In winter they are gregarious.

During migration, or in any more extended flight, either high overhead, or close over the land or water, or even on their return from the mainland to the shore to feed, they advance in the shape of a wedge, and in the latter case if one such party be alarmed, a 'signal whistle' is given, which those that come after are guided by, and uttering it in repetition for those that follow, to be taken up again by them in turn, deviate to a safer track. If frequently thus disturbed, they soon profit by experience, and resort to a different route.

Their flight, which is not very rapid, is executed with regular strokes of the wing, quickened if necessary according to circumstances. They alight somewhat suddenly, closing the wings, and dropping nearly to the ground, then sweeping up once more a little, and then settling down. They always face the wind, should it be at all high: in doing this, thy fly past their resting place if they come down the wind to it, and then turning back and alighting with their heads in that direction. They often stand on one leg, or rest themselves by lying down.

They make their food in winter of small marine insects, crabs, and other minute crustacea, mollusks, worms, and other such, and when the flowing tide covers the sand where these are to be procured they retire inland even to a considerable distance; but as soon as ever the ebbing waves have again retired back so far towards their fixed goal as to leave the sandy margin once more uncovered, back, almost to a moment, do the flocks return, taught by some sense which is out of the range of sight, but which 'He that planted the eye' has likewise implanted, as He has every other proper gift in His creatures, according to their several needs. In summer they pick up flies and different insects, in addition to such of the other kinds of food enumerated here, as may then come in their way, and also bilberries, whortle-berries, lichens, blades of grass, and the tender tops of twigs. They drink often, and are fond of bathing themselves.

The loud, clear whistle of the Curlew is exceedingly pleasant to such as delight in those retired scenes in which it is heard, and with which, as I have said, it so well harmonizes. It is uttered by the bird when on the wing, and its name I suppose has been considered to resemble it. It may be heard high in the air during migration, and also in the spring, at which season the male serenades his mate, rising slowly aloft, and wailing out his quivering cry. If an intruder approaches the nest or its intended site, he is assailed by both birds, who dash at him with noisy screams, and beat about him within a few yards. They also, if driven to a distance and there followed, endeavour to entice their enemy away further by running and skulking in a deceptive manner.

The nest, if any be made in some slight hollow, consists only of a little dry grass, twigs, or leaves, or is placed in the middle of a tuft of the former, among heather or rushes.

The eggs, laid in April and May, are four in number, and they differ much both in their ground colour and the spots. They are of a pale dull green, blotted all over with two shades of brown. They are very large for the size of the bird. They are placed 'quatrefoil' in the nest, the narrow ends inwards. The young run about almost as soon as hatched, but are not able to fly for a considerable time. Until then they are assiduously attended to by their parents. If approached, they hide themselves among the inequalities of the ground, and lie very close, the old birds endeavouring the while to attract the enemy away.

REDSHANK.

COESGOCH, OF THE ANCIENT BRITISH.

**COMMON REDSHANK. REDSHANK SANDPIPER. RED-LEG.
RED-LEGGED HORSEMAN. RED-LEGGED SANDPIPER. STRIATED SANDPIPER.
GAMBET. GAMBET SANDPIPER. SANDCOCK. POOL SNIPE.**

Scolopax calidris,   PENNANT. MONTAGU.

Scolopax—A Woodcock.   *Calidris*—........?

THIS bird is found in Europe, in Iceland, the Ferroe Islands, Lapland, Norway, Sweden, Denmark, and the Islands of the Baltic Sea; also in Holland, Germany, Italy, Hungary, Greece, and Spain. In Asia it appertains to Persia, Siberia, and Japan; and is said also to belong to North America, about Hudson's Bay, but the Prince of Canino, Lucien Buonaparte, doubts this; and again to Africa, in which latter it is well known and plentiful. With us it is indigenous, but local.

In the winter they frequent the sea shore, delighting in the sandy or muddy flats which are in many places left uncovered by the falling tide of the 'ever sounding and mysterious main;' and in spring they repair to fenny places and marshes, and the borders of lakes, ponds, and pools.

They travel northwards in the month of March and April, to their breeding haunts, and southwards from July to the end of September. They move in the evening or by night, the adult birds singly or in pairs, the younger either in families or flocks. It is rare to see more than three or four old ones together. The former are said to progress farther northward than the latter. They are shy birds, and sometimes try to escape notice by remaining motionless under cover of the uneven surface of the ground.

In running along the sands they exhibit a dipping motion, as may be seen in other birds of the class. 'The ordinary posture of the young Redshank is with the head sunk back between the shoulders, the back of the neck being bare of feathers.' This species is tamed without much difficulty. 'Its attitude when walking is very graceful and elegant; when running it moves about with a wonderfully light step, hardly touching the ground with its feet. It rarely runs, unless it is provoked to do so. It wades, reaching its head down under water at full length, but does not dive or swim by choice. The flight of the Redshank is generally performed with quick motions of the wings, which are not opened at full length, although the bird floats frequently some distance on the wing during the pairing season, in fine still weather. When alighting, it is very beautiful to see this bird, just before coming to the ground, turn up its wings, as pigeons are known to do, and shewing thus the white under surface.'

They frequent the same spots, and take the same flights day after day, and resting on the margin at full tide assemble again on the rocks, sands, or mud banks, as soon as left uncovered; viz., when the tide is at its height they assemble in flocks on the uncovered places, but immediately that its fall permits their return to their feeding places they disperse in quest of prey. In the latter case twenty or thirty may keep together, but in the former, flocks of some hundreds are crowded together. They are reckoned good eating.

These birds sometimes perch on trees. They can swim well if necessitated to do so. In winter they assemble in flocks, often from a dozen to fifty, and upwards, from one hundred and fifty to two hundred, and are then difficult to approach, being always on the look-out and ready to take wing on the slightest alarm. If fired at, they almost seem as if they saw the flash of the gun in time to avoid its discharge. If disturbed while the young are yet unable to fly, they are very vociferous, wheeling about an intruder with a slow quivering flight, the wings depressed for a more than ordinary space of time, and frequently stooping close down, as if to buffet him, whistling shrilly while doing so, with their red legs stretched out behind or drooping, as if languidly, under them, and at times feigning to be wounded. Indeed at any time, especially if approached unawares, they utter a wild scream of alarm, more or less loud, which, if not intended, is yet taken as a signal by other birds about. Their flight, if suddenly disturbed, 'is at first irregular and tortuous, but soon becomes tolerably steady. It is rapid, but rarely protracted.'

They feed on grasshoppers, beetles, marine insects, and worms, and in search of these bore with their bills in the mud or sand, jumping up and so pressing them in by the weight of their bodies. They likewise eat portions of weeds and mosses.

The call note of the Redshank is only a 'dgæ, dgæ,' or 'liddle, liddle.' It is loud and clear, merry and not unmusical, and also at times is plaintive and garrulous, but ordinarily more clamorous and as if scolding. When a number are assembled together it becomes a sort of chatter.

The nest, of a little coarse grass, is made by the marshy margins of lakes and other uncultivated watery places, on a heap of flags, or in some slight depression, or sheltered by a bush or tuft of herbage, as also, it is said, occasionally on heaths. Sometimes, often indeed, the bare earth alone is used for the purpose.

The eggs, deposited early in May, are pale reddish white, tinged with green, and blotted, spotted, and speckled with dark red brown, most at the larger end; some varieties with bluish grey. They are four in number, and are placed informally in the nest. The young are hatched in from fourteen to sixteen days, and immediately quit the nest, under the tutelage of the female bird, the male taking no care of them; they soon are fledged and able to provide for themselves.

COMMON SANDPIPER.

PIBYDD Y TRAETH, OF THE ANCIENT BRITISH.

SUMMER SNIPE.   SPOTTED SANDPIPER.   SAND LARK.   SAND LAVROCK.

Tringa hypoleucos,   PENNANT.   MONTAGU.

Tringa—........?   *Hypoleucos.   Hypo*—Under.   *Leucos*—White.

The Common Sandpiper is generally known throughout this country —from Cornwall, Devonshire, Dorsetshire, Hampshire, Kent, Essex, Cambridgeshire, and Oxfordshire, where small parties occasionally pass the summer near Brighthampton, Witney, Mr. Stone writes me word, to Norfolk, Durham, and Northumberland, and from Wales to Scotland, being plentiful on the inland lakes—Loch Awe and others, in Caithnesshire, Sutherlandshire, and elsewhere.

The Summer Snipe visits us in April, about the 20th., and leaves us by about the end of September, or earlier—in August—according to the state of the season. They arrive singly or in pairs, and travel by night. Before starting they fly about in a restless manner, uttering their whistling note.

It is a bird of lively and active habits, and it is pleasant to watch it running nimbly, in the summer time, along the water's edge, by the side of a still lake or pond, or the bank of the rapid or the slow stream, the large or the small river, or treading lightly over the beautiful leaves of the water-lily, which float so buoyant themselves on the crystal surface. It is seldom seen on the shore of the sea, but the situations mentioned are all alike congenial to its taste, whether in a hilly or a flat country, an open or a wooded district. It can both swim and dive well; even the young, if need appear to be, take fearlessly to the water, and remove underneath the surface to a considerable distance. One has been known thus to seek and find safety from the pursuit of a Hawk. The wings are used in progression underneath.

It is almost constantly in motion, and has, like so many others birds, a habit of flirting its tail up and down, while the head and neck are thrust forward in a nodding manner, or again retracted during the search for food. If disturbed during the period of incubation, 'the female quits the nest as quietly as possible, and usually flies to a distance, making at this time no outcry; as soon, however, as the young are hatched, her manners completely alter; the greatest agitation is expressed on the apprehension of danger, and every strategem is tried, such as feigning lameness, and inability of flight,

Redshank

Common Sandpiper

to divert the attention of the intruder from the unfledged brood:' both parents indeed are clamorous at this season, ignorant of the worldly maxim that 'speech was given to us to conceal our thoughts.' These birds perch at times on roots and stumps by the water side. Small flocks of a dozen or fourteen may at times be seen together, or up to twenty or thirty; but they do not associate very closely or determinedly, each individual following its own inclination, both when on the ground and in flying off, or alighting.

It flies with ease and celerity; if to a distance, at a moderate height; but if otherwise, it proceeds a little way, and commonly settles on the opposite side to that which it had left. 'Its flight,' says Selby, 'is graceful, though peculiar, being performed by a rapid motion of the pinions, succeeded by an interval of rest, the wings at the same time being considerably bent, and forming an angle with the body; and in this manner it skims with rapidity over the surface of the water, not always flying in a straight line, but making occasional sweeps.' When settling down, the wings are at some seasons kept up stretched over the back, and in this position it runs along the sand, uttering the while its plaintive whistle. Sandpipers may at times be seen running along the grass by the river side, stretching themselves out, and ruffling their feathers in an odd sort of manner.

They feed on worms and insects, such as flies, gnats, and water spiders, and on minute snails, but rarely. In search of some part of their food, they thrust their bills into the mud.

The note, a clear pipe, is, though pleasant to the ear, a mere 'wheet, wheet, wheet,' uttered when the bird is put up, as well as when perched on some stone, branch, or stake, near the water-side. Meyer likens it to the syllables, 'heedeedee, heedeedee.' It is repeated a great number of times—as many as forty or fifty—by the bird when on the wing.

Nidification commences about the middle of April.

The nest is slight—a collection of a few leaves or a little moss, dry grass or leaves, in a hollow in a bank, in a tuft of grass, or tussock of rushes, upon a bed of gravel, or even on a bare rock, the eggs being kept together by only a very slight inequality in the surface. It is generally thus sheltered or protected, on one side at least, and is usually built near the water's edge, but sometimes in an adjoining field, always above the highest water-mark. It is well hidden in a tuft of grass or rushes, or among the lower branches of willows and osiers, so as to be difficult to find. The same pair, if undisturbed, will return for several successive seasons to their accustomed building-place.

The eggs, four in number, are of a reddish white or cream yellow tint, spotted and speckled with dark brown, and other marks of a lighter hue. Some are of a clear very light blue ground colour, with minute brown spots all over; others with large blots of deep brown. They are, as the eggs of other waders, admirably adapted, both by their form and their position in the nest, to occupy the smallest possible degree of space, as rendered expedient by their large size in proportion to that of the bird. The young are hatched in about fourteen days, and leave the nest almost immediately. They quickly learn to hide themselves in the nearest covert, and in about a month are able to shift for themselves.

The plumage in this species is of a silky texture.

AVOCET.

PIG MYNAWYD, OF THE ANCIENT BRITISH.

SCOOPER. COMMON AVOCET. SCOOPING AVOCET. CROOKED-BILL.
YELPER. COBBLER'S-AWL DUCK.

Recurvirostra avocetta,   FLEMING. SELBY.

Recurvirostra. Recurvus—Crooked—bent.
Rostrum—The beak of a bird.   *Avocetta*—............?

THIS bird, unique, as far at least as our country is concerned, in the singularity of its appearance, is in Europe plentiful.

In Yorkshire, two were formerly obtained on Skipwith Common, near Selby; several have been met with near Spurn Point, and on other parts of the coast, and the banks of the Humber.

Sir Thomas Brown has recorded that Avocets were common in his time in Norfolk; and within the present generation, as many as twenty are said to have been received within one month of one year, in Leadenhall market. They used to frequent the marshes at Winterton; a pair were taken at Yarmouth, the 22nd. of April, 1852; two also in the month of June, 1851. It used to be more common there on Breydon, but has of late years become more rare. It has been known to breed at Salthouse. One was obtained in the spring of 1837. They were formerly also met with on the Durham coast. A specimen was shot some years since at Croxby Lake, Lincolnshire, as the Rev. R. P. Alington has informed me, by the late Theophilus Harneis, Esq., of Thorganby Hall. In Cornwall, two have been killed at Swanpool, near Falmouth, one of them in November, 1845; others formerly have been noticed in Gloucestershire and in Shropshire.

In Sussex, Markwick says that it was not uncommon in his time, 1795, on the coast in summer; and he met with a pair which had young, in a marsh near Rye. It also visited the shore at Bexhill. A. T. Dodd, Esq., of Chichester, saw a flock of five at Pagham harbour, near there, and procured three of them. In Surrey, one at Godalming is recorded. In Kent, Romney Marsh used to be a locality for it; and the muddy flats at the mouth of the Thames, in that county, and 'over the water' in Essex. In the former-named a nest of young ones was found in 1842, by Mr. Plomley, and two young ones procured the following year; one was shot at Sandwich, the 22nd. of April, 1849. Donovan mentions that they were formerly common in the Cambridgeshire Fens. In Devonshire, one was obtained near Plymouth, in November, 1854, as John Gatcombe, Esq., has been kind enough to send me word. One near Kingsbridge, previously, in 1847.

In Ireland, as stated by the late William Thompson, Esq., of Belfast, it is a very rare visitor. In Scotland, it is in like manner an occasional straggler. In Orkney, it is stated by Edmonston to have occurred.

The mouth of the Severn, in Gloucestershire, is given as another of its 'quondam' localities; also Shropshire, Fossdike, in Lincolnshire, and the Dorsetshire coast.

It is of migratory habits, arriving in this country, that is, when it does arrive—for, though formerly a regular and frequent visitor, it is not so now—in the month of April; and leaving again in September. Its migration is performed during the night.

It prefers muddy shores to those of a sandy or rocky kind; also salt marshes, to which it resorts while the tide covers its other feeding-grounds, but leaves again for the latter when it has ebbed sufficiently. The Avocet walks in an easy and graceful manner, and is able also to run very fast; 'which,' says Meyer, 'it does invariably close to the water's edge when pursued, standing every now and then still, raising its head sharply, and lowering it again, and at last if the pursuit is kept up, it flies up high in the air, and leaves the neighbourhood. Swimming may also be ranked among its capacities, during which exercise it nods with its head at every stroke; but it seems to like to float rather than to swim.'

'The flight of the present species is very different from that of most others of its family, owing in part, to its bending its wings into perfect arches during their movements; the wings are either beaten in quick succession, or more moderately, accordingly to the pleasure of the bird. During the breeding-season, they fly great distances, low, over the surface of the water, but pursue their migratory journey at a great elevation. The form of the Avocet, when on the wing, is particularly strange, in consequence of the head being drawn close to its body, with the beak bent somewhat downwards, and the legs projected out very far behind. On alighting, it opens its wings for a moment high above the back, and then closes them very carefully.'

When the female is frightened off the nest, she flies round and round with drooped legs and extended neck, counterfeiting every sign of disablement, and crying out with alarm, or the desire to distract attention. They are quick and active in their movements. Avocets are sociable birds among themselves, but shy in their general character. They travel usually in small numbers, but sometimes unite in large flocks. They build in companies. Montagu writes, 'The singular form of the bill led Buffon, according to his absurd atheistical tendency, to suppose it to be 'one of those errors or essays of nature, which, if carried a little further, would destroy itself: for if the curvature of the bill were a degree increased, the bird could not procure any sort of food, and the organ destined for the support of life, would infallibly occasion its destruction.'

They feed on aquatic insects, embryo crustacea, shrimps, and worms, and in search of these wade deep or not as the case requires, but usually keep near the edge. The manner in which they obtain their prey appears to be by scooping with the concave part of the bill, from side to side in a zigzag manner in the sand, and also in the water. A good deal of gravel is swallowed with the food.

The note or pipe is likened to the syllables 'kwee, kwee,' or 'twit, twit.'

The nest is said to be made in a hollow on some dry spot in a marsh, or on the bank, just above high-water mark, among the short grass, or other marine vegetation. It is lined with a little of those materials. The eggs are described as being usually two, but sometimes three or four in number, brown or greenish white, spotted and speckled with black. The young are hatched in eighteen days, and leave the nest almost immediately. If chased, they hide themselves, with much success, among the scanty cover.

Avocet

Black-Tailed Godwit

BLACK-TAILED GODWIT.

RHOSTOG, OF THE ANCIENT BRITISH.

COMMON GODWIT. GODWYN. YARWHELP. YARWHIP. LESSER GODWIT.
JADREKA SNIPE. RED GODWIT. HUDSONIAN GODWIT. SHRIEKER.

Limosa melanura,   LEISLER. TEMMINCK.

Limosa. Limus—Mud.   *Melanura. Melas*—Black. *Oura*—A tail.

THIS species extends pretty generally, though unequally, over Europe
—so far north as Iceland, Lapland, and Greenland, and south again
to Spain, Switzerland, Italy, and Holland; Asia, to which continent
Temminck assigns Japan and the Sunda Isles as localities for it, as
well as the vicinity of Mount Caucasus and Persia; and Africa, about
Tangiers, Tunis, and other parts of the north.

It most affects the countries that are nearest to the sea, and attaches
itself to moist and swampy places, low meadows, where a rank vegetation
prevails, and other such.

In England it is generally distributed, though by no means abundant.
It breeds occasionally, though sparingly, in the Cambridgeshire and
Norfolk Fens, near Buckenham and Oby; so it is also said to have
done on the edge of Hatfield Chase, near Thorne, Yorkshire—a very
likely place in former times for any such birds. It is common about
Breydon, near Yarmouth, in Norfolk; it belongs also to the Northumbrian, Lincolnshire, and Yorkshire coasts. In Suffolk, two in full
summer plumage were shot in a fen near Wisbeach, May 4th., 1850.

In Cornwall, one was shot at Swanpool, near Falmouth, by Mr. May,
December 12th., 1846; another at Grade, July 14th., 1853. In Surrey,
it has occurred near Godalming; in Devonshire, it has been obtained.
In Bedfordshire, at Cardington; also in Derbyshire, one on Sinfin Moor.

In Orkney it is a rather rare winter bird, during which season it
appears in small flocks.

In Ireland it is an occasional visitant, and has been obtained near
Dublin, in October.

Its haunts in winter are the oozy banks of the larger estuaries, and
the mouths of rivers.

They arrive in March in the places where they intend to rear their
young. They move by night, and then unite in companies of perhaps
forty or fifty individuals, but at other times are unsociable among
themselves, as well as shy, excepting when interested for their brood,
whom they endeavour to obtain security for by flying about any intruder.
The young birds shew great dexterity in hiding themselves.

They are highly esteemed for the table, and are both shot and taken
in snares.

'In flight it opens its pointed wings at full length, and beats the air
in regular succession; but when hurried, its wings are only half opened,
and the strokes become very quick, whereby its speed is very much
increased. Its walk is not unlike that of the Stork, and when at rest
it invariably stands on one leg.' When asleep, it generally 'puts its
head under its wing.'

The Godwit feeds on insects and their larvæ, and worms, obtained
by boring in the soft sand and mud with its long bill, not only when

the surface is uncovered, but also under the water, immersing the head for the purpose. It follows its vocation early in the morning and late in the evening, and, of course, longer during moonlight nights.

The note has been compared to the syllables 'grutto, grutto, grutto.'

About the beginning of April they arrive at their nesting-places, and begin to lay early in May, in the rough parts of swamps, and low meadows near water, the nest being composed of dry grass, and other wild plants, and hidden among any coarse herbage.

The eggs are four in number, of a deep green or light olive brown colour, faintly blotted with spots of a darker shade.

As soon as the young are able to flutter about, the old ones leave them to themselves.

The plate is after a design by the Rev. R. P. Alington.

DUNLIN.

Y PIBYDD RHUDDGOCH. LLYGAD YR YCH, OF THE ANCIENT BRITISH.

PURRE. DUNLIN SANDPIPER. SEA SNIPE. PLOVER'S PAGE.
STINT. LEAST SNIPE. SEA LARK.

Tringa variabilis,   SELBY. JENYNS.

Tringa—........?   *Variabilis*—Variable.

THE Dunlin, or Purre, the former the name that used to be given to the bird in its summer, and the latter in its winter plumage, as if two species, has had its specific name assigned to it as indicative of the great difference between its appearance in the one and in the other season: I do not however see but that the other Sandpipers have an equal claim to the title on the like account.

It is very abundant in the Arctic regions of America, and the islands of the Polar sea, and thence through the United States to Florida, Carolina, Cayenne, Mexico, and Domingo, and others of the West Indian Islands; as also in Europe from the Ferroe Isles, Iceland, Greenland, Lapland, and Norway, and so on to the southern countries of the continent. It likewise belongs to Asia, being common in Asia Minor and the region about the Caucasus, as also in the islands of the Indian Ocean—Japan, Sunda, and Timor. So, too, from the north coast of Africa, even, it is said, to the Cape.

The Purre is one of the commonest of our Sandpipers, being found throughout England, Scotland, and Wales.

In Ireland, it is also plentiful, as likewise in the Shetland Islands, and the Orkneys.

This species advances to the north in the spring, and retreats southwards in the autumn, travelling, it is related, 'early in the morning or late at night, when they fly close to the ground along the seashore, or high in the air across the water, flying in a straight line at a quick pace.

About the middle of April, or nearer to its end, or in the beginning of May, they betake themselves to the moors to nest, attaching themselves to the same grounds as the Plovers and the Snipes, and towards the end of August again return to the sea-side, though found at times also by the margins of lakes and rivers. They approach dwelling-houses without fear, if such happen to adjoin the places that are congenial to their habits. They frequent the coast, and especially those parts which are sandy and humid, or where mud prevails.

'In Scotland and its islands,' says Selby, 'this bird may be considered as indigenous, and great numbers are known to breed not only upon the sea-coast, but in the marshes of the interior. A few also remain in Northumberland, which may be called the southern limit of the permanent residence of the species. It is not to be supposed, however, that the multitudes that people our northern shores are the offspring of such only as breed in this latitude; they are principally composed of migrants from countries farther northward, to which the great body retires during summer.' I may, however, here observe that many pass the summer, at all events, so far south as Yorkshire, their nests having been found on Stockton Common, near York, and they have also been known to build on Thorne Moor, near Doncaster, and on the high moors near Halifax; one was shot at Brodsworth, near Doncaster, in the spring of 1844. In Cambridgeshire, the Rev. Leonard Jenyns records that they were seen now and then in summer time, in the fens, and that in the beginning of July, 1824, they were particularly abundant in that district.

They assemble in large flocks, thousands being sometimes to be seen at once, before they disperse for the winter into smaller companies; and very pleasant it is to watch them as they sweep out over the sea, and then round in again not far above the surface, displaying in their winter plumage, a light and dark appearance alternately: in thus coursing along they all move in a simultaneous manner, as if under the guidance of some leader.

The Dunlin is very careful of her nest and its contents, and in more than one instance has been known to suffer herself to be taken with the hand sooner than forsake it. More commonly, if it be approached, the male, and not unfrequently the female also, will fly towards any intruder, and alighting near him, use every endeavour, as by pretending lameness and disability, to cheat him of a knowledge of its situation, but an opposite result to that intended is sometimes hazarded. The Dunlin is not a shy bird, and is easily reconciled to confinement. It is good to eat in the autumn, on its first return to the sea.

They run along the sands in a sprightly manner, and very fast on occasion, in a horizontal position of body, the head being carried in the same way, and retracted with the neck, continually flirting up the tail. They skim over the surface of the sea with great rapidity in a semicircular course.

They feed on small beetles, gnats, sand-flies, and other aquatic insects and their larvæ, worms, crustacea, and mollusks, for which they probe with the bill; and in quest of these run nimbly along the sands by the edge of the sea, coursing, now here, now there, and then flying off to some short distance for a fresh search. They frequently wade in a little way, or rather, are often overtaken by the light foam of the spent wave, which their instinct tells them will in a moment be withdrawn, in obedience to the Divine command imposed

Dunlin

Land-Rail

on every element, and which, as it must obey, need therefore not be feared. During the full tide they rest on some rock or other eminence, or remain gathered together on the beach, awaiting the time when they shall be able to return again to their feeding-places.

The ordinary note, which is frequently given utterance to, is only a weak scream, a 'kwee, kwee;' but the male bird sings his best to the female to amuse her while sitting on the nest, or sounds a timely alarm if any danger be thought to approach. While at rest on the ground, the cry is softer than when on the wing. They frequently give a scream on first taking flight.

The nest is usually located under the shelter of some tuft or small bush in any dry spot, on marshy moors and heaths, mosses or salt marshes, as well as by the sea. It is often concealed, intentionally or unintentionally, with great success, so as to be very difficult to find. Sometimes, however, it is fashioned upon the open grass which grows fresh and verdant here and there among the dark heather, 'lonely, lonesome, cool, and green.' A few bits of moss, withered heath, or grass, form its careless lining, if there be any in it, the same materials being for the most part merely rounded into form—a natural cradle.

The eggs are four in number, of a greenish white, greenish grey, or dull green colour, blotted and spotted with a darker and a lighter shade of brown, most so towards and at the larger end. Some have the ground a light blue inclining to dull white, others a clear light green, richly spotted with light brown. They are deposited in the nest with the smaller ends inwards.

The young leave the nest as soon as hatched, and hide themselves in the most recondite manner.

These birds naturally vary very much in the intermediate stages of their plumage, between that of summer and that of winter.

I procured, in May, 1842, a very elegant specimen of this bird, shot near Bridlington Quay, displaying to great advantage the two plumages of summer and winter.

The engraving is after a design by my friend the Rev. Richard Pye Alington, Rector of Swinhope, Lincolnshire.

LAND-RAIL.

RHEGEN Y RHYCH. RHEGEN YR YD, OF THE ANCIENT BRITISH.

CORN-CRAKE. DAKER HEN. MEADOW-CRAKE.

Crex pratensis,	SELBY. JENYNS.
Crex—........?	*Pratensis*—Pertaining to meadows.

ONE would think that this bird, so difficult to make get on the wing, and which seems of such feeble powers when it has been at last, evidently against its will, forced to do so, could never sustain, or, at all events, would never voluntarily undertake so lengthened and laborious a flight as that which must be necessary to cross from the continent to this, its temporary island home. But such a thought is contradicted by the fact, and glad are many, no doubt, with myself, that so it is. Every one must recall with pleasure the 'Old Times,' when first he heard, and first remarked, as on first hearing he could not fail to do, the curious creaking cry of the Corn-Crake.

Its favourite haunts are low meadows of mowing grass, clover fields, willow beds, fields of growing corn, and any such like fastnesses as can afford it a secure hiding-place.

They conduct their migration by night, and arrive in England about the last week in April, reaching the northern parts of the kingdom about the beginning of the first week in May, but some have been seen by the end of April. Their arrival in the south seems to be rather later, namely, in the second week in May. Their departure takes place early in October, but one is recorded to have been killed near London, in December, 1834; one near Yarmouth, in Norfolk, in January, 1836; and one in Ireland on the 29th. of March, but whether it was a newly-arrived bird, or one that had stayed through the previous winter, cannot be affirmed. Instances have occurred of some individuals remaining throughout the winter, but only exceptions to the general rule.

They assemble together, in certain places, before going away. On their first arrival, they are in poor condition, but soon become in better case. Forty were once seen by a farmer, in the parish of Mod-bury, Devonshire, in the month of October, collected together previous to leaving; he shot seventeen, but the next day the others had all dis-appeared. Individuals have been occasionally taken on ships at sea.

The Land-Rail has a great aversion to being put up, and, being of a shy and timorous nature, skulks and runs about most per-tinaciously in its covert, doubling backwards and forwards both rapidly and cleverly, rather than do so. If alarmed unawares into flight, it will suddenly drop, after flying a few yards, and take to its legs for security; it is in consequence very rarely seen, in pro-portion to the comparative abundance in which it unquestionably exists. I remember last year dislodging one close to me, which, though apparently it must have lurked almost under my feet, I could not discover: it is still more difficult to make it rise a second time. If closely followed it will at times take refuge in trees, running without difficulty among the branches, and hiding among the leaves.

The late Bishop Stanley, in his 'Familiar History of Birds,' gives the two following curious accounts of torpidity in this species, the latter quoted from the 'Edinburgh Journal,' volume viii:—'We have two instances of dormant Corn-Crakes, which are also migratory summer birds. A farmer at Aikerness, in Orkney, about mid-winter, in demolishing a mud wall, there called a hill-dyke, found a Corn-Crake in the midst of it, a bird which is plentiful in summer, but departs, like Swallows, at the close of that season. It was apparently lifeless, but being fresh to the feel and smell, it began to move, and in a few hours was able to walk about, and lived for two days in the kitchen; but, refusing all food, it died. The other occurred at Monaghan, in Ireland, where a gentleman, having directed his labourers, in winter, to remove a large heap of manure that had remained undisturbed for a great length of time, perceived a hole, which was supposed to have been made by rats; it penetrated to a great depth, but at its termination, instead of rats, three Corn-Crakes were discovered, as if placed there with the greatest care, not a feather being out of its place, and apparently lifeless. The birds, on examination, were however, considered to be in a torpid state, and were placed near a fire in a warm room. In the course of a short time, a tremulous motion was observed in one of their legs, and soon after, a similar motion was noticed in the legs and wings of the whole, which at length extended itself to their whole bodies, and finally the birds were enabled to run and fly about the room.'

This is an exceedingly good bird for the table, and, as such, has come under the protection of the Game Laws. Thirteen couple have been known to have been killed in one day in Devonshire, fifteen couple in one day in Sussex, and seven couple at the same place the following day. Mr. Selby mentions his having shot eight or ten in the course of an hour in a single field. Old Drayton, in the 'Poly-olbion,' quaintly says of the Rayle, that it 'seldom comes but upon rich men's spits,' and two are said to be a present for a queen; but any very great value must not be put upon such legendary assertions, for we have most of us heard, and doubtless at the time we did hear it, believed, that 'four and twenty Blackbirds' made a 'dainty dish to set before the king.' Certain, however, it is that the bird before us is of very superior quality. It is capable of being kept in confinement.

It flies in a slow manner, with the legs dangling down, and in general but for a short distance, seeking only the nearest sheltering covert. At times it perches upon walls, showing an awkward capability of climbing, analogous to that exhibited by the Water-Hen. It can run with almost incredible swiftness, and threads its way in an astonishing manner among the grass without any apparent disturbance of it.

The food of the Land-Rail is composed of worms, snails, slugs, insects, grass seeds, and portions of vegetables. Sir William Jardine found a mouse in one.

The well-known note of the Corn-Crake, whence this its name, 'crake, crake; crake, crake,' is begun to be heard when summer is at last fully established, simultaneously in general with the arrival of the bird. The male it is that gives utterance to the dissonant cry, and by imitating it he may be enticed pretty near. It is uttered most frequently from the top of a clod of earth or a stone, but also otherwise at times. It is mostly heard in the evening or the morning, but occasionally also throughout the day, until the hen begins to sit. In like manner it is not unfrequently continued through part of the calm still summer night, 'till morning comes again,' at least from about eight o'clock in the evening till about twelve or one. A curious ventriloquism is resorted to at pleasure, making the sound at one moment appear close to the listener, and the next a long way off.

The nest is placed among long grass or corn, in a furrow or some slight hollow, and is lined with a few of the leaves and stalks of the neighbouring herbage.

The eggs, commonly seven or eight, or ten, or even eleven in number, are of a pale reddish brown. Two broods are wont to be reared in the year, the first being hatched between the beginning or middle of June, or later towards the end.

The young quit the nest when hatched, and in rather less than six weeks are able to fly. The female sits very close, and often suffers in consequence, from the unwitting scythe of the mower. She leads the young about almost as soon as hatched.

MOOR-HEN.

DYFRIAR, OF THE ANCIENT BRITISH.

WATER-HEN. COMMON GALLINULE. MOAT-HEN. MOOR-COOT.
MARSH-HEN.

Gallinula chloropus,   PENNANT. MONTAGU.

Gallinula—........?   *Chloropus.* *Chloros*—Green. *Pous*—A foot.

THIS is a well-known bird throughout the continent of Europe.

Its haunts are among rushes, reeds, sedge, osiers, or brushwood of any kind, by the sides of ponds, lakes, moats, streams, and rivers, preferring such of the latter as are more 'slow and still,' or those parts of them that are so.

The Moor-Hen, if unmolested, though of a shy nature, soon becomes very familiar and tame, and will feed with domestic poultry, little heeding the approach of man. It is in fact, even in its wild state, so to speak, a 'demi-semi' domesticated species. I have seen them on waters where they are not disturbed, heedless of near approach, and tolerant of passers-by on an adjoining public road. The Rev. R. P. Alington has had them come of their own accord into his hall, and pick up crumbs, and on being disturbed, they would quietly run out of the door, stop, turn a wistful glance of regret back, and commence feeding outside.

Pennant mentions a pair which would come to him to feed with poultry when called; and there are some now so tame on the ornamental waters in St. James' Park, that they will come close to those who offer them food.

If they have not oftener been known to come to doors, to forage with fowls, it is only because they have met with discouragement instead of the contrary. In gardens they will do, it must be allowed, considerable damage sometimes both to fruit and vegetables.

They increase in numbers very rapidly, as will appear only natural from the account to be presently given of the number of broods produced in the year. The old birds nevertheless are very combative among themselves, and extremely tenacious of their territorial rights. If protected they will keep long to the same situation. They are excellent eating.

These birds have the power of submerging their bodies beneath the water, while only the bill, or little more than the bill, is kept above it. This has been conclusively proved by W. H. Slaney, Esq., of Hatton Hall, Shropshire, in the 'Zoologist.' They have also been known, when pursued, to dive to the bottom and remain there till almost dead, sooner than be taken. I remember once hooking one accidentally when fly-fishing, as it was swimming from one side of the brook to the other. They take part of their food also below the surface, as is proved by their having been captured by means of bait set for fish—'the thief caught with the mainour.' The one just mentioned, was, I think, diving at the time. They spend most of their life in the water.

The flight of this species is, for the most part, low as well as slow, with the legs drooping down. During the fine warm nights of summer they may, at times, be heard, that is the male birds, flying about and uttering their note over-head at a considerable height in the air. If disturbed in open water, the Moor-Hen will take to its wings, but if near its nest, or in the proximity of cover, will, if it does not use that mode of escape, resort to diving, and after the latter, especially if pursued by a dog, will seldom rise to the surface again, but remain submerged, the bill only being kept up for the purpose of breathing. For a conclusive essay on this power possessed by various water-birds.

They seem, when in such situations during the daytime, to like to keep near the trunk, at least in fir-trees. They are then easily approached quite close, and only quit on being alarmed. If surprised on the land they will either run or fly to the nearest cover or water, or combine the two motions, and then hide in a hole, or under or among the vegetation. They progress beneath the water by the united action of both wings and legs, the expanded membrane of the toes assisting their advance. They are good swimmers, and run expertly also over the water-plants. It is pretty to watch them picking out their steps along a railing, as they may at times be seen to do, and still more so when on the bending boughs of some small tree which give way beneath their weight, but on which they nevertheless keep their hold and adroitly balance themselves, although their feet are so ill-adapted, from their size, for such performances that they can afford but very little comparative help. It is curious also to see how cleverly they will thread their way out from the middle of a thick bush, without any apparent ruffling of their feathers. When walking, or swimming, they frequently toss up their heads, and have a constant habit of flirting the tail. The former motion is also constantly practised when the bird is feeding on the water, as it pecks first on one side and then on the other in succession. The young, when only a very few days old, begin to forage for themselves. They take to the water instinctively.

They feed severally in the morning or the evening, on the water or the land, on water-insects, larvæ, slugs, worms, grasshoppers, grain, small mollusks, seeds, grasses, water-cresses, and other plants, the latter being of especial service in hard weather, when they are frozen out from their other and ordinary sources; but even with this provision they appear weak and languid in very hard winters, whether from the severity of the cold, or the failure of a sufficient amount of their more proper food.

The note is a mere cry or sort of chirping call, moderately loud.

The nest, which is large, is strongly put together, though only of rough workmanship, and is commonly found well concealed among reeds, long grass, or the roots of trees, just above the water's edge, on the margin of a stream or by a bank.

'During the breeding season,' says Dr. Stanley, 'they are constantly adding materials to their nests, making sad havoc in the flower gardens; for though straw and leaves are their chief ingredients, they seem to have an eye for beauty, and the old hen has been seen surrounded with a brilliant wreath of scarlet anemones. As in this case, so do they usually build their nests on stumps of trees or convenient bushes, by the side of the water, and artlessly formed, as it is, of a few rushes, one might suppose it would be easily discovered, which would be the case but for the caution adopted by the bird, who, before she quits her eggs, covers them carefully up, for the joint purpose of concealment and warmth.

The eggs are usually five, six, seven, or eight in number; nine or ten have, however, been often seen in one nest. They are of a reddish or yellowish white colour, spotted and speckled all over with reddish brown; they vary exceedingly in size. Three broods are commonly reared in the year, sometimes, it has been thought, even four; the first eggs are laid the end of April, or in May, and are, in early seasons or localities, hatched in the latter month, but otherwise the beginning of June.

Incubation continues three weeks. The young soon leave the nest, still attended by their mother, who leads them to the water, but, for a time, they return to it at night for shelter. The hen takes the young at times under her wings: she has been seen to fly down with a young bird in each foot, from the nest built a few feet over the water on the branch of a tree.

The plumage in this species is close and thick-set.

COOT.

JAR DDWFR FOEL, OF THE ANCIENT BRITISH.

COMMON COOT. BALD COOT.

Fulica atra,   PENNANT. MONTAGU.

Fulica—........?   *Atra*—The feminine of *ater*—Black.

THE Coot is widely distributed throughout the continents of Europe, Asia, and Africa.

Its natural resorts are large and small lakes and ponds, and sluggish rivers, where reeds and rushes, the spontaneous growth of the alluvial soil, furnish umbrageous recesses suitable to its desire of privacy; but it also at times visits the low parts of the coast, especially during hard frosts, when the inland waters are frozen up.

It is, to a certain extent, migratory; many remain with us throughout the year, but still more come towards winter from the north, and of these also the chief number seek the more southern parts of the island. The spring movement takes place in March and April, and the autumnal one in October and November. The birds proceed by night to or rather towards their destination, beginning to move about dusk, and halting by the break of day at any suitable place of repose and refreshment. The flocks preserve no special order in their flight, and their voices may be heard aloft in still weather, at such times indicative of the approaching change of weather.

They are shy, except in the breeding-season, and give instant notice, made use of at the same time by other birds in their neighbourhood, of the approach of any danger. They will live long in confinement, being easily tamed, if a sufficiency of water exists for their habits. Sir Thomas Browne wrote about two hundred years ago of these birds:—
'Upon the appearance of a Kite or Buzzard, I have seen them unite from all parts of the shore in great numbers, when, if the Kite stoops

near them, they will fling up and spread such a flash of water with their wings, that they will endanger the Kite, and so keep him off again and again in open opposition.' Messrs. Shepherd and Whitear, in their 'Catalogue of Norfolk and Suffolk Birds,' observe that they practise this habit also to defend themselves or their young from the frequent attacks of large and predaceous Gulls. Coots are frequently to be seen in the markèts for sale, but they are not considered good birds to eat. They have the same power that the Moor-Hen has of keeping the body sunk beneath the water, while only the bill is kept out to breathe, and even the very young birds not only dive, but practise this mode of hiding themselves when pursued.

The Coot dives with great quickness and ease, rising sometimes as much as a hundred yards from the spot where it had gone down. They are very powerful and strong on the wing, though they seem to dislike getting up, and are at times seen at a considerable height, and make extended migrations. In flight they carry the legs stretched out behind them. If alarmed to get up from the water, they scurry and flap along, the head and neck straight out, and their feet pattering upon the surface, and a large number together make a very considerable noise. They move about on dry land actively and well, and are said to be able to perch on trees, but prefer to keep, which they mostly do, on the other element.

'When the bird is by chance seen to walk on the ground,' says Meyer, 'its appearance is not very elegant, owing to the formation and backward position of the legs, and the attitude it necessarily requires to keep its balance, which is by carrying its breast high, back arched, and tail lowered.' They are said to make use of their feet as weapons of defence, if attacked at close quarters. They roost at night either on a congeries of rushes in the middle of a piece of water, at a small distance from the land, or ascend some height, or mount into a tree, which they do with ease and readiness.

They will readily feed on grass if other food be scarce; grain they devour with avidity. Small fish, aquatic insects, and water-plants form their ordinary supplies; and they also pick the buds, blossoms, and seeds of different plants, and corn, too, when seeking food at night on the land. In the early part of the year, when the plants that have their roots below the water have not as yet reached the surface, these birds, acting on the principle that 'if the mountain will not come to Mahomet, Mahomet must go to the mountain,' are in the habit of frequently diving to procure them, where they only then can be procured. They remain a considerable time under water in search of food.

The call is only a harsh wild 'crew,' or 'kew,' the origin probably of the name, uttered either singly or several times in succession. This is the similitude of it as given by Meyer; but it is rarely indeed that the note of any bird can be properly expressed in the syllabic form. The male bird also in the spring, when the hen is sitting, gives utterance to a strong, loud, and shrill twanging cluck. The young keep up a constant noise, unless any one approach, when they instantly become still.

The nest, not unfrequently deferred to be made until May, is a large structure, and, though of rough workmanship, very strong in its composition, so as to keep the eggs dry, albeit in such close proximity to water. It is built by the edges of islands in, or by the

Moor-Hen

Coot

borders of lakes, ponds, and rivers, and is generally placed among, and loosely attached to flags and reeds; sometimes on a tuft of rushes, and composed of the former plants: the finer portions are placed inwards. Mr. Hewitson says that they are sometimes accumulated so much as to rise from half a foot to a foot above the water, going down also to a depth of from one foot and a half to two feet; the width is about a foot and a half, and the interior nearly flat, just sufficiently hollowed to retain the eggs. Bewick mentions an instance where the nest of a Coot, built among some rushes in a lake at Belsay, the seat of Sir W. Middleton, in Northumberland, having been dislodged by the wind and driven about, the hen bird still continued to sit on the eggs, and hatched the young as if nothing had happened. Such instances occasionally occur, the nest being either built on a floating mass of sedge or rushes, or composed itself of moveable materials.

The eggs are from six or seven, to ten or even fourteen in number, of a light dull yellowish, or greenish pale brown, or stone-colour, spotted with small rust-coloured spots. If the first hatch be taken or destroyed, a second is produced, but in less numbers.

The young almost immediately leave the nest to run about, and after a few days entirely forsake it, unless the weather is unseasonable, in which case they return to it at night for a week or two, the old birds carefully tending them as long as necessary. The hen covers them with her wings.

The plumage is well adapted to resist water.

MUTE SWAN.

ALARCH, OF THE ANCIENT BRITISH.

TAME SWAN. DOMESTIC SWAN.

Cygnus mansuetus,   GOULD.

Cygnus—A Swan.   *Mansuetus*—Accustomed.

THOUGH this species is that which we only see preserved as an ornament on the lakes, rivers, and ponds of the nobility and gentry of the country, and is not known in a wild state, yet as there is no reason why it should have been imported for the purpose in preference to any of the others, and from the latter, commonly met with as they are, one would more naturally look for the supply to be obtained, it seems to me that the fact of its being now found as it is, ought to be accounted for by the probable supposition that wild birds obtained in this country were the original source of the present race; on this account, therefore, rather than because its establishment in the kingdom has become 'un fait accompli,' I consider that it has a fair title to the place which it holds as a British bird. It is stated, however, that it was first brought into England by King Richard the First from

Cyprus. By an Act of Edward I. no one but the king's son was allowed to keep one unless possessed of five marks. Taking their eggs was to be punished with imprisonment for a year and a day, or at the king's will.

It is found in the wild state in Europe—in Russia, and the southern parts of Scandinavia generally, Prussia, Lithuania, Poland, Hungary, Germany, Holland, France, and Italy; in Asia—in Siberia, Persia, and the countries between the Black and the Caspian Seas.

Water is their element, whether that of the sea, the river, the lake, or the pond. If frozen out, they are obliged to take ' ton deuteron ploun,' and keep in the neighbourhood, or by any springs, if such there be, that have withstood the frost.

There are Swanneries of greater or less size in various parts of England, and in numberless places a pair of these noble, stately, and graceful birds are to be seen. As many as forty are mentioned by Mr. Knapp, the author of the 'Journal of a Naturalist,' as having been counted by him on a Swan-pool that then existed, but no longer exists, near Lincoln; and twice that number might recently be seen on the Swannery of Lord Ilchester, at Abbotsbury, in Dorsetshire.

In their wild state they are shy, but, as is expressed by their duplicate names, and is also well-known, are thoroughly tameable, so as to come when invited, and take food from any one accustomed to give it to them, or even from strangers, when used, if so I may express myself, to the sight of them.

Bewick writes, 'At the setting in of frosty weather, the Wild Swans are said to associate in large flocks, and thus united, to use every effort to prevent the water from freezing: this they accomplish by the continual stir kept up among them; and by constantly dashing it with their extended wings, they are enabled to remain as long as it suits their convenience, in some favourite part of a lake or river, which abounds with their food. The Swan is very properly entitled the peaceful Monarch of the Lake: conscious of his superior strength, he fears no enemy, nor suffers any bird, however powerful, to molest him; neither does he prey upon any one. His vigorous wing is as a shield against the attacks even of the Eagle, and the blows from it are said to be so powerful, as to stun or kill the fiercest of his foes. The wolf or the fox may surprise him in the dark, but their efforts are vain in the day.'

Part of the above statement is, however, to be taken 'cum grano salis,' for while engaged with their young, and in guardianship of them, Swans are full of spirit, and anything but peaceful, and their great strength makes them powerful and dangerous foes to man, dog, or other supposed enemy. It has been said that a fair blow of the wing will break a man's leg. Meyer mentions one which he knew attack a man with great fury, and fracture his arm with one stroke. When different pairs of Swans, with their families, are on the same piece of water, each keeps within the limits of its own district, and resists any encroachment by the others.

The old birds associate with their young through the winter, but drive them away in the spring. Swans have been known to live fifty years. The male bird swims higher out of the water than the female.

The noise made by the sounding pinions of these great birds, may be heard at a long distance, as they wend their way to or from their feeding grounds. They fly in a straight line, and at the height of three or four hundred feet, that is, the wild birds; the tame ones only attain to a much lower elevation. They walk in an ungainly manner, and evidently are not at home on the dry land. Every one must have observed the elegant manner in which the Common Swan arches up its wings, when sailing about on the water; and it seems, so I am told, that the attitude is peculiar to it, and is not exhibited by the wild species.

They feed on water-plants, their roots and leaves, insects and their larvæ, and occasionally swallow fish. They take some water each time that they browse.

The Swan has obtained the character, contradicted by its name, as well as, except in some very small degree, by fact, of being a bird of song. It has especially had assigned to it the office of singing before it dies, a dirge at its own departure, the echoes of which die away over the form that has then ceased to utter it. Some saturnine epigrammatist thus turned the idea into a medium of satire—

> 'Swans sing before they die—
> Methinks, 'twere no bad thing,
> Would certain persons die before they sing.'

The usual note is rendered, by Meyer, by the words 'maul, maul.' The Swan has, however, a low, soft, and not unmusical voice, formed of two notes, uttered in the spring and summer, when engaged with its young.

The Swan disposes its nest on the ground near the water side, or on some mound on an island in the river or lake. It is made of rushes and flags, and if the water threatens to rise, more materials, which the male bird brings, and the female works in, are added to the deposit under the eggs, which are thus gradually raised further out of danger.

The nest, when the first egg is laid, is small in size, but, as by degrees a larger family is expected, the mistress adds to the size of it by clutching at every suitable material in its vicinity, and this even to a greater extent than appears to be, or indeed is, at all necessary. Instinct suggests this for a wise purpose; but where reason would say 'hold, enough,' the former displays its inferiority by not knowing where to stop.

The eggs are from five or six to seven or eight in number, older birds laying the larger, and younger the fewer numbers respectively. They are of a dull greenish white colour.

Incubation continues for from five to six weeks. After being hatched for one day, they follow the guidance of their parents to the water, and have but little instruction, beyond that instinctively given them by nature, in the art of swimming about and feeding themselves. Still, 'The attention, says Meyer, 'bestowed by the old birds upon the young is incessant; and when fatigued by the strength of the stream, or requiring to be removed to a far distance, too great for their young capacity, the hen bird takes the young ones on her back, which she accomplishes by lowering herself a little in the water, and occasionally assisting them to ascend with her foot, and in this manner they are carried in safety to some desirable spot. The shape of the Swan's back, which is very flat, is well adapted for this purpose; and when her wings are raised, the young ones repose in the most beautiful and safe cradle imaginable.'

Mute Swan

Smew

SMEW.

Y LLEIAN WEN, Y LLEIAN BENGOCH, OF THE ANCIENT BRITISH.

LOUGH DIVER. WHITE NUN.
WHITE MERGANSER. WHITE-HEADED GOOSANDER.
SMEW MERGANSER. RED-HEADED SMEW.

Mergus albellus,   PENNANT. MONTAGU.

Mergus—A Diver.   *Albellus. Albus*—White.

THE Smew is an exceedingly elegant and handsome bird, though its plumage is plain, consisting only of the two primitive colours, so to call them.

It occurs in Iceland, Sweden, Russia, Holland, France, Germany, Switzerland, Greece; also in Asia, in Persia, Kamtschatka, and Siberia, Asia Minor, about the Caucasus, and in Japan. It is known, though only as a straggler, in America, in the Fur Countries, and the United States: it belongs to Greenland.

It frequents the coast as well as rivers and inland waters, giving a preference, it would seem, to the latter, and not, like so many other birds we shall soon have to give account of, to the 'deep, deep sea.'

In Yorkshire one was killed at Sutton-upon-Derwent, near York, in May, 1852, as the Rev. George Rudston Read, Rector of that place, has informed me; several have been shot near Doncaster in hard winters; a few near Leeds; one at Swillington, January 24th., 1838; also at Gledhow. One, a female, at Barnsley, in January, 1854. Others near York, the males more rarely, the females and young less so. The same remark applies to Oxfordshire, and indeed no doubt everywhere else. In the month of January, 1838, however, three adult males were killed at one shot on the Isis, near the seat of the famous University, the foundation of the Great Alfred, my own 'Alma Mater.'

The Hon. T. L. Powys has met with the Smew on the River Nene, in Northants, near Stoke Doyle, on the 5th. of January, 1850. In January, 1849, as Arthur S. H. Lowe, Esq., of Highfield House, near Nottingham, has written me word, several were seen near there, and four were shot: only three had been known in the preceding thirty years. Three or four, G. Grantham, Esq. mentions to me as having been procured near Lewes, on the Sussex coast, one of them in February, 1855, between Cuckmere Haven and Seaford. In Hertfordshire one was shot near Watford. In Cambridgeshire the Smew has occurred near Ely on the 7th. of December, 1849. In Surrey, near Godalming. In Suffolk, near Woodbridge.

In Cornwall this species is rare, and only occurs in severe winters; thus, one on the River Truro in 1845; a second in Penryn Creek, February, 1846; a third there in 1848; and a fourth at Swanpool, on the 29th. of January, in that year. Specimens have also occurred at Gwyllynvase, near Falmouth—one on the 29th. of January, 1848. In Derbyshire, I am informed by Fitzherbert Wright, Esq. that one visited the lake at Osmaston Manor, near Derby, for about a week in the winter of 1857-8. In Norfolk young birds are not uncommon near

Yarmouth in hard winters: the adult bird is more rare. In the county of Northumberland Bewick mentions three females killed on the Tyne at one shot, in January, 1820, after a severe frost. In Cambridgeshire, Willughby mentions having had one from Cambridge, and the Rev. Dr. Thackeray has another, bought in the market there, in April, 1825.

The Smew has been observed in Sanday, Orkney, and is believed to breed in that part.

In Ireland it is an occasional winter visitant. It is a Scottish species likewise in the same manner, in Caithness and East Lothian.

They come to us in winter. Their movements are southwards in the autumn, and northwards in the spring.

They are shy and careful birds, and take wing with great readiness when apprehensive of danger. One has been kept on the water in St. James's Park, London.

They feed on small fish, crustacea, and water-insects.

They fly quickly, and are excellent divers, but walk in a laboured manner.

The nest of the Smew is made of dry grass, and lined with the down of the bird herself. It is placed on the ground, upon the banks of lakes and rivers, not far from the water, or in a hollow in a tree.

The eggs are said to be eight or ten, or from that to fourteen in number, and of a yellowish white colour.

SHIELDRAKE.

HWYADYR EITHIN. HWYAD FRAITH, OF THE ANCIENT BRITISH.

COMMON SHIELDRAKE. SHELDRAKE. SHELLDRAKE. SKELLDRAKE. BURROW DUCK. SKELGOOSE. SKEELING GOOSE.

Tadorna Bellonii,	STEPHENS.
Tadorna—........?	*Bellonii*—Of Bellon.

THE Shieldrake is a bird of very wide dispersion. In Europe it is known in Sweden, where it breeds; also in Iceland, Norway, Germany, Italy, Spain, France, and Holland. In Asia, its range extends from Kamtschatka and the southern parts of Siberia to Persia, Tartary, China, and Japan. Bewick mentions that Captain Cook has noticed them at Van Diemen's Land, and that they have been seen in great numbers on the Falkland Islands.

This species is strictly a maritime one, though it has sometimes occurred inland; but such instances form the 'exception, not the rule.' It has been shot in Northamptonshire, the Hon. T. L. Powys has written me word, and he also mentions two killed near Oxford. In Cambridgeshire it used to be not uncommon. In Yorkshire, it has occurred near Doncaster, also near York, Driffield, and Thirsk, one namely at Gormire, but rarely; frequently on the high moors above Huddersfield. Several have been found near Sutton-on-Derwent, where they have appeared in small flocks. They used to breed on the banks of the Humber. In Nottinghamshire, near Retford. In Northumberland, they build on the coast, where there is sand above high-water mark.

In Lincolnshire, the Rev. R. P. Alington informs me that the Shieldrake occurs on the sea-coast, near Summercoats, and breeds in a rabbit-warren on the sandhills of the sea-bank in that parish, likewise at Humberstone. In Norfolk, at Sandringham, the seat of J Motteux, Esq.: they are not uncommon, and breed among the low sand-hills on the coast. In Cornwall, it has been met with at Gwyllynvase, Carrick Roads, and Swanpool, near Falmouth, in the south, but rarely, in the north also sparingly. In Oxfordshire, they occur in most years, in the neighbourhood of Weston-on-the-Green, as stated by the Revs. Andrew and Henry Matthews; likewise in Dorsetshire and Hampshire. In Devonshire not numerous.

They occur in Ireland, and are indigenous, but rather rare; also on the shores of Scotland, quite to the north; in Sutherlandshire, Caithness, and elsewhere. In Orkney, too, they arrive early in the spring, and remain till the autumn, a few only staying throughout the winter. Also in Shetland; and in Wales, Llandudno, etc.

Their proper home is the neighbourhood of the sea, but they are occasionally, and not very unfrequently, met with inland. They remain with us throughout the year, and always in pairs. They move southwards in the autumn, returning to the north in the spring; the former in September, and the latter in March.

A. E. Knox, Esq. mentions that a friend of his knew a brood of young Shieldrakes come from the rabbit-burrow in which they had been bred, at the whistle of the gamekeeper, to receive food. If the nest be approached by an unwelcome intruder, the young ones hide themselves: 'the tender mother drops at no great distance from her helpless brood, trails herself along the ground, flaps it with her wings, and appears to struggle as if she was wounded, in order to attract attention, and tempt a pursuit after her. Should these wily schemes, in which she is aided by her mate, succeed, they both return, when the danger is over, to their terrified motionless little offspring, to renew the tender offices of cherishing and protecting them.' When however the young are older, they fly straight away from them, as if aware that by diving and otherwise they could then better take care of themselves, as indeed is the fact. The young broods collect together, it seems, in troops of from thirty to forty, accompanied by the old birds.

This species, though naturally extremely wild, is very readily brought into a state of domestication, and will come to a call. Some that have wandered away have returned even after an absence of several months. The richness of its well contrasted plumage renders it a great ornament. They have been known to breed in the reclaimed state, but not often: one at Lord Derby's paired with a duck; another also, a male, whose mate had died, paired with the widow of an Egyptian Goose on the lake at Sir Oswald Mosley's, of Osmaston Manor, near Derby, so I have been informed by Fitzherbert Wright, Esq.

They walk in an easy and handsome way, with the neck bent in a graceful manner. They fly strongly and quickly, in a straight line. They dive well.

These birds feed on marine vegetables and worms, sandhoppers, small shell-fish, the lesser crustacea, insects, and the fry of fish, as

Shieldrake

Red-Breasted Merganser

also on grain and seeds when 'to be obtained in lieu of the former.

The note is a shrill whistle.

Incubation lasts about thirty days. These birds are believed to pair for life: they unite in the second year, when the complete plumage has been assumed. The male takes the place of the female on the nest in the morning and evening, when she leaves it to feed.

The Shieldrake builds in rabbit-holes and other hollows in the earth, often as much as ten or twelve feet from the entrance. Some down, plucked from their own breasts, is the lining with which the nest is fitted, the remainder being dry grass.

The eggs are ten or twelve, or even more; it is said thirteen or fourteen in number, but these, in such cases, may possibly have been the produce of two birds. They are nearly perfectly white, having only a very faint tinge of green, and are smooth and shining.

RED-BREASTED MERGANSER.

RED-BREASTED GOOSANDER.   SAWBILL.   HARLE.

Mergus serrator,   PENNANT. MONTAGU. BEWICK.

Mergus—A Diver.   *Serrator. Serra*—A saw.

THE Merganser is a common bird in Europe—in Norway, Sweden, Lapland, Iceland, and the Ferroe Islands, as also in Holland, Germany, Switzerland, France, and Italy. It likewise is found in Asia, in Siberia, about Lake Baikal, and along the courses of the larger rivers, and eastward to Japan. In America it belongs to Greenland, the Fur Countries, the shores of Hudson's Bay, and Newfoundland.

They frequent the coast, its bays and estuaries, and the lower parts of rivers, namely, where they disembogue themselves into the sea, but sometimes advance upwards, and reach inland waters, though seldom beyond the influence of the tide. They breed, however, on fresh-water lakes.

In Northumberland these birds occur along the coasts, Holy Island and the Fern Islands being favourite localities; also on the shores of Durham.

In Lincolnshire the Rev. William Waldo Cooper shot one in the Ancholme, in the winter of 1853-4. In Northamptonshire the species has occurred on the River Nene. In Suffolk one near Ipswich, as T. J. Wilkinson, Esq., of Walsham Hall, has written me word. In the adjoining county of Norfolk one, a male, an adult bird, was seen at Lowestoft, in the third week of July, 1852, as recorded by J. H. Gurney, Esq., of Easton, in the 'Zoologist,' page 3599. In the usual way it is also seen in those parts in the winter months, but old males are seldom obtained except in severe seasons. Many specimens were procured along the coast of Essex and the two last-named counties in the winter of 1829-30. They are not uncommon near Yarmouth, and generally on the Norfolk coast in severe weather, but the immature birds are much more common than the adult.

In Yorkshire, a fine female specimen was shot near Richmond on the 12th. of December, 1854; a female also at Barnsley, in January of the same year. Some have occurred near Hebden Bridge; also near Doncaster—one in 1837. Individuals too near York as well as at Huddersfield, and at Swillington, near Leeds—January 24th., 1838, several were procured in the year 1830. One at Thornton, near Pocklington, in the winter of 1861-2. In Cambridgeshire, a pair were shot at Pricwillow, in 1854. A female in Burwell Fen, in summer; others have been sold in the Cambridge market. In the sister county of Oxford, a fine specimen of this bird was killed on Otmoor, in February, 1838, and in the winter of 1841, two others fell to the gun near Cassington. A pair, male and female, were killed near Reading, in 1795. Three were shot, adult birds, a male and two females, at Terrington Marsh, Norfolk, on the 7th. of December, 1849. In Essex, two on the Thames, near Barking, the beginning of January, 1850.

In Cornwall, one was obtained near Penryn Creek, Falmouth, in December, 1846, and a second specimen in November, 1847; others on the Truro river and its branches. The species has occured also in Kent, by the Thames; in Worcestershire, on the Severn, near Worcester; likewise in Lancashire, Dorsetshire, and Surrey, near Chertsey, in November, 1842, one was shot out of a flock of thirty-four. In Devonshire it is occasionally procured in immature plumage.

In South Wales, Mr. Dillwyn has noticed its occurrence at Swansea. It has also been met with in North Wales. In Montgomeryshire three were seen at Bronafron, on the River Severn, January 2nd., 1850, one of which was shot.

They also breed in Scotland, in Sutherlandshire, on all the lochs, as near Scowrie, and elsewhere; likewise in Argyleshire, on Loch Awe, where the nest was found by Sir William Jardine, Bart., and Mr. P. J. Selby, in June, 1828; in Rosshire, at Loch Maree, and in East Lothian, more frequent in winter, and the like in Caithness. They also remain throughout the year in Orkney, Shetland, and the Hebrides, and rear their young. Pennant has mentioned their breeding in the Isle of Islay, and Mr. Macgillivray found the nest in Harris.

In Ireland specimens have been obtained in Meath and other parts. There also the birds are indigenous.

They come to us in winter, when 'the winds whistle cold' and even the hardiest sea-birds are glad to betake themselves to comparative shelter.

These birds are extremely shy and wary, especially during the breeding-season. They go in flocks. They too, have the power of submerging the whole body in a gentle and imperceptible manner, the bill only being kept out.

They swim and dive with the greatest expertness, and are able, it is said, to remain two minutes under the water, making rapid progress beneath the surface. They can walk fast, but are ungraceful in their movements. They fly in a buoyant and easy manner.

Their food is chiefly made of small fish, but also of beetles, water-insects and their larvæ, worms, and frogs.

The note sounds most like the words 'curr, curr.'

The places chosen by this species for nesting are the vicinage of the sea, and the neighbourhood of lakes and rivers, among reeds and rushes.

GREAT CRESTED GREBE.

GWACH GORNIOG. TINTROED, OF THE ANCIENT BRITISH.

TIPPET GREBE. CARGOOSE. LOON.

Colymbus cristatus,   LINNÆUS.

Colymbus—A Diver.   *Cristatus*—Crested.

THE Great Crested Grebe is very plentiful in Holland and Germany, and belongs also to Iceland, Sweden and Norway, Italy, France, and Russia.   In Asia it has been observed about the Caucasus and in Siberia, Asia Minor and Japan.   Also in Africa, both north and south.   It belongs likewise to North America, advancing southwards from the Fur Countries, as far as Mexico, through the States.

This singular-looking bird is indigenous in many parts of the country, *videlicet*, in Lincolnshire, Norfolk, Shropshire, and Wales.   Its occurrence has been noticed in Cumberland.   In Yorkshire, one was procured near Doncaster, the beginning of 1837, one or two near Sheffield, others at Sutton-on-Derwent and Hornsea Mere, where they used to breed.   They are sometimes obtained in Oxfordshire, in the neighbourhood of Weston-on-the-Green.   One in Berkshire, near Hungerford, in February, 1808.   In Hampshire, one was seen on the Southampton Water, the end of March, 1849; three shot in the winter of 1866-7. In Surrey one, a young bird, was captured near Reigate, on the 28th. of February, 1849.   An adult male was shot in the month of June, on the Lincolnshire fens, Mr. William Felkin, Junior, of Carrington, near Nottingham, has informed me.   It has occurred also on Croxby Lake.   In Sussex, three near Battle, one of them the beginning of March, 1848.   In Northamptonshire, one was shot on the 27th. of January, 1855, on the River Nene, as I am informed by the Hon. T. L. Powys; he adds, that it has also occurred at Blatherwycke Park, the seat of Augustus Stafford, Esq., M.P.   In Norfolk four were shot near Yarmouth, on the 14th. of April, 1851; they are common on the Broads, and breed there: twenty-nine were collected in the same county, in the months of April and May, 1851, by Richard Strangways, Esq.; one at Diss Mere, the end of July, 1834.   One of these birds, a male, was shot in February, 1850, at Blyth, in Northumberland.   One on the 27th. of November, 1852, near Henley-upon-Thames, in Oxfordshire. In Cornwall, they are not uncommon off the coast in winter, one was shot on the river Helford, near Falmouth, in February, 1856.   Also in Devon, but not common, one shot by R. Cameron, Esq.

In Wales, Mr. Dillwyn has noticed the species in Glamorganshire.

In Scotland, it is considered rather a rare winter visitor, in Caithness, etc.   In East Lothian it is described as not uncommon on the Forth, in winter.   They breed in the Hebrides.

Great Crested Grebe

Dabchick

In Ireland, it is a perennial resident on the larger lakes, but is only occasionally seen.

Their haunts are lakes, ponds, rivers, and creeks of the sea, if these indeed are bordered with reeds and other such covert. In winter frost and ice send them down to the mouths of rivers and the coast.

Towards evening this species becomes active and lively, having previously been disposed to float about quietly, with the head drawn back on the plumage.

They migrate in small and large flocks of from seven or eight to fifty or more, during the night, taking advantage of calm weather. When 'Gaffer Winter' is creeping on, they pass to the south, and in March return in pairs to their intended breeding-places.

The skin of the breast of this Grebe has become a fashionable substitute for fur, and several were exhibited accordingly in the Great Exhibition of 1851. One of these birds has been kept on the water in St. James' Park, London. They appear to go in small flocks of eight or nine.

They can fly well, and to a distance of two or three miles or more; but during the time they are engaged with their nest, they resort **exclusively to diving**, in which they are perfect adepts, for security, raising the head only above water to breathe, after a stretch of a couple of hundred yards. They do not excel in walking or running, but swim admirably, and dive with remarkable quickness: they float low. The female, 'if disturbed from her charge, seldom rises within gunshot, and if a boat be stationed to intercept her, will tack about and alter her course under water, without rising to breathe.'

Their food, procured by diving, is made up of small fish and young fry, crustacea, water-insects and their larvæ, small frogs, tadpoles, and parts of plants; and 'it is a remarkable fact that the specimens obtained of this species invariably prove to have feathers in their stomachs, from the breast of the bird itself.'

The note sounds like the words 'cuck, cuck, cuck,' and 'craærr, craærr.'

The Loon breeds in fresh water, and makes its nest, such as it is, early in the year—in the month of April. It is a very large and careless mass of weeds, flags, and other water-plants, partly sunk under, and partly raised above the water, the top being slightly hollowed. The general width is about a foot or a little over; the height about half as much.

The eggs are three or four, and occasionally five. Four appears to be the usual average number, but one of them is generally addled. They are concealed by fragments of rushes placed over them, and if these be removed others are added. Their colour is white or greenish white.

Yarrell says, 'The parent birds are very careful of their young, taking them down with them for security under their wings when they dive.' According to Meyer, the birds pair for life, and haunt the same nesting-place year after year, both assisting in the work of nidification. The young swim about as soon as hatched, scrambling up at times on their mother's back, and then again darting and gambolling about.

If the nest or eggs be taken, the bird continues laying over and over again.

DABCHICK.

HARRI GWLYCH DY BIG, OF THE ANCIENT BRITISH.

DOBCHICK. LITTLE GREBE. BLACK-CHINNED GREBE. DIDAPPER.
DUCKER. DIPPER. SMALL DOUCKER. LITTLE DOUCKER. LOON.

Colymbus Hebridicus, GMELIN.

Colymbus—A Diver. *Hebridicus*—Belonging to the Hebrides.

The Dabchick is very generally distributed over the British Islands, and though more commonly seen perhaps in winter than in summer, appears both in the extreme north and the farthest south at all seasons.

Its natural home is the water, both the open lake and the village pond, the gently flowing river and the still pool, the narrow streamlet and at times the edge of the open sea. In winter, when the frost has shut the door of its natural larder, it betakes itself to the salt-water, if within reach, and is then to be found in bays and sea-side pools.

In some parts of the country the Dabchick disappears, so it is said, in winter. In Yorkshire it is constantly seen at that season, as well as in summer, except indeed when its usual places of haunt are frozen up, and then, as a matter of course, it is obliged to quit them for a time. In frosty weather they are compelled from the larger pieces of standing water to the running stream.

This Grebe is naturally shy, but becomes accustomed to the sight of passers by the water that it inhabits, and its quick movements in diving may be watched not far off with little disturbance of its proceedings. They occasionally, as I have said, enter the sea close to the shore in those places where their accustomed haunts are adjacent to it.

The Dabchick, like some other birds previously mentioned, has the power of sinking its body under the water, the head only and the tail being kept out, and of then wholly submerging itself, if need be, and diving off to some distance, when it rises as suddenly as it went down, and with a shake of the head, urges itself on its way. If suddenly startled, it is curious to see how 'instanter' it vanishes with a quick plash, and this is even more especially to be admired, if it has risen to the surface after having been before alarmed, when, if the cause of disquietude is still visible, its descent again seems but a continuation of its upward movement. It is able to remain underneath the water for an almost incredible time, if need be, and when anxious to escape from threatening danger, rarely resorts to flight, though it will do so at times, but endeavours to conceal itself after the first alarm among the tangled plants that fringe the margin, or carpet the floor of its native element.

If alarmed they dive, this, as just said, being the mode of escape they prefer to attempt. They are spirited birds, and when taken will attack any object within their reach. The young, when hatched, presently take to the water, and swim about with their parents to be fed, diving also with innate readiness.

I have only seen these little things fly close over the water, with trailing legs, dappling the surface as they have gone along. They have however been observed flying at a height of from six to ten feet. Their flight is tolerably rapid. It is on and below the surface of the water, however, that they are most at ease, and every movement is characterized by the most consummate dexterity and facile quickness and agility: the most expert waterman that sculls his skiff on the Thames or the Isis, is but an humble and unskilful imitator of the Dabchick. In moving straightforward the wings are used to aid their progress, as if in the air, and in turning 'it has an easy gliding motion, feet and wings being used as occasion requires, sometimes on one side and sometimes on the other.' This species walks but indifferently, as may readily be imagined from the position of the legs, so very far back.

It is pleasant to watch the parent bird feeding her young.—Down she dives with a quick turn, and presently rises again with, five times out of six, a minnow, or other little fish, glittering like silver in her bill.. The young rush towards the spot where the mother has come up, but she does not drop the fish into the water for them to receive, until she has well shaken it about and killed it, so that it may not escape, when for the last time in its own element. I have seen a young chick, which had just seized, out of its turn I have no doubt, the captured prey, chased away by her, and pursued in apparent anger, as if for punishment, the following one having the next fish willingly given to it without any demur. I have noticed the old bird feeding the young one so late as the 14th. of September. Small fish or fry comprise their ordinary food, together with shrimps and marine insects, when sojourning for a while by the sea. Plants are also made use of, and some of the feathers of the bird itself are swallowed. A Dabchick was found dead at Witchingham, in Norfolk, apparently choked by a bull-head fish, which it had been swallowing, the spines being seen sticking in its throat.

The note of this interesting species is a lively, pretty, and sonorous, though somewhat shrill chirruping, quickly repeated. It is uttered when on the wing in the spring, as well as when on the water at other times. It has been likened, and not ill, to the sound made by drawing a stick across a rail.

The nest of the Dabchick, which is placed at a little distance, often as much as twenty or thirty yards, from the water, on or among any plants that grow near the sides of rivers, lakes, and ponds, is composed of short pieces of roots, reeds, rushes, and flags, and a considerable quantity of these is occasionally put together, sometimes to the height of a foot or more; when dry the whole naturally becomes very brittle. It is seldom raised more than an inch or two above the water, so that, except in hot seasons, it generally is quite soaked with water.

The hen bird may be seen pecking about her while on the nest. It is related that until the latter is finished she is in the habit of sitting at night on a similar but smaller tuft which she has raised by its side.

The eggs are four, five, or six in number, oval in shape, tapering towards each end, and dull white in colour. The bird is in the habit of covering them over with weeds when leaving the nest for a time, at least, as soon as they are all laid, and it would further appear that the covering is not then removed, but that she sits on both it and the eggs: they become a good deal stained in consequence. The period of breeding is about the middle of May.

The young take to the water immediately on being hatched.

GREAT NORTHERN DIVER.

Y TROCHYDD MAWR, OF THE ANCIENT BRITISH.

NORTHERN DIVER. IMBER. GREAT DOUCKER. RING-NECKED DIVER.

Colymbus glacialis,	PENNANT. MONTAGU. BEWICK.
Colymbus—A Diver.	*Glacialis*—Of or belonging to ice.

THIS Great Diver is in Europe found in Iceland, Spitzbergen, the Faroe Islands, Russia, Norway, Sweden, Denmark, Lapland, Finland, Holland, Switzerland, Germany, and France, but in the latter only rarely in comparison with the former, and in Italy a single specimen is the only one that has occurred.

The sea is mainly the resort of this species, but it is occasionally found on rivers, and breeds on the larger ones and inland lakes;—this chiefly within the polar circle. St. Kilda's 'lonely isle' is one of their more southerly stations.

They are very shy in their natural habits, nevertheless they have been kept for some time in confinement, when well supplied with water. They are courageous as well as powerful birds, and the blows that they are able to give are formidable from their size and strength.

Montagu says, 'A Northern Diver taken alive, was kept in a pond for some months, which gave us an opportunity of attending to its manners. In a few days it became extremely docile, would come at the call from one side of the pond to the other, and would take food from the hand.' The young, when only a day or two old, are led to the water by their mother.

The following account is quoted by Yarrell, as given by Mr. Thomas Nuttall, of Boston, who kept another for some time:—'A young bird of this species which I obtained in the Salt Marsh at Chelsea Beach, and transferred to a fish-pond, made a good deal of plaint, and would sometimes wander out of his more natural element, and hide and bask in the grass. On these occasions he lay very still until nearly approached, and then slid into the pond and uttered his usual plaint. When out at a distance he made the same cautious efforts to hide, and would commonly defend himself in great anger, by darting at the intruder, and striking powerfully with his dagger-like bill. This bird, with a pink coloured iris, like albinos, appeared to suffer from the glare of broad daylight, and was inclined to hide from its effects, but became very active towards the dusk of the evening. The pupil of the eye in this individual, like that of nocturnal animals, appeared indeed dilatable, and the one in question often put down his head and eyes into the water to observe the situation of his prey. This bird was a most expert and indefatigable diver, and remained down sometimes for several minutes, often swimming under water, and, as it were, flying with the velocity of an arrow in the air. Though at length inclining to become docile, and showing no alarm when visited, it constantly betrayed its wandering habits, and every night was found to have waddled to some hiding-place, where it seemed to prefer hunger to the loss of liberty, and never could be restrained from exercising its instinct to move onwards to some secure or more suitable asylum.'

These birds have the faculty of sinking the body below the surface of the water if suddenly alarmed, the head and neck alone being extant. When diving for food, one minute appears to be the usual length of time that they remain below; less, of course, if successful in their pursuit. It is said, however, by Meyer, that they can remain underneath the surface for the long space of three minutes and a half, and that when pursued, the bird manages to dive with ease for one hundred and fifty or a couple of hundred yards. In swimming and diving the legs only appear to be used in general, and not the wings, though the latter are also, according to Audubon. They progress with very great speed if pursued, and dive with instantaneous quickness. They resort to this mode of escape in preference to attempting flight, no doubt for the reason elsewhere spoken of. Mr. Selby asserts, from observation, that they can swim at the rate of more than seven miles an hour. They consort together in small parties of four or five. They are often to be seen floating and drifting on the water as if asleep, the head pillowed back among the feathers. In the roughest weather they are equally at ease, and fish among the heavy surf with fearless confidence. They cannot walk, properly speaking, but are only able to shuffle along, neither can they rise on the wing from the ground. Even on the water they are obliged to scurry forwards for some distance before being able to get up. This is 'accompanied by a frequent repetition of its call-note. When a party of six or eight of these birds rise together, they mount high in the air, and follow one another in a line.'

They fly in a strong and able manner, and Dr. Richardson observes that when on the wing they advance swiftly. If their nest be threatened, they exhibit natural alarm, and wheel in circles round the intruder.

They feed on small crabs and crustacea generally, frogs, insects and their larvæ, flat-fishes, herrings, sprats, and other kinds of fish. The smaller ones they gorge whole, the larger they are obliged to swallow piecemeal. They destroy, as will readily be conceived, a great quantity, so that where they are sojourners, their absence rather than their presence is desiderated by the fishermen. Fourteen perch were found in the throat of one. In stormy weather they suffer much from want of food, their prey having probably removed into deeper water.

The note, which is loud and plaintive, is said by Meyer to resemble the words 'who, who,' or 'whee, whee,' frequently repeated. Other sounds are also uttered, both of a deep and a high character. One is a clear 'kawk.'

The nest of this fine bird is placed close to the water's edge, so as to admit of an immediate retreat, if necessary, to that element.

The eggs are two, or sometimes, according to Audubon, three in number. Their colour is a dark olive greenish brown, with a few spots of a darker shade, or purple reddish.

Both birds take their turns in sitting, and when the young are hatched, continue an equal and watchful care over them as long as it is required.

The plate is from a drawing by John Gatcombe, Esq., of Wyndham Place, Plymouth. It is one of the best figures of a bird I have ever seen.

GUILLEMOT.

GWILYM, OF THE ANCIENT BRITISH.

SKOUT. WILLOCK. SEA-HEN. FOOLISH GUILLEMOT. QUEET.

Colymbus Troile,   LATHAM. STEPHENS.

Colymbus—A Diver.   *Troile*—........?

FAIRLY launched now on the waves of the mighty ocean, a volume indeed of water, the land and the intermediate shore, along whose margin we have hitherto lately wandered together, and which though belonging to both belongs to neither, 'nec tellus est, nec mare,'—taken leave of, yet still, as will be seen, I have not 'cast off the painter,' and I hope that by means of this ultra-marine telegraph, a clear understanding may still be kept up by my readers, of the forms and features of the wild birds of the wild waters, whose portraits in their turn I now proceed to give. In other words, having completed, in the preceding volumes, the History of the British Land Birds, Waders, and others which pertain more or less to both land and sea, I now enter upon that of those which may the most strictly speaking be called sea-birds. Truly in following them, though only with the eye of the mind, we shall 'see the works of the Lord and His wonders in the deep.'

The present species is frequent in Greenland, and about Hudson's Bay, in North America, from whence some individuals advance as far south as the United States.

In Europe, they occasionally make their way from Nova Zembla, the Ferroe Islands, Iceland, Norway, and Holland, by the Straits' of Gibraltar to Italy and Sicily; and in Africa, in like manner, are found along the northern shores. In a few instances the species is recorded to have occurred on the lakes of Switzerland.

The Guillemot is ubiquitous on our coasts, being frequent in Yorkshire from Burlington to Yarmouth Roads, and thence to Dorsetshire, and so on all round the island.

In Scotland, they breed in vast numbers on the Island of Handa, and the high cliffs of the Moray Firth, and in Caithness; common also in East Lothian, on the Bass Rock, etc., as too, in Sutherlandshire and elsewhere; so they do also on the Fern Islands, off the Northumbrian coast, and at Flamborough Head, in Yorkshire. A few formerly bred on the cliffs at Hunstanton, Norfolk; some used to do so also near Tenby, in Wales.

They are equally abundant in the Orkney and Shetland Islands, and the Hebrides. So too in Ireland are they plentiful on all parts of the coast, and in Guernsey and Sark.

The Foolish Guillemot is so called because it shews but little apprehension of danger, and allows a near approach.

In the places where these birds 'most do congregate,' numbers sit side by side in rows, 'and when one flies away, all successively take wing in such regular order that, when seen at a certain distance, they appear as if they were actually strung together; they never take wing in a body, but always one after another. Again, when they can be seen sitting in a long string on the edge of some cliff, their behaviour is most amusing, for the birds keep complimenting each other right and left where they sit, and also welcome the new comers by bowing to them, and uttering their call notes, which sound like the words 'curr' long drawn out, 'ærrrrrr, merrrrrr, girrrrrr,' etc.

These birds are of sociable habits, both as regards their own kind and other species, except, as mentioned presently, in the matter of nidification, so to call it where no artificial nest is made.

In the eighth volume of the 'Magazine of Natural History,' I wrote some years since—'I lately happened to have an opportunity of observing a Guillemot diving in very clear water, and was much struck with the great similarity of its wings both in their shape and in its manner of using them under the surface, to the fins of a fish, 'remigium alarum;' and in the water, instead of the air, the analogy loses none of its force.'

They are excellent divers, and though bulky birds, swim in a lightsome manner. They fly quickly, mostly at a low height, the wings being beaten with short repeated strokes: they have some difficulty in rising from the surface. 'During the breeding-season they are generally compelled to make a circuitous flight before they can attain a sufficient elevation to reach the ledge of rock selected for that purpose.'

They feed on sprats, young herrings, anchovies, sardines, and other fish, mollusca, testacea, and sea-insects.

Mr. Couch observes of the Guillemot, in his 'Illustrations of Instinct,' 'I have watched with much interest the proceedings of this bird when capturing the stragglers of a school of young mullets, and the admirable skill with which their dispersion was prevented, until a full meal had been secured. It is the nature of this bird, as well as of most of those birds which habitually dive to take their prey, to perform all their evolutions under water with the aid of their wings; but instead of dashing at once into the midst of the terrified group of small fry, by which only a few would be captured, it passes round and round them, and so drives them into a heap, and thus has an opportunity of snatching here one and there another, as it finds it convenient to swallow them, and if any one pushes out to escape, it falls the first prey of the devourer.'

Towards the end of March or beginning of April, they assemble in countless thousands, with a view to lay and hatch their eggs, and at times even darken the sea with their prodigious numbers. When the work of incubation is over, they repair in small parties to the sea.

The Guillemot makes no nest, but lays her single egg upon the barren rock. Countless numbers of these birds breed together on the rocks or cliffs that abut upon the ocean, thinking there to find that security, which indeed they would find were it not for the superiority of mind over instinct. They often build in the same places as the Kittiwake, Herring Gull, Puffin, and Razor Bill, but each in distinct ranks. Incubation continues for a mouth. The old bird is believed to convey her young down to the sea on her back.

The eggs are very large in proportion to the size of the bird, and more than ordinarily narrowed at one end and widened at the other. They vary in an extraordinary manner, and a description of the principal varieties only would be almost endless, 'adeo sunt multa.' Some are entirely white, others more or less spotted with brown, and others again bluish green, blotted and streaked with dark reddish brown or black. Some are entirely green. 'The shape of the egg, which is very tapering, prevents it from rolling off into the sea; for when moved by the wind, or other circumstances, it only rolls round its

Great Northern Diver

Guillemot

own circle, without changing its first immediate situation.' If the first egg be taken a second is laid, and if the second, a third.

In their breeding-places they choose separate ledges of rock for themselves, apart and quite distinct from the other kinds which rear their young in the same situations.

The young are able to take to the water when about five or six weeks old.

Theodore Compton, Esq. has given me a drawing of the present species for the use of this work.

PUFFIN.

PWFFINGEN, OF THE ANCIENT BRITISH.

COULTER NEB.   SEA-PARROT.

| *Mormon Fratercula,* | GOULD. TEMMINCK. |
| *Mormon*—A hobgoblin. | *Fratercula*—..........? |

IN giving to the world this my 'Book of Mormon,' the historical part is illustrated by a figure which, though not one of the 'Golden Plates,' will, I hope, more truly corroborate the fidelity of the account I furnish from the salt sea, than did those of the impostor of the 'Salt Lake,' that which he gave to the deluded followers of his wretched deception.

The Puffin is extremely abundant in Iceland, Lapland, and Norway, as well as in other parts of Scandinavia, and thence goes north to the Faroe Islands, Nova Zembla, and Spitzbergen, and is met with in the Arctic circle. In America, it belongs to Labrador, Baffin's Bay, Hudson's Bay, and many other parts, advancing southwards as far as Georgia.

They are seen in immense multitudes in the Shetland Islands, and not a few resort annually to the Fern Islands, on the coast of Northumberland. They breed also on the cliffs of the Moray Frith; and in Wales, near St. David's, the Great Orme's Head, etc.

In Yorkshire, the Puffin is very common at Flamborough, and breeds there. One was found dead in the canal near Barnsley on the 7th. of July, 1856. Two others had been taken alive previously, and one shot, in the same neighbourhood. They breed also on the north coast of Devon, and are seen at times in the south.

Fifty years ago they used to be very abundant on different parts of the Isle of Wight, Hampshire, and bred there. One of these birds was found dead in Whitecliff Bay, on the 4th. of January, 1853, after some stormy weather; others have been observed on the coast; one also on the third of that month in Seaford Bay, Sussex, where several had been procured the previous December. In Dorsetshire, one was taken on the rocks under Portland, in January, 1851; five others were found dead on the Chesil Bank, on the 27th. of February, in the same year, after gales from the south-west. Likewise, in February and March, 1853, the Welsh coast about Morfa, Bychaw, and Harlech, was strewed with dead Puffins. They are occasional visitants to Yarmouth, Norfolk, and the coast, in autumn. One was found near Ely, in Cambridgeshire, in a fen, the 18th. of February, 1852.

In Cornwall, one was shot on the beach near Falmouth, January 27th., 1850; one near St. Looe, in March, 1845, and another in January, 1846. It has occurred also at Gwyllynvase and Swanpool, but the species is not common: it is said to be more numerous at the Scilly Islands. In the county of Berks, a specimen of this bird was taken alive in Northbrook Street, Newbury, March 16th., 1816.

In Scotland, in Sutherlandshire, the Puffin is numerous in Handa, and other parts; likewise in Caithnesshire; at Puffin Island, in the Firth of Forth; the Bass Rock, off East Lothian, and others of the Scottish Islands. So also in the Orkneys they are very abundant, but only throughout the summer, moving southwards as winter is about to commence. In the Shetland Islands, too, they are to be seen in immense numbers; as also at St. Kilda and the Hebrides generally. So again on the Fern Islands off the Northumbrian shores; likewise in Guernsey and Sark.

They are common birds in Ireland, and have breeding-haunts around the coast. They occur in Anglesea, and Priestholm Islet off its coast, as also in different parts of Wales, as at St. Margaret's Island, near St. David's; likewise in the Isle of Man.

They come northwards early in April, and depart towards the latter end of August, or beginning of September, but generally between the 10th. and the 20th. of the former month, according as they are farther north or south. Selby writes, 'It is only known to us as a summer visitant, and that from the south, making its first appearance in the vicinity of the breeding-stations about the middle of April, and regularly departing between the 10th. and 20th. of August, for the south of France, Spain, and other parts of Europe, where it passes the remainder of the year.'

These curious and grotesque-looking birds are able to inflict a severe bite with their strong bills, and do so if proceeded against in their nests. They assemble in their native countries in such vast numbers, that Mr. Hewitson describes a flock seen at the distance of a mile, as having the appearance of a dark cloud.

They sit on the ledges of the rocks in long rows, bowing towards each other, and putting themselves into various amusing attitudes. They are restless birds, and continually keep moving or looking about, turning the head first in one and then in another direction. They are rather wary, and take wing or dive on the approach of suspected danger; they are, however, readily tamed, and soon become familiar. Like the next species, whose cognomen sufficiently indicates the keenness of its bite, the vernacular name of the one before us bespeaks the fact that its neb or bill is as strong and sharp as a coulter.

The Puffin has but indifferent capabilities for walking, leaning on the whole length of the leg and foot, but swims and dives well. It also flies swiftly, in general for a moderate distance, but for some miles on occasion, and in a straight direction, usually near the water, the wings being opened wide and quickly beaten.

Their food consists of sprats and young fish, sea-insects, and the smaller crustacea—shrimps, crabs, and others, as also, it is said, sea-weed. The young are fed with fish until able to leave the nest and fish for themselves. Meyer thus writes, 'The shape of the Puffin's beak is such as to make the bird to lodge within it several small fishes at a time, which it carries securely while still continuing to catch more;

and thereby the trouble of going for food for the nestling is considerably simplified; the bird may frequently be observed returning to the breeding ground, laden with fishes, several of which project out of of its beak, giving it the appearance of having moustaches.'

The note is a low 'orr,' 'orr.'

The Puffin breeds in precipitous places on the coast and its adjacent islands, seeming to give a preference to such as are covered with a formation of mould. The nest is made both on cliffs and high rocks, and on the short verdure which obtains on any level places on the sides or summit of such, or among stones and boulders. At first indeed, strictly speaking, there is little or no nest, but as incubation advances, a few grasses may be seen commingled with some feathers of the owners of the hard couch. These birds either take possession of a rabbit-burrow, often contending with the proper owners for it, or dig a hole themselves, as a receptacle for their eggs, frequently to the depth of three feet, and often in a curving direction, and with two entrances. A natural cranny or fissure in the rock will equally serve the purpose, or a time-worn hole in an old wall or ruin. They often build in company with the Razor Bill, Herring Gull, Kittiwake, and Guillemot, but in separate ranks.

The egg is deposited at the farther end. Mr. Selby adds that when engaged in digging, which operation is generally performed by the males, they are sometimes so intent upon their work, as to allow themselves to be taken by the hand; and the same may also be done when the bird is sitting on its egg. The young are hatched after a month's incubation. In about a like period of time, or a week or two more, they come to their full feathers, and are able to quit their native burrows, and enter on their ocean of life. Meyer says that where both birds have been killed, others have been known to take charge of the egg or young.

Only one egg is laid, and its colour is white, sometimes spotted with pale grey.

These birds begin to assemble in April, and the building-time is at the end of May or beginning of June.

RAZOR-BILL.

CARFIL GYLFINDDU, OF THE ANCIENT BRITISH.

RAZOR-BILL AUK. BLACK-BILLED AUK. AUK. MURRE. FALK.
MARROT. SKORT. COOTER.

Alca torda,   PENNANT. MONTAGU. BEWICK.

Alca—........?   *Torda*—Quære, a corruption from *Tarda* slow.

THIS bird is plentiful on the shores of the islands in the Arctic seas of Europe, Asia, and America, from Canada, Labrador, and Greenland, to Iceland, Norway, and Kamtschatka. It is seen also in Denmark, Holstein, Prussia, France, and Spain, and has occurred

Puffin

Razor-Bill

on the northern coast of Africa, namely at Tangiers. In America a few occasionally go as far south as New York.

The Razor-bill breeds in Yorkshire, at Flamborough Head, the well-known promontory near Burlington; also on the Fern Islands, the rocky cliffs of the Moray Firth, and other suitable places, the Great Orme's Head, off the Welsh coast, etc., etc. It occurs occasionally at Yarmouth, Norfolk, and along the coast, the young birds more commonly, and the old ones less so at all times of the year except in summer.

The species has occurred in Oxfordshire—for this I have the authority of the Hon. T. L. Powys. In Cornwall it is not uncommon near Gwyllynvase, Swanpool Bay, and Falmouth. One found dead by Mr. Cocks on the 3rd. of January, 1849. A young bird was shot there by Mr. May, January 9th., 1849. In Hampshire it has occurred at the Isle of Wight, not uncommonly I believe: also in Devonshire and Dorsetshire.

In February and March, 1853, the beach about Morfa, Bychaw, and Harlech, in North Wales, was strewed with dead birds of this kind.

It is plentiful in the Orkney and Shetland Islands, also in Scotland, in Sutherlandshire, about Handa and other parts; in Caithnesshire, etc. Many migrate southwards in the winter from the more northern parts, and these in turn are succeeded by others from still colder regions.

They are common in Ireland.

The Razor-bill is a migratory species, and begins to move southwards about the end of September, continuing its travels through November and December, according as the weather up to that period has been more or less severe. In March and April it returns northwards again. According to Meyer, 'During these migrations an interesting circumstance may be observed, namely, that when the several divisions or groups of a flock descend upon the sea to rest themselves, the parties that are behind· alight some distance in advance of those that first settled, so that when the first-arrived parties have recruited their strength, and taken wing again, the later-arrived groups having alighted so much in advance, have had time to rest themselves also, and are prepared in their turn to follow in the train of their former leaders as soon as these have passed over.'

They may often be seen far from land, 'cœlum undique et undique pontus.' The parent birds appear to be much attached to their young.

They fly strongly, rather fast, and well, but for the most part near the surface of the water, rising up only to gain a rock or cliff, the wings being quickly beaten. The birds that compose a flock keep at some distance from each other. On the land their motions are awkward and slow, and if pursued they make use of their wings to further their advance. They swim and dive with great ability.

They feed on young herrings, sprats, and other small fish, as also on crustacea, obtained by diving to a considerable depth.

The note is likened to the syllables 'arr' and 'orr,' also to 'hurr-ray.'

Any slight hollow or cranny in a rock of the cliff overhanging the sea, or even the bare unsheltered surface of the rock itself, a preference being given to the most precipitous places, is chosen by the Razor-bill as a deposit for its single egg. This in the month of April. Even here, however, it is exposed to accidents of different kinds, and is not unfrequently thrown down by a high wind, or some other bird, great numbers frequenting from the like cause of predilection the same breeding-places, or is broken by a chance stone or mass of earth dislodged from above: such landslips overwhelm also, at times, the bird itself. They often build in company with the Kittiwake, the Puffin, the Herring Gull, and the Guillemot, but each kind keeping to itself.

The old ones shew much attachment to their young. The latter are able in July to provide for themselves, but the descent to the sea is not always accomplished with safety. It sometimes happens that in throwing themselves down from the edge of the cliff, to which they are led by their parents, and instructed, as it were almost what to do, they fail in clearing every obstacle below, and the force of the fall in such case is fatal. They are also at times the victims of the onslaughts of Falcons.

They lay towards the end of May, or the beginning of June. The egg is subject to almost endless variety. Its prevailing colour is white, blotted and spotted with blackish brown and reddish brown.

CORMORANT.

COMMON CORMORANT. CRESTED CORMORANT. CORVORANT. GREAT CORVORANT. CRESTED CORVORANT.

Pelecanus carbo, PENNANT. MONTAGU. BEWICK.

Pelecanus—A Pelican. *Carbo*—........?

THE Cormorant is a bird of almost universal distribution, and belongs to each of the four quarters of the globe. It is also accommodating in the situations it frequents, and makes itself equally at home on sea or land, both near the shore and farther from it, in barren and rocky places, as well as in those that are wooded, the neighbourhood of buildings, and the most lonely wilderness, rivers and lakes, fresh-water and salt.

Mr. John Dutton has favoured me with some particulars of these birds. He says they always dip their wings in the water on first taking flight from their resting-places.

They often collect in parties of thirty or forty, and occasionally in very large bodies, more than a thousand having been observed together at one time.

On the land they are dull and heavy. They are only to be seen to advantage on the water. They roost indiscriminately on rocks or high trees, houses and other buildings, posts, or logs of floating timber, and may often be noticed perched on a rail or withered tree by the water side. They now and then follow the course of a river for severa miles inland, both by flight and swimming. Sir William Jardine says, 'We have known several birds take up a regular station, remaining to fish on the river, and roosting during night on its banks, upon some overhanging trees, and where inland lakes or waters are situate at no great distance from the sea, they are constantly frequented.'

Under the head of 'Sporting by Steam,' a curious circumstance is related in the 'Zoologist,' page 3712, by the Rev. G. Gordon, of one of these birds having been struck down and killed by the funnel of the engine of an express train, as it was crossing the Loch of Spynie, in Elginshire, on the 20th. of September, 1852. It had a flounder ten inches long in its bill at the time, and both bird and fish were taken up.

Young Cormorants become perfectly tame, and are readily trained in this country, as well as in China, where, as is well known, the practice is a regular and established one, to catch fish for their owners, the precaution being taken of placing a ring round the neck of the bird, to prevent the prey from being totally swallowed. I was invited once or twice the last few years by my friend Captain Arthur Brooksbank, of Middleton Hall, to go with him and Captain Salvin, to see the tame Cormorants of the latter thus fish in the Driffield streams below Wansford in my former parish of Nafferton, and was able on one of the occasions to accept the invitation. A sight well worth seeing it was. Montagu mentions one which never seemed to be so happy as when permitted to remain by the side of its master. Some kept by Dr. Neill used to roost with the poultry, but to usurp the best places. One of them laid two eggs while in the domesticated state. Sir Robert Shafto Adair, Bart., reported to Mr. Yarrell the circumstance of a pair of Cormorants having fed and brought up a nest of young Ravens, whose own parents had been destroyed. They provided them with a constant supply of fish.

Nothing is more interesting than to see a Cormorant fishing, so well does he swim, and so quickly does he dive. There he is, long and low in the water, like a pirate craft, and equally swift for his size. To pursue is to capture, and to overtake is death. Nor is he ever becalmed, wind-bound, or without the weather guage; or if he floats indeed on a surface unruffled by a breath of air and as smooth as glass, he has oars which are never motionless, and his upright head is unceasingly on the look out. Now he raises his body, and down below and onwards he plunges, as if in the act of making a sommersault: you cannot help but look with interest for his re-appearance, and on a sudden he starts up after a lengthened dive, where you perhaps expected him, or still more likely in a different spot—a fish you may be almost sure he has.

In the old days of the flint-and-steel guns, the first flash used to send the Cormorant down, so quick was his eye, and even now it is difficult to get within shot. They fly strongly and well, though not very fast, and at a considerable height, if over the land. They may often be seen standing on the shore or rocks apparently to dry their wings, previous to which the one kept by Montagu was observed to beat the water violently with its wings without moving from the spot, then shake its whole body, ruffle its feathers, at the same time covering itself with water, and this many times together with short intervals of rest. They are able to perch on trees. The young dive instinctively even from the very first.

It is curious to watch the Cormorant swallowing, or attempting to swallow a fish, eel, or other, too large to be got down at once; sometimes as much as half an hour is passed in the attempt, before a successful issue is come to: at last down it goes, and always head

Cormorant

Green Cormorant

foremost. Fish are its natural food, and those of the size of a herring or mackerel it can swallow whole. One has been seen to carry an eel it had caught to a rail it had previously been sitting on, strike it with three or four hard blows against the rail, and then after tossing it up into the air, catch it by the head, and swallow it at once. Colonel Montagu says, 'If by accident a large fish sticks in the gullet, it has the power of inflating that part to its utmost, and while in that state the head and neck are shaken violently, in order to promote its passage.' He adds, speaking of a tame bird he had, 'to a gull with a piece of fish it will instantly give chase: in this it seemed actuated by a desire to possess the fish, for if the gull had time to swallow it no resentment was offered.'

The note of this species is a harsh 'kree,' 'kraw,' or 'krell.' The young ones have a querulous cry.

The Cormorant naturally prefers an elevated situation for its nest, though in default of such it is obliged to put up with a lowly one. It is well for those of a higher rank in creation than the bird when they can thus readily accommodate themselves to the circumstances in which they are placed. Many pairs congregate together.

In the former case the tops of lofty cliffs are built on, or, as the next best, high trees. Failing these, a bed of rushes is made to serve the purpose on the mainland; or the top of a low island rock is resorted to.

The nest, which is large, is composed of sticks or sea-weeds, heaped up to the height of a couple of feet. The finer portions of grass forming the interior.

The eggs, small in proportion to the size of the bird, are of a pale bluish or greenish white colour, without polish, and of an oblong shape.

Three, four, or five are usually laid, but sometimes six. This in the month of April or May.

As soon as the young are able to fend and forage for themselves, which is as soon as they can fly, they are conducted to the sea by their parents, and then left to their own resources. This is when they are about three weeks or a month old.

The engraving is from a spirited drawing sent by Theodore Compton, Esq.

GREEN CORMORANT.

CRESTED CORMORANT. SKART. SCARF. CRESTED SCARF. SHAG. SHAG CORMORANT. CRESTED SHAG. COMMON SHAG. GREEN SCOUT.

Pelecanus cristatus,	PENNANT.

Pelecanus—A Pelican.	*Cristatus*—Crested.

THIS species is common on the northern shores of Europe, those of Norway and Sweden, Lapland, Finland, Russia, Iceland, and the Ferroe Isles, and is not unfrequent about the islands of the Mediterranean—Corsica, Sardinia, and Cyprus; also in Asia, both on the coasts and lakes of Siberia, and Kamtschatka; so too in America.

In the county of York a young bird of this kind was shot by the keeper of Andrew Lawson, Esq., at Rawcliffe, near Boroughbride, towards the end of October, 1848. They used to breed at Flamborough Head—not so now. In Oxfordshire one was obtained on the River Isis, near Oxford; and in Berkshire one near Pangbourne, in September, 1794. In July, 1851, a pair of these birds, in immature plumage, were killed at Burton Joyce, on the River Trent, six miles from Nottingham, as Mr. John Felkin, Junior, informed me, and one of them was obligingly presented to me by that gentlemen. A specimen was shot near Oxford in the beginning of 1851.

In Surrey it has occurred near Godalming. In Hampshire, in Stokes Bay, in the autumn of 1832. It is thought very rare at Yarmouth, in Norfolk, and the specimens which occur are chiefly seen in the autumn, and mostly immature. In Cornwall one, a young bird, was shot near Pennance Point, Swanpool, Falmouth, in 1854. One killed at the mouth of the Yealm, April 2nd., 1852. It is not an uncommon species in those parts. They used to be common in the cliffs in the Needles, Isle of Wight, formerly, but are now as rare. Building-places exist in the Isle of Man, and at St. Bees' Head.

In Scotland the Green Cormorant breeds in many places along the coasts of Kircudbright and Sutherland, etc., for instance, on Whiten-Head, Handa, and others; the Bass Rock and the Isle of Man. So also in Orkney are they common; as likewise in Ireland.

This kind keeps exclusively to the sea, unless indeed in such exceptional cases as those already enumerated.

On the ground these birds walk but indifferently. They sit in an upright posture, resting partly on the tail, but sometimes, Meyer says, lay down flat. They seem fond of spreading and flapping their wings, as if to dry them, when perched, as they often continue to be for a considerable time, on a low rock or sand-bank. They swim and dive in the most perfect manner. The head, or rather the neck, is carried very erect, and the body sunk low in the water. They do not remain swimming for a long time together, but either fly about, or repair to the rocks or the land for a change.

These birds return home regularly about sundown, from their feeding places, flying in a straight line, and low over the water, if the weather be fine, but at a good height if it be rough or lowering.

The old and young birds appear to keep in separate flocks or companies.

They feed on fish, and dive after them to a depth of from one hundred to one hundred and fifty feet.

These Cormorants make their nests on the ledges and shelves of cliffs or caves over the sea, lower down than the other species. Many pairs, a score or more, frequent the same place. They return to it annually for the breeding-season. Montagu mentions his having counted thirty together on a small rock. The bird sits upright on the eggs.

The nest is a mass of sea-weed, softened off internally with the finer sorts or grass.

The eggs are three, four, or five in number, and their original colour is white; but they soon become stained and discoloured.

Male; weight, about four pounds; length, two feet four or five inches. Bill, at the base of the under mandible, yellowish green, the remainder dusky black; iris, green. There is a rich dark green crest on the head in the spring, which is erected and even bent forwards at the pleasure of the bird. In some specimens it consists of only one, two, or three plumes, but in others is much more developed, probably with more mature age; their length upwards of two inches, and bent forwards. In autumn and winter the crest is absent. Crown, neck, and nape, rich dark bronze green, the plumage of a silky texture. In some individuals a few white feathers have been noticed. Chin and throat, rich dark green, the pouch under the chin is yellowish green with specks of black; breast, rich dark green, the plumage silky. Back on the upper part, dark green, with purple, green, and bronze reflections, the feathers narrowly edged at the tip with black.

The wings expand to the width of three feet eight or ten inches; greater and lesser wing coverts, dark blackish green, showing reflections of purple, green, and bronze, the feathers narrowly edged with velvet black. Primaries, black; secondaries, black; tertiaries, black. The tail is short, wedge-shaped, and black in colour. It contains twelve feathers; they are strong and elastic, forming, as already noticed, a support for the bird when on land. Legs and toes, dusky black; the middle claw is serrated; webs, black.

The female resembles the male, but is less in size; weight, three pounds and a quarter; length, about two feet three inches.

The young bird is at first covered with black down, which soon gives place to the regular plumage, namely, head, crown, neck, and nape, greyish black tinged with green; chin and throat, white. Breast above, greyish brown, on the middle and lower part greyish white, the sides dusky; back, brown, tinged with dull green; the black edge to the feathers is wider than in the old bird. The tail dusky, each feather edged with pale grey, the tips white; upper tail coverts, dusky.

Sir William Jardine mentions one of these birds which he saw of a light grey appearance. A cream-coloured specimen was shot off the coast of Iona, in the summer of 1854, by Mr. Colin Mc' Vean, as Henry F. Wood, Esq., of Southfield Square, Bradford, has obligingly sent me word. All such occasional varieties pay the penalty of 'shewing false colours,' and are sure to receive a shot.

The engraving is from a figure made by John Gatcombe, Esq., of Plymouth. Theodore Compton, Esq., has also obliged me with a drawing of the bird.

GANNET.

COMMON GANNET. SOLAN GOOSE. SOLAND GOOSE.

Sula alba,   FLEMING.

Sula. Sulao—To rob or spoil.   *Alba*—White.

THE Gannet, in Europe, is frequent in Norway, Sweden, the Ferroe Isles, and Iceland, and thence advances to Portugal, Spain, and the Mediterranean generally. It thus occurs on the northern shores of Africa. In Asia it is equally common, and is also assigned to South

Gannet

Common Tern

Africa and Madeira. In America it extends from Greenland and Labrador to the United States, as far south as Carolina it is said, and probably still further.

Gannets breed in immense numbers on Ailsa Crag, in the Firth of Clyde; the Bass Rock, in the Firth of Forth; the Stack of Souliskerry, near the Orkney Islands; Borea and St. Kilda, in the Hebrides; Lundy Island, in the Bristol Channel; and the Skelig Isles, off the coast of Ireland.

The Solan Goose has not unfrequently been met with quite inland.

They migrate southwards towards winter, and northwards again in the spring; the latter towards the end of the month of March or the beginning of April, 'Over the sea, over the sea,' and occur with us mostly in the summer, but some have been met with in February and March. Many in March, 1807, and in February, 1808.

Great numbers of Gannets are taken for the sake of their feathers and down, which are very valuable. They are sold for as much as one and eightpence each. They are also eaten by those who can get no better food. They are tameable birds, and will live for many years if kept by a piece of water.

Montagu points out a very curious peculiarity in the formation of the Gannet. I give the subjoined extracts from his account:—

'In the act of respiration, there appears to be always some air propelled between the skin and the body of this bird, as a visible expansion and contraction is observed about the breast; and this singular conformation makes the bird so buoyant, that it floats high on the water, and not sunk beneath its surface as observed in the Cormorant and Shag. The legs are not placed so far behind as in such of the feathered tribe as procure their subsistence by immersion: the Gannet, consequently, has the centre of gravity placed more forward, and, when standing, the body is nearly horizontal like a Goose, and not erect like a Cormorant.

Having, by the dissection of a specimen of the Gannet for preservation, noticed the slight and partial adhesion of the skin to the flesh of the whole under part of the body, we availed ourselves of the opportunity of paying more attention to the structure of this bird, and by experiments endeavoured to discover to what extent, and upon what principle, the inflation of the body was performed.

The appearance of so singular a conformation, brought to recollection what Buffon relates of the Pelican; who remarks, that from the lungs the air passes through axillary pipes, into a thick vesicular cellular membrane, that covers the muscles and envelopes the whole body. The structure, however, of the Gannet, although probably intended for similar purposes, is very different from that of the Pelican, according to the relation of that naturalist.

By comparative anatomy it has been clearly demonstrated, that birds in general are provided with air-vessels in different parts of the body, and that many of their bones are not destitute of this contrivance, admirably fitted for increasing their levity, and consequent buoyancy, as well as progressive motion through that element in which they are intended principally to move; and that too, with a velocity that far surpasses all other parts of animated nature. Mr. John Hunter, (in the Transactions of the Royal Society,) proves that the air-cells in the parts already mentioned, have a free communication with the lungs, by means of openings on their surface, through which the air passes readily into them.

Thus far have the scientific researches of that anatomist contributed to our knowledge on this subject. No one appears to have noticed the phenomena attendant on the construction of the Gannet, or to what further extent this circulation of aërial fluid is carried in some particular species of birds, a circumstance which demands our highest admiration, when we contemplate the advantages of such a structure in conducing to the comforts, and perhaps to the very existence of such animals.

From what has been already observed, it will not be unreasonable to conclude that the Gannet is endowed with such singular properties for very different purposes than those of long and continual immersion, of which we have before stated it appears to be incapable. But such a power of inflation must contribute greatly to lessen the concussion in its rapid descent upon water, in order to seize its prey. Besides, as the enlargement of the surface, without materially adding to the specific gravity, must greatly contribute to its buoyancy both in air and water, it is well adapted for residing in the midst of the most tempestuous sea, floating on its surface in the most perfect security, and following those shoals of fishes on which depend its whole existence. Thus when all other birds are compelled to seek shelter in bays and creeks, the Gannet is enabled to brave the severest weather in all seasons without attempting to near the shore. This contrivance may also be of the most important service to an animal which is constantly exposed, even in the most inclement season, and cannot quit its station without starving. Nothing could possibly conduce more to its security against intense cold, or be better adapted to preserve the necessary temperature of animal heat, than the intermediate air dispersed between the skin and the body, since that element is found to be a non-conductor of caloric. Upon this principle, what animal can be more securely protected against cold, or retain its vital heat so effectually as the Gannet of such birds as are almost surrounded with a body of confined air, divided by cells, and intersected by membranes between the skin and the body, and that skin so amply covered with a light porous substance filled also with air and impervious to water. The Gannet is capable of containing about three full inspirations of the human lungs divided into three equal portions, the cellular parts under the skin on each side holding nearly as much as the cavity of the body.

Now as a full or extraordinary inspiration of the human lungs has been considered to occupy a space of about sixty cubic inches, ('Philosophical Transactions,' volume lxix, page 349,) so the Gannet is capable of containing not less than one hundred and eighty cubic inches of air at one time, subject to the will of the bird under certain impressions.'

These birds roost on rocks along the coast, or on lonely islets in the open sea, or on the water itself in default of the former. Vast numbers congregate together. The following occurrence was recorded in the 'Sherborne Journal:'—'A servant of the Rev. F. J. C. Trenon, Rector of Langton, observed, on the 23rd. ultimo, an unusual commotion among the Swans in the Fleet, near Langton, which proved to be a battle between a Gannet and two full-grown male Swans, the latter both attacking at the same time, and following up the contest most vigorously with the former, who defended himself most resolutely for a very long time, and ultimately defeated the Swans, beating them both off, and laying them prostrate, totally disabled, helpless, and seemingly seriously injured. The Gannet, much exhausted by the protracted struggle, was easily caught alive, and very little the worse for fighting.'

It is described as a beautiful sight to watch the Gannet hawking for, and stooping on its prey. It flies with great power, agility, and freedom, the wings being quickly beaten, or at times skims along in a steady sailing manner: thus coursing on at a greater or less height, on catching sight of a quarry, it is down upon it, like a thunder-bolt, straight, or in a slightly slanting direction, the wings partly closed, dashing the water into foam as it plunges, and soon re-ascends, in the most lightsome manner, some yards from the place where it went down, rarely without its prey. The time that elapses between the plunge and the emersion, is about fifteen seconds. Sometimes after the bird has arrested its flight for a stoop, on perceiving either that it has been mistaken in the supposed object, or that the intended prey has already disappeared, it sails away on a fresh voyage of discovery.

Selby says that Gannets are long-lived birds, some that had been recognised from particular marks having been observed to return to the same stations for upwards of forty-eight years.

When engaged with their nests they become very tame, and will allow themselves to be stroked with the hand, without any sign of displeasure or alarm, beyond the utterance of a low guttural note. It is said that they are unable to rise from the water, except against the wind, and consequently that they may be taken in that situation by being run down upon in a boat.

They feed on fish—herrings, pilchards, anchovies, sardines, and sprats especially, such being found near the surface: they are swallowed head foremost.

The note is a dull 'grog, grog.'

Great numbers of these birds build together in the same situation, on the sides of precipitous cliffs and rocks, the nests being placed almost close to each other. These are made of sea-weed and grass.

The egg, for there is only one, is white, or with a pale tinge of blue.

Both parents sit; the period of incubation being about six weeks.

COMMON TERN.

TERN. GREATER TERN. SEA SWALLOW. GULL TEASER.

Sterna hirundo,	PENNANT. MONTAGU. BEWICK.
Sterna—........?	*Hirundo*—A Swallow.

IT would appear that this species is not so common as is imported by its name, other kinds having been confounded with it in the first instance.

It visits Germany, France, Spain, Holland, Switzerland, Italy, and the Mediterranean, from Norway, Spitzbergen, and other places of the north. In Asia it is seen in Asia Minor; and in Africa on the west coast, in Madeira, and the Canary Islands. In America, in Greenland and about Hudson's Bay, and so southwards to New England and other parts.

In Cornwall it occurs about Gwyllynvase, Newlyn, where it breeds, Swanpool, and Falmouth, but it is not common there, though generally elsewhere. It is however not unfrequently seen quite inland, as in Oxfordshire, especially in the spring months. In Worcestershire one, a young bird, was shot near Worcester, on the banks of the River Severn, in October, 1846. In Monmouthshire another was obtained on the 12th. of the same month; others were seen. Some large flocks had occurred a few years before. In Surrey this bird has been frequently shot at Frensham Pond, near Godalming. Two at Chertsey, October 6th., 1846. One was killed at Bushy Park, and others nearly forty miles up the Thames.

It is very common on the Yorkshire, Lincolnshire, and Norfolk coasts. Specimens, too, have occurred inland in the first-named county, at Leeds, though rarely, Huddersfield, Hebden Bridge, and Barnsley, by the margins of reservoirs and the course of canals. In Derbyshire one near Melbourne, May the 25th., 1845. It has been met with near Oxford. In Cambridgeshire it is found in the Isle of Ely during the summer months. Some were shot at March, the 7th. of May, 1850. The species is observed all along the south coast; in Kent most numerously, it is stated, about Winchelsea, Dungeness, and Romney Marsh; Dorsetshire, Devonshire, and Cornwall; so in Essex, Norfolk, Suffolk, Durham, and Northumberland, as also not unfrequently in the Solent, Isle of Wight, Hampshire.

It is common in Ireland; also in Scotland, in the Firth of Forth, and along the coast; and has occurred in different years in Dumfriesshire; likewise in the Hebrides; also in Wales, at Llandudno, etc.

The Common Tern breeds near Skinburnness, on Rockcliffe Saltmarsh, by Solway Firth, and a few on Solway Moss. Many on Foulney Island, on the Lancashire coast. Priestholm Isle, off the coast of Anglesea, is another nesting place, as also the Fern Islands, on the Northumbrian coast, and the Isle of May in the Firth of Forth, the Firth of Clyde, as likewise in the Orkneys.

They frequent low coasts, the borders of lakes, and the mouths of large rivers, and follow the course of the latter.

These birds arrive variously in different parts of the country in April, May, or June, and remain till the end of August, or through the month of September, or to the beginning of October. They migrate, it is said, by day, and travel slowly.

All the varied movements of the Sea Swallow in flight are performed with that striking ease and grace which are characteristic of these birds, whether on a calm summer day when the glassy surface of the sea shimmering in the sun is broken only by the leaping of the shoals of fish over which the Terns hover, or later on in the waning year when the 'winds their revels keep.'

Their food consists of small sea-fish, and, in fresh water, of minnows and any other small kinds. They sometimes pursue the Sea Gulls, and make them drop what they had caught for themselves, and then seize it before it reaches the water. They also capture insects, running about in pursuit of them on the ground.

The Common Tern lays its eggs on sand, rocks, or shingle, making little or no nest beyond scooping out a slight hollow: what there is, is placed either by the sea-side or in marshes, on islands, or by the sides of lakes and rivers.

The eggs are variously of a pale blue, pale yellow, green, brown, white, or light dull yellowish or stone-colour, blotted and spotted with grey, dark reddish brown, and blackish brown: three in number. They are laid from the latter end of May to the beginning of July.

The male bird assists the female in the task of sitting during the day, she taking charge of the clutch at night; in fine weather, however, the heat of the sun seems to be thought sufficient warmth, and the bird leaves them to its rays. Ten or twelve pairs of these birds breed together. The young come forth in fifteen or sixteen days, and are able to fly when about three weeks old. The old ones display much anxiety for their safety, and are very clamorous when any one approaches their station, flying round, and frequently even striking against him.

BLACK-HEADED GULL.

YR WYLON BENDDU. BRAN Y MOR, OF THE ANCIENT BRITISH.

BROWN-HEADED GULL. BROWN GULL. LAUGHING GULL. RED-LEGGED
GULL. PEEWIT GULL. SEA CROW. BLACK-CAP.
HOODED MEW. PICKMIRE.

Larus ridibundus,   PENNANT. MONTAGU. FLEMING.

Larus—A ravenous sea-bird.   *Ridibundus. Rideo*—To laugh; in allusion
to one of the vernacular names of the bird.

THIS graceful and lively bird is well known in many parts of the world. In Europe, it is a native of Russia, Sweden, Holland, France, Germany, Italy, and Switzerland. In Asia, of Siberia, Syria, Armenia, and Arabia. In America, of Greenland and the shores of Baffin's Bay and Davis' Straits. In Africa, it is found in Egypt and along the northern shores.

In spring and summer these birds dwell by marshes, rivers, lakes, and ponds, and for the remainder of the year resort to the sea-shore and the mouths of the larger rivers.

They arrive at their summer quarters generally in the month of March, but some about the middle or latter end of February, and leave again the end of July or beginning of August. Many must leave the country in the autumn, and return again in the spring, the numbers of those seen in the latter season and the summer being so very great.

These birds are easily kept in confinement in suitable places, such as walled gardens, but continue shy and timid. T. E. Wilkinson, Esq., of Walsham Hall, has written me word of his having kept one of them alive and well for nearly a year, and it was at last killed by a dog, having unfortunately wandered out of its bounds.

They may be seen at times perched on low bushes, the top of a boat-house, or the upright stump of a tree, in the places where they build.

The young were formerly considered good eating, and some proprietors used to make from fifty to eighty pounds a year by their sale.

Their flight is easy, noiseless, and buoyant, and they sometimes hover for a short time over their prey, and then dash on it into the water. They do not usually resort to swimming. On the land they run about in a light and graceful manner.

They frequently hunt for insects in the twilight, and have been seen so late as between nine and ten o'clock at night, and heard returning from their forage at still later hours.

They feed on small fish and insects—cockchaffers, May-flies, beetles, and moths; as also on slugs, worms, shrimps, butts, and other crustacea, and, if need be, on water-plants. The first-named, if of the fresh-water kinds, they hawk for at a height of ten or twelve feet in the air, and on descrying the object, they lower their course, and, skimming the surface, pick it up. They almost always follow the course of the stream, and in winter advance up rivers in the morning, going downwards again towards night. In the spring months they resort to ploughed lands, following the plough in quest of worms and insects; and in summer repair to water. 'During the heat of the day, many of them disperse up and down throughout the corn, pasture, and fallow fields, in search of food. These they beat with great diligence, traversing them again and again, at a height of about ten feet as before. When any suitable object meets their eye, they immediately round to, alight on the ground, and generally keeping their wings extended upwards, seize it.' The ghost-moth is a favourite object of pursuit on the still summer evenings, when it hovers over the grass or swarms about trees.

'It is indeed a most amusing and interesting sight to witness the elegant evolutions of these beautiful birds when in pursuit of these large moths, oftentimes brushing the surface of the ground with their downy breasts, and generally capturing with facility the moth as it hovers at a distance of from one to two feet from the earth. Occasionally, however, the bird misses its aim, and the moth, by the rapid motion of the Gull, is struck to the ground. The bird, however, nothing dismayed, hovers for a few seconds over the retreat of its fallen prey, and if it perceives it embedded in the grass, pounces upon it, or if disappointed flies off in search of another prize.' May-flies also they course after over the streams almost like Swallows.

The same writer from whom I have made the above quotation, Mr. Archibald Jerdon, adds, in the 'Zoologist,' page 246, 'I have repeatedly seen numbers of them flying about long after sunset, and lately I have remarked that they come abroad in the evening apparently for the purpose of catching insects, which they do on the wing, after the manner of the Swallow tribe. On the 22nd. of this month, I watched the proceedings of a number of these birds by the banks of the Jed, between nine and ten o'clock. There was a small grove of trees at a short distance from the river, to which some of them resorted, flying from one extremity to the other, and returning again, all the while seemingly engaged in the pursuit of insects of some kind. Their motions were much the same as those of Swallows, although somewhat slower; they sometimes remained hovering and suspended while catching an insect, so long and so near the trees, that I thought they were going to alight. Others of them scoured the fields and the water-side, and others again followed the course of the river; but all apparently intent on the capture of some winged prey.'

The note is a hoarse cackle, 'cack, cack, cack, cack,' which has been likened to a laugh, from whence one of the trivial names of the bird. Where large numbers dwell together a great din is produced.

They are very anxious about their young, and stoop and dash at an intruder again and again. As soon as the brood are able to fly, they scatter about the neighbourhood, to feed on moist meadows and such places, whence they are shortly conducted by their parents to the nearest coast.

This pretty-looking bird resorts to fenny districts and the sides of pools and inland waters and their islands to breed, and vast multitudes congregate together for the purpose, as well both near the sea as farther from it, and on the lands adjoining the sea itself, if low and marshy.

The nest is flat, and a composition of grass or the tops of reeds and sedge, placed, perhaps, on a tuft of rushes or other such herbage.

If the first set of eggs be taken a second is laid, and a third if the second, but in such cases they are less each time in size. They are valued as food, and in some places are farmed for the purpose.

The eggs, two, three, or sometimes, it is said, four in number, are laid the middle or end of April, or beginning of May, chiefly at the latter season, and are hatched the end of May or early in June. They vary exceedingly in colour and markings; some are light blue, others yellowish, and others green, red, or brown. Some have scarcely any spots, and others are thickly covered with marks of different shades of brown and reddish brown. One beautiful variety has been described, the ground-colour a very light greenish white, blotted with two shades of rich brown. In some intances they are found entirely white.

The young birds leave the nest and betake themselves to the water as soon as hatched.

Sir William Jardine writes, 'They are particular in the choice of a breeding-place, at least some which we would think suited for them are passed or deserted, and others more unlikely are selected. We possess a reedy loch which was for many years a haunt of these birds, but the edges were planted and they left it; ten years afterwards, and when the plantation had grown up, a few pairs returned, and in time increased to a large colony, when an artificial piece of water was made by damming up a narrow pass in an extensive muir, nearly two miles distant; thither the Gulls resorted the following spring, leaving their ancient ground; and they have been increasing in numbers for some years past.'

The colour of one of the birds in full plumage is a white body, light grey wings, and a black head. The young ones are quite mixed with brown, with no black head; and I observe when they first return in the spring of the year, that nearly half the birds have white heads, which gradually turn black while they stay. This leads me to the conclusion that they do not get the black head until about a year old.

Black-Headed Gull

Great Black-Backed Gull

GREAT BLACK-BACKED GULL.

GWYLAN DDU A GWYN, OF THE ANCIENT BRITISH.

WAGEL. COB.

Larus marinus,   PENNANT. MONTAGU. SELBY.

Larus—A ravenous Sea-bird.   *Marinus*—Belonging to the sea—marine.

THIS fine bird occurs in Europe, in Sweden, the Ferroe Islands, Denmark, France, Italy, Germany, Holland, Norway, and Iceland. In America, in Greenland, Baffin's Bay, Labrador, and as far south as Florida. In Asia, in the vicinity of the Caspian Sea.

It is with us a not uncommon though not numerous species; seen throughout the year on the shores of the Island, but for the most part singly or in pairs.

They breed abundantly in the Orkney and Shetland Islands, also on the Bass Rock, in the Frith of Forth, and one or two other stations on the Scottish coast, and the northern islands of the same; Souliskerry in the Orkneys; and in Shetland; so too on Lundy Island and Steep Holme, in the Bristol Channel; and near St. David's, as also, according to Mr. Yarrell, on the low lands of the estuary of the Thames.

In Yorkshire, I have seen the Black-backed Gull near Burlington, and it is not uncommon on the coast. It has occurred at times about Huddersfield and Barnsley. So in Norfolk, at Yarmouth, and along the shore; as likewise in Suffolk, Durham, and Northumberland, also in Devonshire and Dorsetshire. In Surrey it has been seen at Godalming. In Lincolnshire, at Tetney.

In Cambridgeshire one was bought at Cambridge, in the market. In Oxfordshire, small parties of four or five have been frequently noticed. In Cornwall the species is not uncommon at Falmouth, Penryn River, and other parts. In Kent and Essex along the banks of the Thames.

It is a tolerably common species in Ireland, as near Dublin, etc., and a resident throughout the year. So, too, in Scotland, as in Sutherlandshire on the friths, and in Caithnesshire, East Lothian, etc. In Wales, in Caermarthenshire, near Tenby, Llandudno, and Laugharne.

In Orkney it is described by Dr. Baikie and Mr. Heddle as being pretty widely distributed. Also in Shetland, Guernsey and Sark.

These birds seldom advance farther inland than the estuaries.

It is curious that this Gull should be very shy, while the Wagel, the same bird, so called at a different and younger period of life, is not by any means so much so.

These are powerful birds, and at the same time bold and daring, and stout opponents. They may be kept in confinement, and Mr. Yarrell has furnished an account of one as sent to him by the Rev. Robert Holdsworth, which was hatched successfully from an egg taken by the crew of H. M. Revenue Cutter, Vigilant, and lived for many years quite tame, near Dartmouth. It swam in the river every day, and looked out for the fishermen returning from sea, who were in the habit of feeding it.

The eggs are eaten and considered good by the inhabitants of the northern islands.

These birds float aloft at times on almost motionless pinions, wheeling round and round in a chain of circles. Their ordinary flight is rather slow, but powerful, and they wing their way along without much seeming effort. They sail buoyantly on the water, and swim well.

They feed on fish, and anything that is capable of being fed upon, and are said even to attack and destroy lambs. One has been seen to drop on a Guillemot which had just been shot, and begin to devour it. Smaller birds are therefore, as might be hence supposed, not objected to. They drive away the lesser Gulls from any prey they may have discovered.

The note is a mere 'kac, kac, kac,' given in a loud, rough, and harsh tone, capable of being heard at a great distance. It is uttered most in the spring-time.

The Great Black-backed Gull builds chiefly in marshes and low undrained moors, as also in and on the cliffs and rocky islets of the sea-coast and of inland lakes, making its nest of dry grass, sea-weeds, and sticks. Many resort to the same place. The nest is of large size. Both male and female assist in its construction.

The eggs are three in number. They are considered very good to eat, and great numbers are taken for the purpose, the first and second clutch being removed, and the bird then laying a third time. Their colour is yellowish brown, with a tinge of green, a little spotted with bluish grey and dark brown.

Male; weight, nearly five pounds; length, two feet six inches or over. The bill, which is large and very strong, is pale yellow, the lower angle of the under mandible orange red, with a dusky black spot in the middle on each side; the tooth of the upper bill dusky in winter. Iris, pale yellow; the eyelids bright red; there is a dark mark before the eye in winter. Head, crown, neck, and nape, white; in winter the former streaked with a little grey; chin, throat, and breast, white; back, dark leaden grey.

The wings reach in extent to the width of five feet nine inches; greater and lesser wing coverts, leaden grey; primaries, nearly black, the first and second ending with a triangular-shaped white patch, longest in the former, the second with a black spot in the white near the tip, the third with a short white tip, the fourth with a short white tip, succeeded by black, and this followed by a narrow clouded bar of greyish white, the others tipped with white, the inner webs being leaden grey; secondaries, leaden grey, ending in white, forming a bar across the wing; tertiaries, leaden grey, also ending in white; greater and lesser under wing coverts, white. Tail, white; upper tail coverts, white; under tail coverts, white. Legs and toes, pale yellowish red.

Female; length, two feet three or four inches.

In the young the bill is black; iris, dark blue; head, crown, neck, and nape, dull white, mixed with greyish brown; chin, throat, and breast, also dull white, but paler in the markings. Back, greyish brown, the feathers dark in the middle, the edges greyish white.

Greater and lesser wing coverts, mottled and spotted with pale greyish brown and greyish white; primaries, black; greater and lesser under wing coverts, dull greyish white, with some pale brown marks. The tail has the middle feathers black, tipped with white, the side feathers mixed with black and white. Legs and toes, dull greyish white, with a red tint.

HERRING GULL.

GWYLAN BEUWAIG, OF THE ANCIENT BRITISH.

SILVERY GULL. PEE-OL.

Larus argentatus,   BEWICK. FLEMING. SELBY.

Larus—A ravenous sea-bird.   *Argentatus. Argentum*—Silver.

THIS bird has an extensive European range, occurring in Iceland, the Ferroe Isles, Norway, Sweden, and Denmark, Holland, France, Italy, and Turkey. It belongs also to Africa, and is seen at Madeira; so too in Asia, in Asia Minor and along the shores of the Black Sea; and is also an American species, observed in Greenland and at Melville Island, Mexico, and thence to Labrador, and on Whitehead Island, in the Bay of Fundy, also about New York and Philadelphia.

The Herring Gull is common on our coasts, and remains throughout the year.

I have received several particulars respecting this species from John Dutton, Esq. He writes—'The Herring Gull is exceedingly common on the coasts of Hampshire and in the Isle of Wight. They build in great numbers in Scratchell's Bay, and in the cliffs under the Needles lighthouse. It is a fine sight to see them from the top of those grand cliffs, towering aloft in graceful circles, their beautiful snow-white necks contrasting finely with the blue of their blacks. They build on the ledges of the cliffs, and frequently in the beds of samphire, which grows in abundance there.'

The Herring Gull, which is readily tamed to a certain extent, so far as to follow a gardener while digging, to pick up any dislodged insects, has been known to breed in confinement, namely near Fermoy, in the county of Cork, as recorded in the 'Zoologist,' page 1395; another pair at Walthamstow, for three successive years; also at Quy Hall, the seat of J. T. Martin, Esq., two eggs were laid, and one young bird reared: another kept in a garden made a great friend of a terrier dog. Montagu mentions one which thus lived in confinement for thirteen years.

Mr. Hewitson gives the following, as communicated to him by the Rev. W. D. Fox:—'At Colbourne, in the Isle of Wight, a Herring Gull made its escape about thirty years ago from a garden where he had been kept a prisoner. From that time, however, to the present, he has returned all but daily to visit the place of his former captivity, though at the distance of six or seven miles from that part of the coast where they resort. Here he is regularly fed, and is so tame with the man who has regularly attended to his wants, that he would eat out his hand, but will not allow any further familiarities. In the breeding season he is accompanied by his mate, who will not venture to descend, but remains hovering and screaming over him whilst he is feeding below.'

These birds utter loud cries at the approach of danger, and so become sentinels for other species.

They fly rather slowly, and at a low height, sweeping down, and catching up any prey from the water. They walk about much on the sea-beach in search of food.

This species is very indiscriminate in its choice of food, swallowing alike small fish, small crabs, shrimps, crustacea, and mollusks generally, starfish, the eggs of other sea-fowl, wheat, small birds, rats, mice, cockchaffers, worms, in fact any thing eatable. It gives preference, however, when it has a choice, to fish, and is very bold in approaching boats and nets, so as to have acquired in Italy the name of Fisherman—'Pescatore del onda.' It is said also to trample the soft sand, to bring its prey to the surface.

In the 'Naturalist,' vol. iii, page 28, George Donaldson, Esq. writes of one kept in a garden:—'At this period, however, he acquired a taste for Sparrows, and scarcely a day passed on which he did not regale himself with four or five of them. His system of catching them was this:—He was on the best terms with a number of Pigeons which this gentleman had, and as the Sparrows fed along with them, he mixed in the group, and by stooping assumed as much as possible their appearance, and then set at the Sparrow as a pointer dog would do his game; the next instant he had his prey by the back, and swallowed it without giving it time to shut its eyes. The sporting season began with him about the middle of July, as the young birds were leaving their nests; and as numbers of them were produced in Mr. Kemp's garden, and others came to practise there, they found it very slippery ground, for the enemy was upon them in a moment. At the expiration of three years, his plumage was assuming a lighter shade, although the grey feathers on the under part of his body were quite apparent. He pursued his old system of snatching and swallowing with great success, and arrived at so much perfection in the art that he caught his prey often while flying past, and occasionally sprang from the ground, and struck a bird down with his wing, which he had no difficulty in afterwards capturing. On one occasion, while standing near a pump well in the garden, he pounced upon a rat, which had come there for the purpose of drinking; it squeaked on being caught, and Mr. Kemp, who was standing close by, looked immediately, and had scarcely time to see it suddenly disappear head foremost,—a rule which he had strictly observed, with both the living and the dead.' Another, kept by the same gentleman, devoured successively two clutches of young ducks, the first nine in number, and the second five.

The note is very loud and piercing, and is frequently repeated in the spring. Its alarm cry resembles the syllables 'kak-ka-kak,' interrupted by a shrill scream of 'pew-il,' or 'pee-ol.'

The Herring Gull makes a nest of dry grass and sea-weed on the ledges and small grassy or stony spaces that occur along the side of a cliff, and towards the top. They often build in close proximity to the Kittiwake, Razor-bill, Puffin, and Guillemot, but still distinct.

Great numbers of these birds breed together, and in close neighbourhood also with other species.

The eggs are two, or more properly three, in number. They are of a light olive brown colour, spotted over with darker brown of two shades; some deep olive green, blotted over with blackish brown. They are laid about the middle of May, and the young take wing about the 20th. of July.

The male bird keeps watch about the female when sitting, and comes to her assistance and defence if occasion requires.

KITTIWAKE.

GWYLAN GERNYW, OF THE ANCIENT BRITISH.

Larus Rissa,　　　　　TARROCK. MONTAGU. FLEMING. SELBY.

Larus—A ravenous sea-bird.　　*Rissa*—.........?

THE Kittiwake is plentiful in many parts of Europe, as Norway, Sweden, the Ferroe Islands, Iceland, Nova Zembla, and Spitzbergen, in the north, and on the French coast: in Italy it has also occurred. It is common in Greenland, and on the continent of America, from the United States to Labrador and the farthest north, inconceivable numbers congregating, Captain J. Ross, R.N., observed in suitable places. In Africa, specimens have been procured at Tripoli, and on the west coast; and in Asia, near the Caspian Sea, and on to Kamtschatka in the north.

They breed in immense numbers on the northern coasts of Scotland, the Bass Rock and that of Glass, St. Abb's Head, in Berwickshire, Caithnesshire, Fowls-Heugh, near Stonehaven and Montrose, Aberdeenshire, Troup Head, the Isle of May, in the Frith of Forth, the Moray Firth, and other places; so too in the Shetland Islands. Also in Yorkshire on the cliffs about Flamborough, and so formerly at Scarborough and the Fern Islands off the coast of Northumberland. In Hampshire, at the Isle of Wight; and in Devonshire, Dorsetshire, and Cornwall.

The Kittiwake is common along the Yorkshire coast, and some have been seen about Sheffield, Huddersfield, and York. In Cornwall it is not uncommon about Falmouth, Swanpool, Gwyllynvase, and other places; as too in Norfolk, about Yarmouth, and along the coast. One, of which William Brooks Gates, Esq. has informed me, was killed at Pattishall, in Northamptonshire, during the severe frost in January, 1854; and one the second week in February, 1855. The bird is seen on the River Nene in that county almost every winter; so likewise in Oxfordshire the bird is a common visitor at that season. In Surrey one was shot on Wandsworth Common, in February, 1851; and another at Hatch, near Godalming. In 1846, March 30th., one was caught near King's Newton, Melbourne, Derbyshire. It is more or less common on the coasts of Durham, Northumberland, Devonshire, Dorsetshire, and Hampshire, both the mainland and the Isle of Wight.

Herring Gull

Kittiwake

It is a common species in Ireland. Also in Guernsey and Sark. In Orkney it is very abundant, and in Shetland equally so. It breeds also near St. David's, and other places in Wales, and is common in those parts.

They are summer visitors here, but some have been seen, though sparsely distributed, in winter. A young one was shot in Devonshire, in the month of November; and Montagu mentions three washed up on the shore in the month of March, 1806. Meyer also mentions his having obtained an adult bird, in perfect winter plumage, on the 19th. of January, 1837; and an immature bird on the 22nd. of February. Mr. Yarrell speaks of some seen by him at that season on the Dorsetshire and Hampshire coasts; and Sir William Jardine writes of the species as being seen also in winter, though rarely, in Scotland, on the coasts; sometimes too in the Frith of Forth; and of one as shot near Edinburgh, in January, 1843. The greater part of our native birds of the present kind would seem to retire to the eastern parts of Europe for the winter. This species has been kept in confinement, but requiring, as it does, a fish diet, it is more difficult to be preserved than the others which are of an omnivorous character.

They are naturally fearless birds, and far from shy, and are readily kept in confinement. A Gull, believed to be one of these, and which lived for twenty-seven years, used to go away in summer, and pair with another of the wild birds, in the cliffs of the Isle of Wight, returning alone afterwards and spending its time either on a small piece of water, or sitting on the railings of some cottage, or else flying about the country, so tame withal that it would come into the houses and eat from the hands of persons whom it knew, though not from others. Great numbers are shot in some places in the north for the sake of their feathers.

They both swim and fly well and easily, but are indifferently able to walk or run on the land, owing to the shortness and the position of the legs.

They feed on sea productions—fish, shrimps, and other crustacea, and the like.

The note of this Gull is considered to be expressed by its name, 'kittie-weeik,' and is very often uttered, most distinctly when the bird seems angry or alarmed. All the sea-birds' cries are in themselves harsh and discordant, but no doubt they sound 'most sweet voices' in one another's ears, as much so as those of the Nightingale or the Thrush are supposed by us to do to those of their own kinds.

The Kittiwake lays its eggs high up on or in any small ledge or cleft on the side of a steep and rocky cliff by the sea. These are often so narrow and apparently insecure, that Selby says the young seem instinctively aware of their perilous situation, whence sometimes the least movement would precipitate them into the waves beneath, and are observed seldom to change their attitude in the nest till sufficiently fledged to be able to provide for their own safety. Immense numbers of these birds build together, so much so as completely to whiten the places where they assemble for the purpose, and to give them the appearance of being covered with snow. They often are found in company with the Razor-bill, Guillemot, and Puffin.

The nest is a mixture of grass and other dry herbage with sometimes the addition of sea-weed.

The time for laying is the latter end of May, or the beginning of June.

The eggs are usually two, but occasionally, though very rarely, three in number. They differ much in their colouring and markings; the prevailing tint is stone-colour with a tinge of olive, much spotted with grey and brown of two shades; or greyish white, faintly tinged with brown, and blotted with dark brown and purple grey.

SKUA.

GWYLAN FRECH, OF THE ANCIENT BRITISH.

COMMON SKUA. SKUA GULL. SQUAW GULL. BROWN GULL. BONXIE. TEASER.

Lestris cataractes,   JENYNS. GOULD. TEMMINCK.

Lestris—A pirate vessel. *Cataractes. Katarasso*—To drive headlong, to dash down.

THIS stout bird belongs to the colder regions of the north and south, as in Europe to Spitzbergen, Nova Zembla, Iceland, the Ferroe Islands, Norway, and Scandinavia generally; in North America, to Labrador, Newfoundland, Hudson's Bay, and the adjacent parts towards the United States; in South America, to the Straits of Magellan, Terra del Fuego, the Falkland Islands, the New South Georgian Islands, and Kerguelin's Land; also to Africa, at the Cape of Good Hope. Specimens have, however, been obtained in more temperate parts, as on the coasts of Germany, Holland, and France.

In Yorkshire, they are occasionally seen on the coast in the autumn and winter, but are never numerous; one, a young bird, was shot in December, 1853, near Scarborough. Sir William Jardine has noticed them at times on the Solway, and far up the Firth of Forth. They similarly appear, wandering southwards in the autumn, on the coasts of Northumberland, Durham, Norfolk, four shot in the Yarmouth Roads, October 7th., 1827, Essex, Kent, one at Greenwich, and another at Sandwich, in the winter of the year 1800, and Sussex. In Cornwall the species occurs, but not commonly, at Falmouth, Penryn River, and other places. Also in Devonshire; in April, 1850, one of these birds was caught near Plymouth in a net, by some fishermen, as R. A. Julian, Esq., Jun., of Laira House, has informed me. One, too, on the River Severn. One on the Cumberland coast, which allowed itself to be seized when in the act of killing a Herring Gull.

The Skua breeds in Shetland, and has three principal stations there, namely, Foula, the Hill of Rona, in Mainland, and the Isle of Unst. In Orkney it is but an occasional visitant. A specimen was shot near Kirkwall in the winter of 1845-6, and another has since been killed near Stromness.

It is likewise an Irish species, but rare. One in Dublin Bay. In Scotland one near Dunbar, in February, 1867. It is very common on the Caithness coast; one at Inverurie, inland, in 1868.

These birds are valued by the inhabitants of the places where they build, as scaring away the Eagles from their flocks; a pair has been seen to drive one from their nest. They are preserved in some of the northern islands on this account. They dash with extreme courage and boldness at any intruder, increasing in the vigour of their attacks as the nest is more nearly approached. Meyer thus writes, 'While the breeding-season lasts, this Skua is exceedingly ferocious, for every intruder, whether man, bird, or beast, is attacked by it, and driven from the locality that it has chosen. Men, when attacked, are obliged to defend themselves stoutly; dogs and foxes are driven off the ground, and the Eagle itself is obliged to take proper warning.'

They have been kept in confinement; one for a period of ten years or more. Many are killed in the north for the sake of the feathers.

The Skua soars at times at a great height, and flies both strongly and rapidly, in an impetuous dashing manner.

They may be considered as a sort of sea-hawk, feeding on fish, and at times on other smaller birds and their eggs. 'They rarely, however, take the trouble to fish for themselves, but watching the Gulls when thus employed, they no sooner observe one to have been successful, than they immediately give chase, pursuing it with fury, and obliging it from fright to disgorge the recently-swallowed fish, they descend after it to catch it, and are frequently so rapid and certain in their movements and aim, as to seize their prize before it reaches the water. It is on this account these birds have been called Parasitic Gulls, because they are supported by the labours of others.' Hence also their other name of Pirate, as shewn above, 'Might versus Right' being their only motto, and that upon whose principle, or what we should call want of principle, they act on every occasion that happens, but still following only the proper instinct of their nature. With reference, however, to this name Bewick properly observes, speaking of one of the other species, 'It may admit of doubt whether the character of parasitic belongs to any of this tribe, least of all to the present bird. What it obtains from other birds is not by fawning or cunning, but by courageous open assault.' They thus attack even the Gannet; but are themselves the objects of the hostility of the Terns. They hold their prey in their claws, and so tear it to pieces. They have, however, been known to swallow a herring whole. They are great favourites with the fishermen, frequently accompanying their boats to the fishing-ground, which is considered a lucky omen.'

The nest of the Skua is of large size, as well as somewhat carefully constructed; the materials used being grasses, lichens, moss, and heath. The bird places it on the tops of the mountains or cliffs in the neighbourhood of the sea, but not on the rocks themselves. They build separately in pairs.

The eggs are only two. They are laid towards the end of June.

Male; weight, about three pounds; length, two feet, to two feet one inch. The bill, which is much hooked at the tip, is dark brownish black. Cere, black; iris, dark hazel brown. Head, crown, neck, and nape, dark umber brown, with slight streaks of yellowish or reddish brown. The feathers of the neck, which are of a pointed shape, are raised by the bird when excited. Chin, throat, and breast, uniform brown; back, dark reddish brown, with lighter-coloured oblong spots.

The wings extend to the width of between four and five feet; greater and lesser wing coverts, dark reddish brown; of the primaries, the first has its outer web and tip blackish brown, the others the same on the tips only, and very pale rusty brown at the base of the

Skua

Manx Shearwater

feathers; the shafts of all of them white and strong. Tertiaries, margined with pale reddish brown. The tail, which is dark brown, is rounded at the end, the two middle feathers a little longer than the others, and darker in colour; the base white. It consists of twelve feathers. Legs, black, strongly and irregularly scutellated in front, and reticulated behind; toes, black. The claws are black, strong, much hooked, and grooved beneath, the inner one the most so.

The female is much less in size than the male, but otherwise similar.

MANX SHEARWATER.

MANX PETREL. MANX PUFFIN. SHEARWATER PETREL. SKRABE. LYRE.

Puffinus Anglorum,	FLEMING. SELBY. GOULD.
Puffinus—........?	*Anglorum*—Of the English.

THE present, as a European species, has occurred in the Mediterranean, Norway, the Islands of Denmark, the Faroe Islands, Iceland, Holland, Italy, and France. In America it extends in its range from Labrador, down by Newfoundland to the south, through the States. In Asia, it has been noticed in Asia Minor. It is included also among the birds of Madeira.

It was formerly very plentiful in the Isle of Man, whence its name.

The Manx Shearwater breeds in the Hebrides, at St. Kilda and Soa; also in Zetland, at Foula and Uist. In Orkney, in the Islands of Papa Westray and Waas.

In England, on Annet, one of the Scilly Islands, and on the coast of Wales, near St. David's. Many which are on sale in Leadenhall market, in the spring of the year, are taken in rabbit-warrens in Wales, Mr. John Dutton being my informant.

In Yorkshire specimens of this bird are occasionally found along the coast in the autumn. In Nottinghamshire one was picked up alive in the parish of Trowell, the latter end of October, 1869, as the Rev. Charles Hudson has written me word. It has also occurred near Yarmouth, but rarely. One or two off the Northumbrian coast, near the Fern Islands. Specimens have been seen off the shores of Dorsetshire and Devonshire, not very unfrequently. In Oxfordshire one was taken alive near Chipping Norton, September, 1839.

In Ireland they are summer visitants, near Dublin and other parts, but locally. They are also Scottish, in East Lothian, Caithness, etc.

They occur, as just mentioned, in the Orkneys, but not very numerously; also in the Hebrides.

They are migratory, arriving in the north in February and March, and departing in the autumn.

In their habits they are somewhat addicted to the twilight, flying abroad when the 'stars glimmer red,' to take their pastime, and seek their daily food.

They roost with the head turned back, and the bill buried in the feathers. They are altogether birds of the sea, except when drawn to land for the purpose of breeding. Flocks of as many as three hundred have been seen together, and they appear to be easily approached. Meyer writes, speaking of their mode of feeding, 'It is very amusing to watch a flock of these Petrels thus employed; the birds are seen swimming on the waves with their heads in the water, all in the same direction, and moving on very rapidly, the hindermost bird always flying up and settling in advance of the foremost, like rooks following a plough. Fishermen, when in pursuit of their calling, watch carefully the movements of these birds, and when they see them thus employed, lower their nets with a tolerable certainty of finding the shoals, of which they are in search, near the surface.'

The eggs and young are in considerable request in the places where they occur, but the natural consequence is, or rather has been, a great decrease in their numbers where they used formerly to abound.

They swim low in the water, and have the same habit as the other, of seeming to run along the top of the waves, scudding lightly over them, and at times as it were, supporting themselves on their webbed feet to pick up food.

They feed on fish—sprats, anchovies, and others, shrimps, cuttle-fish, worms, and other marine productions, and with these converted into an oil the young are fed. It is also made use of as a means of defence, blown from the tubular nostrils.

These birds resort for the purpose of incubation to the highest grassy parts of small rocky islands and the kindred shores of the mainland, as also to sandy places, where they breed in burrows, going to a depth of about two feet. The excavating of these appears to occupy a considerable time. Both birds sit, and that so closely, as to allow themselves to be taken in the hand. They are said to be much attached to their young.

They seem to be very variable in the time of laying, from the end of May to the end of June.

The nest is at most and best but a slight collection of fern leaves and withered stems of other plants: frequently none is formed, but the sand alone suffices the bird.

Only one egg is produced; it is large in size in proportion to the bulk of the bird, perfectly white, and of an oval form, but both ends obtuse.

Male; weight, seventeen ounces; length, one foot two to one foot three inches. The bill, which is furrowed above with a double tube, is blackish brown, the base lighter coloured and of a yellowish brown tint, the tips of both mandibles much hooked downwards; iris, dark brown. Head on the sides and crown, neck on the back, and nape, dusky brownish black, with a slight tinge of grey and a glossy lustre, the sides of the neck mottled with grey and white. Chin, throat, and breast, white, below on the latter, behind the legs, is a brownish black streak. Back, dusky brownish black, with a slight tinge of grey, and a glossy lustre.

The wings, when closed, reach nearly to the end of the tail: they expand to the width of two feet seven inches. Greater and lesser under wing coverts, white; primaries, black; tail, brownish black; under tail coverts, white. Legs, brown behind, in front dull yellowish red; they are laterally compressed; the outer toe brown, the remainder dull yellowish red; the webs rayed with brown.

The young bird is at first covered with greyish black down, except a stripe along the centre of the breast, which is white.

In the bird of the first year the breast is of a deep ash grey, the upper plumage dusky brown, which becomes by degrees darker.

FULMAR.

FULMAR PETREL. PETREL FULMAR. NORTHERN FULMAR.
MALLEMOKE. MOLLY.

Procellaria glacialis,   LINNÆUS. GMELIN.

Procellaria. Procella—A storm.   *Glacialis*—Belonging to ice.

As regards Europe, these birds are plentiful in Iceland, the Ferroe Islands, and Spitzbergen, and have occurred also on the coasts of France and Holland. In America, they are found about Davis' Straits, Baffin's Bay, Hudson's Bay, Newfoundland, the Bay of Fundy, and Greenland, at Grimsey Island.

The Fulmar breeds on Barra, Borrera, and Soay, in the Hebrides, as also at St. Kilda's 'lonely isle,' where they abound in almost incredible numbers, and are said to be the most important to the inhabitants of all their natural productions. Pennant remarks, 'No bird is of such use to the islanders as this: the Fulmar supplies them with oil for their lamps, down for their beds, a delicacy for their tables, a balm for their wounds, and a medicine for their distempers.' The inhabitants frequently risk their lives 'in order to obtain their eggs also, as well as the birds themselves.

In Norfolk, the Fulmar has been occasionally shot in Yarmouth Roads; two were taken twenty miles at sea, December 18th., 1844. Some few specimens on the coast of Durham. In Essex one was obtained at Saffron Walden. In Yorkshire, one was shot at Burlington, in 1849; the species was said not to have occurred there before for forty years. One picked up dead on the beach at Saltburn-by-the-Sea, June 19th., 1869; another at Huddersfield, far inland. Some have been shot in Cornwall, three or four; in Devonshire two. In the county of Derby, one was killed October 25th., 1847, in a field near a pool at Melbourne; it had first alighted on an island in the middle of the water. In Oxfordshire, one was found alive in Weston wood, in the parish of Weston-on-the-Green, on the 20th. of February, 1829; another killed on Port-meadow, near Oxford, in May, 1836. It has occurred occasionally also on the Welsh coast. So also in Ireland, but considered extremely rare. In Scotland, it is recorded as occurring in Caithness-shire.

In Orkney, it appears but rarely; a specimen was shot on the loch of Græmeshall, in Holm, in the month of September, 1846; one at Scalpa, near Kirkwall, in the year 1849.

It is said to be a regular winter visitant in Zetland.

The Fulmar migrates southwards in the autumn.

Fulmar

Stormy Petrel

They are sometimes eaten, but are only indifferent food. They are pugnacious among themselves when assembled together in countless flocks as they are seen sometimes to prey on any common food, and also very fearless at such times, as, for instance, when a whale has been struck, mingling among the men, so as even to require to be thrown out of the way. They are partly nocturnal in their habits, like the others. If in danger, they defend themselves with their powerful bill, and also forcibly eject from it an oil which acts as some protection.

'They are strong and graceful on the wing, flying almost in the teeth of the strongest gale, without any seeming movement of their beautifully-rounded pinions; now swooping along in the troughs of the sea, now skimming on the snowy crests. They are almost constantly on the wing night and day, never alighting on the water except during calm and moderate weather, and then but rarely. They are very bold, flying close to the side of the ship, almost within reach of the hand.' They walk in an ungainly manner when on the land or the floating masses of ice.

They feed voraciously on anything in the shape of food that floats on the water, and when satisfied, sleep on the ice till again called by their appetite to seek for more. The young are fed on an oil, into which these different substances are converted.

The noise that a large flock make is described as almost deafening, 'something between the cackle of a hen and the quack of a duck.'

The Fulmar builds on the small grassy shelves that occur on the front of high and inaccessible precipices, the result of the dilapidations that time works in even the hardest rock. Numberless pairs of these birds build close together.

A slight hollow in the turf, lined with grass and tufts of the sea-pink, forms the nest.

The single egg is of very large size, white, and of a brittle texture.

The young are hatched about the middle of June, the eggs having been laid the beginning of that month.

Male; weight, about twenty-two ounces; length, about one foot seven inches; bill, whitish on the sides, the upper part of the upper mandible greyish white, the tip of the lower one yellowish; it is much and strongly hooked, and also toothed; iris, pale yellow. Head, crown, and neck, white; nape, greyish; chin, throat, and breast, white, with a tinge of pink; back, bluish grey.

Greater and lesser wing coverts, fine bluish grey; primaries, slate grey; secondaries and tertiaries, fine bluish grey; greater and lesser under wing coverts, white. Tail, grey, with white edges to the feathers, rounded at the end, which is paler; tail coverts, white, and reaching beyond the end of the tail. Legs and toes, brownish yellow, tinged with red; the hind toe is very short; claws, slender, curved, and pointed; webs, brownish yellow.

The young in the second year have the tip of the bill yellowish, the remainder greyish; iris, pale dusky: there is a dark spot before it. Head, crown, neck, and nape, greyish brown, the edges of the feathers paler; chin, throat, and breast, pale greyish brown, the edges of the feathers lighter-coloured; back, darker greyish brown, the edges of the feathers paler. Primaries, secondaries, and tertiaries, greyish brown. Tail, greyish brown, the edges of the feathers paler. Legs and toes, pale brownish or greyish yellow; webs, pale brown.

STORMY PETREL.

CAS GAN LONGWYR, OF THE ANCIENT BRITISH.

STORM PETREL.   COMMON STORM PETREL.   LITTLE PETREL.
STORM FINCH.   MOTHER CAREY'S CHICKEN.

Procellaria pelagica,   PENNANT.   MONTAGU.   BEWICK.

Procellaria.   Procella—A storm.   *Pelagica*—Of or belonging to the sea.
Pelagus—The sea.

THIS is the smallest web-footed bird known, the last and least in the latter half of this my 'History of British Birds.'

It has received its name of Petrel from its habit of walking or running on the water, as the Apostle St. Peter did or essayed to do.

These birds are made use of by the inhabitants of the Ferroe and other Islands, to serve for lamps, a wick of cotton or other material being drawn through the body, and when lighted it continues to burn till the oil in the bird is consumed. The quantity of oil yielded decreases as the summer advances, and at last fails altogether, probably from their falling off in condition, and the supply given to their young, they being fed with the same.

They are crepuscular and nocturnal in their habits, and towards night wander forth accordingly over the ocean.

This tiny sea-bird, ever on the wing, as well in the serenest as in the most tempestuous weather, finds equally its home in each and every quarter of the globe. Many is the sad tale it could tell of what it has heard and seen, by day and by night, in the north, the south, the east, and west. Let the imagination, aided by what others have seen and said, set the picture faintly before us in its different points of view.

Now in the north, a thousand miles from land, alone in its wanderings over the vast abyss of the unfathomable ocean, the depth below as pitchy black as the murky night-cloud overhead that will soon enshroud the face of the deep with its darksome mantle till the two elements shall be, as it were, mingled together in one common gloom, the Petrel careers along the driving waves, and revels in the advance of the coming storm. Now it flits round and round; now poises for a moment on its sooty wings; and now is hid behind the brow of a rolling wave. Could we be there while not there—for the very presence of man must take off from the fearful solemnity which can only in its fulness belong to perfect solitude—how utterly lonely the scene, even in the height of a summer's day! and what must it be in the 'wild midnight' of the end of the year, when the short-lived glories of the arctic solstice, that have only gleamed 'too soon to fleet,' have withered and waned into the long and dreary night of the winter of winters? It is indeed in itself the same by day and by night, and yet how great the difference. The 'Northern Lights' themselves are hidden behind a black starless sky, and cutting winds that freeze the life-blood sweep over the wilderness of waters, as if the very Furies were let slip, whirling along the driving snow, or thick showers of heavy rain, whose drops, mixed with spray, sleet, and hail, seem part of the squalls themselves; you hear —even if you are not there you hear—the loud shrieks of each gust of wind, and are aware of every coming blast. Whither is the stray bird to wing its way? Whither is it to 'flee away and be at rest?' Where is it now gone? Where is it next to be seen?

In the offing there rises up the weather-beaten hull of some doomed ship 'lean, rent, and beggared,' which in vain struggles and strains to keep off the fatal lee-shore. She drifts nearer and nearer; you would see at once that her hour has come, and that no human power can save her. Now the darkness lowers still deeper, the mournful sighings of the air tell of the awaking of the winds from their snatched and fitful slumber, and warn that they will soon be sweeping on again with redoubled force, like a troop of gaunt and famished wolves greedy of their certain prey. The black hull looms larger and larger as the tempest-tossed vessel rises on the high wild seas outside, and at last the only barriers between her and the rocky thunder-splitten cliffs, half-way up which the billows are breaking, and recoiling again in boiling surf, are the sunken rocks, 'over which stupendous breakers, lashed into fury by the angry gusts, run riot, mingling the hissing of their seething waves with the furious ravings of the blast.'

It is as nature has foretold, and the signs of the vast power of the air, which she has ushered in with such and so many sublime portents, are quickly fulfilled. The sky above assumes a fierce and fiery appearance, and to windward a huge bank of black cloud rises up and up from the distance, and, as it comes on nearer and nearer, the 'mighty and strong wind,' in the language of Scripture, is driven, as it were out of its dark depths to carry all irresistibly before it. With every fresh burst of the hurtling tempest a harsh screaming sound, as the howl of a legion of evil spirits let loose and borne on its ominous wings, warns of the mischief too late, the cries of the uncaged wind gather strength and wax louder and louder, as if never to be calmed again. Now, for an instant, the vivid lightning lightens up the scene, and reveals the darkness around, above, and below, to leave all still more awful than before, and following it, 'Heaven's artillery,' the thunder-clap, rolls over and echoes away among the clouds, peal upon peal and crash upon crash. Now the gleam has glented by, and, last, night comes on with its gloomy grandeur, and the blackness of the black depth below is taken into the blackness that comes down upon it—all is black. The sea closes over the fated ship, the time of mourning has come, and the wail of the way-worn Petrel is the dirge for those who have perished with her on the 'lone and rocky shore.'

But He who 'rideth upon the wings of the wind,' 'who stilleth the raging of the sea and the noise of his waves,' 'the LORD who sitteth on high,—is mightier.' He says unto the sea, 'Peace! be still:' 'He speaks the word,' and 'there is a great calm.'

So yet once more in milder climates, leaving the dreariness of high northern latitudes for the glory of the serene night of the south, and the ceaseless breaking of the sea on an iron-bound coast for its soft moaning while gently laving the golden sand of a low shore, 'on fine calm evenings, after the smooth surface of the deep has put off the fiery glow imparted by the setting sun, and begins to assume the dull leaden tint of night, then the little Petrel may be seen scouring along upon the face of the sea; now he darts past the fisher's boat as it is rowing along upon its homeward course; is seen for a moment as he flits among the lagging oars, and instantly disappears among the increasing gloom of approaching night. His motions are so rapid, his appearance so sudden, and he looks so extremely diminutive, that it is only a quick eye that will detect his approach at all.'

Such are the scenes in which the Stormy Petrel acts its part.

These birds rise with difficulty from the ground, owing to the great length of their wings, and run along some distance before they can get fairly under weigh. They use their hooked bills to assist them in climbing. They fly very swiftly, and in the most buoyant and light manner imaginable, and are often seen skimming from the top of one wave to another, dipping the bill into the water in search of, or to pick up food, hovering for the moment with up-raised wings. They are able to swim, but seldom alight for the purpose.

They feed on crustacea and mollusca generally, small fishes, and eatable things of any kind that come in their way. They often keep company with ships for many days, possibly for the sake of some little shelter afforded, but more probably to secure stray morsels, either thrown over as waste or purposely cast to them by the sailors.

When engaged with their nests they utter a very peculiar purring or buzzing sound, broken every now and then by a 'click;' also towards evening a frequent shrill whistling noise. Meyer likens the note to the word 'kekereck-ee.' The voices of these birds may be heard, especially towards evening, under the stones, at a depth of three or four feet or more, where they breed on the beach, 'distinctly singing a sort of warbling chatter.'

The Stormy Petrel nestles in rabbit-burrows, the crevices of rocks, holes in cliffs at a great height above the sea, and among loose stones. They also excavate small runs for themselves where the soil is soft, to a distance of three or four feet. The season for laying is late—towards the middle, and sometimes not till quite the end of June, or the first week in July. The young have been found only recently hatched on the 13th. of October.

The egg is white, and somewhat of an oval shape. It is very frequently surrounded about the base with a ring of faint dull-coloured pink or fine rust-coloured spots.

A few pieces of stalks of plants, dried grass, or sea-pinks, with a stray feather or two, are all the nest. The bird sits very close, and will allow herself to be taken sooner than forsake her charge.

"O all ye Fowls of the Air, bless ye the Lord;
praise Him and magnify Him for ever."

INDEX

INDEX OF LATIN NAMES

Numbers in italic type refer to illustrations.

INDEX OF COMMON NAMES

Numbers in italic type refer to illustrations.